Reading Financial Reports

for dummies®
A Wiley Brand

Reading Financial Reports

3rd Edition

by Lita Epstein

for dummies®

A Wiley Brand

Reading Financial Reports For Dummies®, 3rd Edition

Published by: **John Wiley & Sons, Inc.,** 111 River Street, Hoboken, NJ 07030-5774, www.wiley.com

Library of Congress Control Number: 2018956058

ISBN 978-1-119-54395-4 (pbk); ISBN 978-1-119-54398-5 (ebk); ISBN 978-1-119-54396-1 (ebk)

Manufactured in the United States of America

SKY10022886_112620

Contents at a Glance

Table of Contents

Introduction

When I open an annual financial report today, one of the first questions I ask myself is, "Can I believe the numbers I'm seeing?" I never used to think that way. I used to think that any corporate financial report audited by a certified public accountant truly was prepared with the public's interests in mind.

The financial scandals of the late 1990s and early 2000s destroyed my confidence in those numbers, as they did for millions of other U.S. investors who lost billions in the stock market crash that followed those scandals. Sure, a stock bubble (a period of rising stock prices that stems from a buying frenzy) had burst, but financial reports that hid companies' financial problems fueled the bubble and helped companies put on a bright, smiling face for the public. After these financial reporting scandals came to light, more than 500 public companies had to restate their earnings. Yet in almost a repeat of the scandals, the mortgage mess of 2007 showed how financial institutions were still using the same tricks of keeping key financial information off the books to hide financial troubles.

I still wonder what government regulators and public accountants were thinking and doing during these fiascos. How did the system break down so dramatically and so quickly? Although a few voices raised red flags, their pleas were drowned out by the euphoria of the building stock market bubble of the early 1990s and the housing market bubble of the mid-2000s.

These financial scandals occurred partly because Wall Street measures success based on a company's quarterly results. Many analysts on Wall Street are more concerned about whether a company meets its quarterly expectations than they are about a company's long-term prospects for future growth. Companies that fail to meet their quarterly expectations find their stock quickly beaten down on the market. To avoid the fall, companies massage their numbers. This shortsighted race to meet the numbers each quarter is a big reason these scandals happen in the first place.

Since the scandals broke, legislators have enacted new laws and regulations to attempt to correct the problems. In this book, I discuss these new regulations and show you how to read financial reports with an ounce of skepticism and a set of tools that can help you determine whether the numbers make sense. I help you see how companies can play games with their numbers and show you how to analyze the numbers in a financial report so you can determine a company's true financial health.

About This Book

This book provides detailed information on how to read a financial report's key statements — the balance sheet, the income statement, and the statement of cash flows — as well as how to discover and scour a report's other important parts.

When you finish reading this book, you'll understand what makes up the parts of financial statements and how to read between their lines, using the fine print to increase your understanding of a company's financial position. You'll also be familiar with the company outsiders who are responsible for certifying the accuracy of financial reports, and you'll know how the rules have changed since the corporate scandals broke. Although I can't promise that you'll be able to detect every type of fraud, I can promise that your antennae will be up and you'll be more aware of how to spot possible problems. And most important, you'll get a good understanding of how to use these reports to make informed decisions about whether a company is a sound investment. If you work inside a company, you'll have a better understanding of how to use the reports to manage your company or your department for success.

Conventions Used in This Book

I use the words *corporation* and *company* almost interchangeably. Just so we're on the same page, all corporations are companies, but not all companies are corporations. The key difference between them is whether a company has gone through *incorporation*, which is the rather complicated legal process by which a company gets a state charter to operate as a business. To find out more about company structure and incorporation, see Chapter 2.

To help you practice the tools I show you in this book, I use the annual reports of the two largest toy companies, Mattel and Hasbro, and dissect their reports throughout various chapters. You can download a full copy of the reports by visiting the investor relations section of the companies' websites: `www.hasbro.com` and `www.mattel.com`.

What You're Not to Read

Many of the topics I discuss in this book are, by nature, technical — dealing with finances can hardly be otherwise. But in some cases, I provide details that offer more than the basic stuff you need to know to understand the big picture. Because these explanations may not be up your alley, I mark them with a Technical Stuff icon (see the upcoming section "Icons Used in This Book") and invite you to skip them without even the slightest regret. Even if you skip them, you still get all the information you need. On the other hand, if you savor every financial detail or fancy yourself the bravest of all financial report readers, then dig in!

I've also added some sidebars to give you more detail about a topic or some financial history. You can skip those, too, and still be able to understand how to read financial reports.

Foolish Assumptions

To write this book, I made some basic assumptions about who you are. I assume that you

- Want to know more about the information in financial reports and how you can use it.
- Want to know the basics of financial reporting.
- Need to gather some analytical tools to more effectively use financial reports for your own investing or career goals.
- Need a better understanding of the financial reports you receive from the company you work for to analyze the results of your department or division.
- Want to get a better handle on what goes into financial reports, how they're developed, and how to use the information to measure the financial success of your own company.

Both investors and company insiders who aren't familiar with the ins and outs of financial reports can benefit from the information and tools I include in this book.

Icons Used in This Book

Throughout the book, I use icons to flag parts of the text that you'll want to notice. Here's a list of the icons and what they mean.

TIP

This icon points out ideas for improving your financial report reading skills and directs you to some useful financial resources.

REMEMBER

This icon highlights information you definitely want to remember.

WARNING

This icon points out a critical piece of information that can help you find the dangers and perils in financial reports. I also use this icon to emphasize information you definitely don't want to skip or skim when reading a financial report.

TECHNICAL STUFF

This icon highlights information that may explain the numbers in more detail than you care to know. Don't worry; you can skip these points without missing the big picture!

REAL WORLD EXAMPLE

Throughout the book, I give examples from financial reports of real companies, particularly Mattel and Hasbro. I highlight these examples with the icon you see here.

Beyond the Book

In addition to the material in the print or e-book you're reading right now, this product comes with some access-anywhere goodies on the web. You'll probably need reminders about the key parts of an annual report or the best financial analysis formulas to use. Check out the Cheat Sheet at `www.dummies.com/cheatsheet/readingfinancialreports`. You can find other useful information related to reading financial reports at `www.dummies.com/extras/readingfinancialreports`.

Where to Go from Here

You can start reading anywhere in this book, but if you're totally new to financial reports, you definitely want to start with Part 1 so you can get a good handle on the basics before delving into the financial information. If you already know the basics, turn to Part 2 to begin dissecting the parts of a financial report. And to get started on the road to analyzing the numbers, turn to Part 3. If your priority is tools for optimizing company operation, you may want to begin with Part 4. Turn right to Part 5 if you want to know more about company outsiders involved in the financial reporting process.

1

Getting Started with Reading Financial Reports

IN THIS PART . . .

Explore the types of financial reports and get to know the key financial statements.

Discover business types and their tax rules, including sole proprietorships, partnerships, and limited liability companies.

Differentiate between public and private companies, and understand what it means when a company decides to go public.

Understand accounting basics – enough to understand different kinds of profit, and to distinguish debits from credits.

» Reviewing the importance of financial reports

» Exploring the different types of financial reporting

» Discovering the key financial statements

Chapter 1
Opening the Cornucopia of Reports

Financial reports give a snapshot of a company's value at the end of a particular period, as well as a view of the company's operations and whether it made a profit. The business world couldn't function without financial reports. Yes, fewer scandals would be exposed because companies wouldn't be tempted to paint false but pretty financial pictures, but you'd still need a way to gauge a firm's financial health.

At this point in time, nothing's available that can possibly replace financial reports. Nothing can be substituted that'd give investors, financial institutions, and government agencies the information they need to make decisions about a company. And without financial reports, the folks who work for a company wouldn't know how to make it more efficient and profitable because they wouldn't have a summary of its financial activities during previous business periods. These financial summaries help companies look at their successes and failures and make plans for future improvements.

This chapter introduces you to the many facets of financial reports and shows you how internal and external players use them to evaluate a company's financial health.

Figuring Out Financial Reporting

Financial reporting gives readers a summary of what happens in a company based purely on the numbers. The numbers that tell the tale include the following:

- **Assets:** The cash, marketable securities, buildings, land, tools, equipment, vehicles, copyrights, patents, and any other items needed to run a business that a company holds.
- **Liabilities:** Money a company owes to outsiders, such as loans, bonds, and unpaid bills.
- **Equity:** Money invested in the company.
- **Sales:** Products or services that customers purchase.
- **Costs and expenses:** Money spent to operate a business, such as expenditures for production, compensation for employees, operation of buildings and factories, or supplies to run the offices.
- **Profit or loss:** The amount of money a company earns or loses.
- **Cash flow:** The amount of money that flows into and out of a business during the time period being reported.

REMEMBER

Without financial reporting, you'd have no idea where a company stands financially. Sure, you'd know how much money the business has in its bank accounts, but you wouldn't know how much is still due to come in from customers, how much inventory is being held in the warehouse and on the shelf, how much the firm owes, or even how much the firm owns. As an investor, if you don't know these details, you can't possibly make an objective decision about whether the company is making money and whether investing in the company's future is worthwhile.

Preparing the reports

A company's accounting department is the key source of its financial reports. This department is responsible for monitoring the numbers and putting together the reports. The numbers are the products of a process called *double-entry accounting*, which requires a company to record resources and the assets it uses to get those resources. For example, if you buy a chair, you must spend another asset, such as cash. An entry in the double-entry accounting system shows both sides of that transaction — the cash account is reduced by the chair's price, and the furniture account value is increased by the chair's price.

This crucial method of accounting gives companies the ability to record and track business activity in a standardized way. Accounting methods are constantly updated to reflect the business environment as financial transactions become more complex. To find out more about double-entry accounting, turn to Chapter 4.

Seeing why financial reporting counts (and who's counting)

Many people count on the information companies present in financial reports. Here are some key groups of readers and why they need accurate information:

- **Executives and managers:** They need information to know how well the company is doing financially and to find out about problem areas so they can make changes to improve the company's performance.
- **Employees:** They need to know how well they're meeting or exceeding their goals and where they need to improve. For example, if a salesperson has to make $50,000 in sales during the month, he needs a financial report at the end of the month to gauge how well he did in meeting that goal. If he believes that he met his goal but the financial report doesn't show that he did, he must provide details to defend his production levels. Most salespeople are paid according to their sales production. Without financial reports, they'd have no idea what their compensation is based on.

  Employees also make career and retirement investment decisions based on the company's financial reports. If the reports are misleading or false, employees may lose most, if not all, of their 401(k) retirement savings, and their long-term financial futures may be at risk.
- **Creditors:** They need to understand a company's financial results to determine whether to risk lending more money to the company and to find out whether the firm is meeting the minimum requirements of any loan programs that are already in place. To find out how creditors gauge whether a business meets their requirements, see Chapters 9 and 12.

  If a firm's financial reports are false or misleading, creditors may loan money at an interest rate that doesn't truly reflect the risks they're taking. And by trusting the misleading information, they may miss out on a better opportunity.
- **Investors:** They need information to judge whether a company is a good investment. If investors think that a company is on a growth path because of the financial information it reports, but those reports turn out to be false, investors can pay, big time. They may buy stock at inflated prices and risk the loss of capital as the truth comes out, or they may miss out on better investing opportunities.
- **Government agencies:** These agencies need to be sure that companies comply with regulations set at the state and federal levels. They also need to be certain that companies accurately inform the public about their financial position.

- **Analysts:** They need information to develop analytical reviews for clients who are considering the company for investments or additional loan funds.
- **Financial reporters:** They need to provide accurate coverage of a company's operations to the general public, which helps make investors aware of the critical financial issues facing the company and any changes the company makes in its operations.
- **Competitors:** Every company's bigwigs read their competitors' financial reports. If these reports are based on false numbers, the financial playing field gets distorted. A well-run company could make a bad decision to keep up with the false numbers of a competitor and end up reducing its own profitability.

Companies don't produce financial reports only for public consumption. Many financial reports are prepared for internal use only. These internal reports help managers accomplish these tasks:

- Find out which of the business's operations are producing a profit and which are operating at a loss
- Determine which departments or divisions need to receive additional resources to encourage growth
- Identify unsuccessful departments or divisions and make needed changes to turn around the troubled section or kill the project
- Determine staffing and inventory levels needed to respond to customer demand
- Review customer accounts to identify slow-paying or nonpaying customers, to devise collection methods and develop guidelines for when a customer should be cut off from future orders
- Prepare production schedules and review production levels

This list identifies just a few of the many uses companies have for their internal financial reports. The actual list is endless and is limited only by the imagination of the executives and managers who want to find ways to use the numbers to make business decisions. I talk more about using internal reports to optimize results in Chapters 14, 15, and 16.

Checking Out Types of Reporting

Not every company needs to prepare financial statements, but any company seeking to raise cash through stock sales or by borrowing funds certainly does. How public these statements must be depends on the business's structure.

Most businesses are *private companies*, which share these statements only with a small group of stakeholders: managers, investors, suppliers, vendors, and the financial institutions that they do business with. As long as a company doesn't sell shares of stock to the general public, it doesn't have to make its financial statements public. I talk more about the reporting rules for private companies in Chapter 2.

REMEMBER

Public companies, which sell stock on the open market, must file a series of reports with the Securities and Exchange Commission (SEC) each year if they have at least 500 investors or at least $10 million in assets. Smaller companies that have incorporated and sold stock must report to the state in which they incorporated, but they aren't required to file with the SEC. You can find more details about the SEC's reporting requirements for public companies in Chapters 3 and 19.

Even if a firm doesn't need to make its financial reports public, if it wants to raise cash outside a very small circle of friends, it has to prepare financial statements and have a certified public accountant (CPA) *audit* them, or certify that the financial statements meet the requirements of the generally accepted accounting principles (or GAAP, which you can find out more about in the section "Keeping the number crunchers in line," later in this chapter). Few banks consider loaning large sums of money to businesses without audited financial statements. Investors who aren't involved in the daily management of a business also usually require audited financial statements.

Keeping everyone informed

One big change in a company's operations after it decides to publicly sell stock is that it must report publicly on both a quarterly and annual basis to its stockholders. Companies send these reports directly to their stockholders, to analysts, and to the major financial institutions that help fund their operations through loans or bonds. The reports often include glossy pictures and pleasingly designed graphics at the beginning, keeping the less eye-pleasing financial reports that meet the SEC's requirements in the back.

Quarterly reports

Companies must release *quarterly reports* within 45 days of the quarter's end. Companies with holdings over $75 million must file more quickly. In addition to the three key financial statements — the *balance sheet*, the *income statement*, and the *statement of cash flows* (check out the upcoming section "Getting to the meat of the matter" for details on these documents) — the company must state whether a CPA has audited (see Chapter 18) or reviewed (a much less intensive look at the data) the numbers. A report reviewed rather than audited by a CPA holds less weight.

Annual reports

Most small companies must file their *annual reports* within 90 days of the end of their fiscal year. Companies with over $75 million in assets must file their reports within 60 days. The annual report includes the information presented in the quarterly reports and much more, including a full business description, details about the management team and its compensation, and details about any filings done during the year.

REMEMBER

Most major companies put a lot of money into producing glossy reports filled with information and pictures designed to make a good impression on the public. The marketing or public relations department, not the financial or accounting department, writes much of the summary information. Too often, annual reports are puff pieces that carefully hide any negative information in the *notes to the financial statements*, which is the section that offers additional details about the numbers provided in those statements (see Chapter 9). Read between the lines — especially the tiny print at the back of the report — to get some critical information about the accounting methods used, any pending lawsuits, or other information that may negatively impact results in the future.

Following the rules: Government requirements

Reports for the government are more extensive than the glossy reports sent to shareholders (see the preceding section). Companies must file many types of forms with the SEC, but I focus on only three of them in this book:

- **The 10-K:** This form is the annual report that provides a comprehensive overview of a company's business and financial activities.

  Firms must file this report within 90 days of the end of the fiscal year (companies with more than $75 million in assets must file within 60 days). In addition to the information included in the glossy annual reports sent to shareholders (see the preceding section), investors can find more detailed information about company history, organizational structure, equity holdings, subsidiaries, employee stock purchase and savings plans, incorporation, legal proceedings, controls and procedures, executive compensation, accounting fees and services, and changes or disagreements with accountants about financial disclosures.
- **The 10-Q:** This form is the quarterly report that describes key financial information about the prior three months. Most companies must file this report within 45 days of the end of the quarter (firms with more than $75 million in assets must file within 40 days). In addition to the information sent directly to shareholders, this form includes details about the company's market risk, controls and procedures, legal proceedings, and defaults on payments.

- **The 8-K:** This form is a periodic report that accounts for any major events that may impact a company's financial position. Examples of major events include the acquisition of another company, the sale of a company or division, bankruptcy, the resignation of directors, or a change in the fiscal year. When a major event occurs, the company must file a report with the SEC within four days of the event.

TIP

You can access reports filed with the SEC online at Edgar, which is run by the SEC. To use Edgar, go to www.sec.gov/edgar.shtml.

Going global

More companies these days operate across country borders. For years, each country had its own set of rules for preparing financial reports to meet government regulations. Global companies had to keep separate sets of books and report results under different sets of rules in each country in which they operated.

Today most countries have agreed to accept the International Financial Reporting Standards (IFRS; see Chapter 20) developed by the London-based International Accounting Standards Board (IASB). Beginning in 2002, the U.S. agreed to look at ways to converge the IFRS and the U.S. GAAP (see Chapter 18). The U.S. allows companies based outside its borders to file required reports using either U.S. GAAP or IFRS, but U.S.-based companies must still use GAAP to file their reports. The process of converging U.S. standards with international standards is still a work in process.

Staying within the walls of the company: Internal reporting

Not all of an accounting department's financial reporting is done for public consumption. In fact, companies usually produce many more internal reports than external ones to keep management informed. Firms can design their internal reports in whatever way makes sense to their operations.

Each department head usually receives a report from the top managers showing the department's expenses and revenue and whether it's meeting its budget. If the department's numbers vary significantly from the amount that was budgeted, the report indicates red flags. The department head usually needs to investigate the differences and report what the department is doing to correct any problems. Even if the difference is increased revenue (which can be good news), the manager needs to know why the difference exists, because an error in the data input could have occurred. I talk more about reports and budgeting in Chapter 14.

FINDING THE ROOTS OF FINANCIAL REPORTING

Accounting practices can be traced back to the Renaissance, but financial reporting wasn't recognized as a necessity until centuries later.

- **1494:** Italian monk Luca Pacioli became known as the "father of accounting" for his book *Everything about Arithmetic, Geometry and Proportions,* which includes a section on double-entry accounting (see Chapter 4). Pacioli warned his readers that an accountant shouldn't go to sleep at night until his debits equal his credits.
- **1700–1800:** For-profit corporations started to appear in Europe as early as the 18th century. In 1800, only about 330 corporations operated in the U.S.
- **1800s:** As public ownership of stock increased, regulators realized that some standardized distribution of information to investors was a priority. The New York Stock Exchange was the first to jump into the fray, and in 1853, it began requiring companies listed on the exchange to provide statements of shares outstanding and capital resources.
- **1929:** Before the stock market crash, equity investing became a passion. People borrowed money to get into the market, paying higher and higher prices for stock. Sound familiar? Not too different from what occurred just before the 2000 crash of technology and Internet stocks.
- **1933–1934:** Congress created the SEC and gave it authority to develop financial accounting and reporting standards and rules to deter companies from distributing misleading information.
- **1973:** The Financial Accounting Standards Board (FASB) was created to establish standards for financial accounting and reporting. The SEC recognized the generally accepted accounting principles (GAAP) as the official reporting standards for federal securities laws.
- **1984:** The FASB formed the Emerging Issues Task Force, which keeps an eye on changes in business operations and sets standards before new practices become entrenched.
- **2002:** The FASB began work with the International Accounting Standards Board (IASB) to converge international financial reporting systems.

Reports on inventory are critical, not only for managing the products on hand, but also for knowing when to order new inventory. I talk more about inventory controls and financial reporting in Chapter 15.

Tracking cash is vital to the day-to-day operations of any company. The frequency of a company's cash reporting depends on the volatility of its cash status — the more volatile the cash, the more likely the company needs frequent reporting to be sure that it has cash on hand to pay its bills. Some large firms actually provide cash reporting to their managers daily. I talk more about cash reporting in Chapters 16 and 17; Chapter 16 focuses on incoming cash, and Chapter 17 deals with outgoing cash.

Dissecting the Annual Report to Shareholders

The annual report gives more details about a company's business and financial activities than any other report. This document is primarily for shareholders, although any member of the general public can request a copy. Glossy pictures and graphics fill the front of the report, highlighting what the company wants you to know. After that, you find the full details about the company's business and financial operations; most companies include the full 10-K that they file with the SEC.

Breaking down the parts

The annual report is broken into the following parts (I summarize the key points of each of these parts in Chapter 5):

- **Highlights:** These are a narrative summary of the previous year's activities and general information about the company, its history, its products, and its business lines.
- **Letter from the president or chief executive officer (CEO):** This letter is directed to the shareholders and discusses the company's key successes or explains any major failures.
- **Auditors' report:** This report tells you whether the numbers are accurate or whether you need to have any concerns about the future operation of the business.
- **Management's discussion and analysis:** In this part, you find management's discussion of the financial results and other factors that impact the company's operations.
- **Financial statements:** The key financial statements are the balance sheet, income statement, and statement of cash flows. In the financial statements, you find the actual financial results for the year. For details about this part of the report, check out the following section, "Getting to the meat of the matter."

- **Notes to the financial statements:** In the notes, you find details about how the numbers were derived. I talk more about the role of the notes in Chapter 9.
- **Other information:** In this part, you find information about the company's key executives and managers, officers, board members, and locations, along with new facilities that have opened in the past year.

Getting to the meat of the matter

No doubt, the most critical part of the annual report for anyone who wants to know how well a company did financially is the financial statements section, which includes the balance sheet, the income statement, and the statement of cash flows.

The balance sheet

The *balance sheet* gives a snapshot of the company's financial condition. On a balance sheet, you find assets, liabilities, and equity. The balance sheet got its name because the total assets must equal the total liabilities plus the total equities so that the value of the company is in balance. Here's the equation:

Assets = Liabilities + Equities

Assets appear on the left side of a balance sheet, and liabilities and equities are on the right side. Assets are broken down into *current assets* (holdings that the company will use in the next 12 months, such as cash and savings) and *long-term assets* (holdings that the company will use longer than a 12-month period, such as buildings, land, and equipment).

Liabilities are broken down into *current liabilities* (payments on bills or debts that are due in the next 12 months) and *long-term liabilities* (payments on debt that are due after the next 12 months).

The equities portion of the balance sheet can be called *owner's equity* (when an individual or partners closely hold a company) or *shareholders' equity* (when shares of stock have been sold to raise cash). I talk more about what information goes into a balance sheet in Chapter 6.

The income statement

The *income statement,* also known as the *profit and loss statement (P&L),* gets the most attention from investors. This statement shows a summary of the financial activities of one quarter or an entire year. Many companies prepare P&Ls on a monthly basis for internal use. Investors always focus on the exciting parts of the statement: revenue, net income, and earnings per share of stock.

In the income statement, you also find out how much the company is spending to produce or purchase the products or services it sells, how much the company costs to operate, how much it pays in interest, and how much it pays in income tax. To find out more about the information you can find on an income statement, go to Chapter 7.

The statement of cash flows

The *statement of cash flows* is relatively new to the financial reporting game. The SEC didn't require companies to file it with the other financial reports until 1988. Basically, the statement of cash flows is similar to the income statement, in that it reports a company's performance over time. But instead of focusing on profit or loss, it focuses on how cash flows through the business. This statement has three sections: cash from operations, cash from investing, and cash from financing. I talk more about the statement of cash flows in Chapter 8.

Keeping the number crunchers in line

Every public company's internal accounting team and external audit team must answer to government entities. The primary government entity responsible for overseeing corporate reporting is the SEC. Its staff reviews reports filed with the SEC. If SEC employees have any questions or want additional information, they notify the company after reviewing the reports.

REMEMBER

Financial statements filed with the SEC and for public consumption must adhere to the *generally accepted accounting principles* (GAAP). To meet the demands of these rules, financial reporting must be relevant, reliable, consistent, and presented in a way that allows the report reader to compare the results to prior years, as well as to other companies' financial results. To find out more about GAAP, turn to Chapter 18.

With GAAP in place, you may wonder why so many accounting scandals have hit the front pages of newspapers around the country for the past few years. Filing statements according to GAAP has become a game for many companies. Unfortunately, investors and regulators find that companies don't always engage in transactions for the economic benefit of the shareholders, but sometimes do so to make their reports look better and to meet the quarterly expectations of Wall Street. Many times, companies look financially stronger than they actually are. For example, as scandals have come to light, companies have been found to overstate income, equity, and cash flows while understating debt. I talk more about reporting problems in Chapter 23.

- » Exploring sole proprietorships
- » Taking a look at partnerships
- » Checking out limited liability companies
- » Comparing different types of corporations

Chapter 2

Recognizing Business Types and Their Tax Rules

All businesses need to prepare key financial statements, but some businesses can prepare less formal statements than others. The way a business is legally organized greatly impacts the way it reports its financials to the public and the depth of that reporting.

For a small business, financial reporting is needed only to monitor the success or failure of operations. But as the business grows, and as more outsiders — such as investors and creditors — become involved, financial reporting becomes more formalized until the company reaches the point at which audited financial statements are required.

Each business structure also follows a different set of rules about what financial information the business must file with state, local, and federal agencies. In this chapter, I review the basics on how each type of business structure is organized, how taxation differs, which forms the business must file, and what types of financial reports are required.

Flying Solo: Sole Proprietorships

The simplest business structure is the *sole proprietorship* — the IRS's automatic classification for any business that an individual starts. Most new businesses with only one owner start out as sole proprietorships. Some never grow into anything larger. Others start adding partners and staff and may realize that incorporating is a wise decision for legal purposes. (Check out "Seeking Protection with Limited Liability Companies" and "Shielding Your Assets: S and C Corporations," later in the chapter, to find out more about incorporating.)

To start a business as a sole proprietor, you don't have to do anything official, like file government papers or register with the IRS. In fact, unless you formally *incorporate* — follow a process that makes the business a separate legal entity — the IRS considers the business a sole proprietorship. (I talk more about incorporation and the process of forming corporations in the upcoming section titled "Shielding Your Assets: S and C Corporations.")

WARNING

The fact that the business isn't a separate legal entity is the biggest risk of a sole proprietorship. All debts or claims against the business are filed against the sole proprietor's personal property. If a sole proprietor is sued, insurance is the only form of protection against losing everything.

Keeping taxes personal

Sole proprietorships aren't taxable entities, and sole proprietors don't have to fill out separate tax forms for their businesses. The only financial reporting sole proprietors must do is add a few forms about their business entity to their personal tax returns.

Most sole proprietors add Schedule C — a "Profit or Loss from Business" form — to their personal tax returns, but some choose an even simpler form, called Schedule C-EZ, "Net Profit from Business." In addition, a sole proprietor must pay both the employer and employee sides of Social Security and Medicare taxes using Schedule SE, "Self-Employment Tax." These taxes total 15.3 percent of *net business income*, or the business income after all business expenses have been subtracted.

TECHNICAL STUFF

Sole proprietors in specialized businesses may have different IRS forms to fill out. Farmers use Schedule F, "Profit or Loss from Farming." People who own rental real estate but don't operate a real estate business use Schedule E, "Supplemental Income and Loss."

Reviewing requirements for reporting

Financial reporting requirements don't exist for sole proprietors unless they seek funding from outside sources, such as a bank loan or a loan from the U.S. Small Business Administration. When a business seeks outside funding, the funding source likely provides guidelines for how the business should present financial information.

When sole proprietors apply for a business loan, they fill out a form that shows their assets and liabilities. In addition, they're usually required to provide a basic profit and loss statement. Depending on the size of the loan, they may even have to submit a formal business plan stating their goals, objectives, and implementation plans.

TIP

Even though financial reports aren't required for a sole proprietorship that isn't seeking outside funding, it makes good business sense to complete periodic profit and loss statements to keep tabs on how well the business is doing and to find any problems before they become too huge to fix. These reports don't have to adhere to formal generally accepted accounting principles (GAAP; see Chapter 18), but honesty is the best policy. You're fooling only yourself if you decide to make your financial condition look better on paper than it really is.

Joining Forces: Partnerships

The IRS automatically considers any business started by more than one person a *partnership*. Each person in the partnership is equally liable for the activities of the business, but because more than one person is involved, a partnership is a slightly more complicated company type than a sole proprietorship. Partners have to sort out the following legal issues:

- How they divide profits
- How they can sell the business
- What happens if one partner becomes sick or dies
- How they dissolve the partnership if one of the partners wants out

Because of the number of options, a partnership is the most flexible business structure for a business that involves more than one person. But to avoid future problems that can destroy an otherwise successful business, partners should decide on all these issues before opening their business's doors.

Partnering up on taxes

Partnerships aren't taxable entities, but partners do have to file a "U.S. Return of Partnership Income" using IRS Form 1065. This form, which shows income, deductions, and other tax-related business data, is for information purposes only. It lists each partner's share of taxable income, called a Schedule K-1, "Partner's Share of Income, Credits, Deductions, Etc." Each individual partner must report that income on his or her personal tax return.

Meeting reporting requirements

Unless a partnership seeks outside funding, its financial reports don't have to be presented in any special way because the reports don't have to satisfy anyone but the partners. Partnerships do need reports to monitor the success or failure of business operations, but they don't have to be completed to meet GAAP standards (see Chapter 18). Usually, when more than one person is involved, the partners decide among themselves what type of financial reporting is required and who's responsible for preparing those reports.

WARNING

If the partnership seeks funding from a bank or investors, more formal reporting may be needed, such as audited financial statements and business plans.

Seeking Protection with Limited Liability Companies

A partnership or sole proprietorship can limit its liability by using an entity called a *limited liability company*, or LLC. First established in the U.S. about 30 years ago, LLCs didn't become popular until the mid-1990s, when most states approved them.

This business form actually falls somewhere between a corporation and a partnership or sole proprietorship in terms of protection by the law. Because LLCs are state entities, any legal protections offered to the owners of an LLC are dependent on the laws of the state where it's established. In most states, LLC owners get the same legal protection from lawsuits as the federal law provides to corporations, but unlike the federal laws, these protections haven't been tested fully in the state courts.

Reporting requirements for LLCs aren't as strict as they are for a corporation, but many partnerships do decide to have their books audited to satisfy all the partners that the financial information is being kept accurately and within internal control procedures determined by the partners.

Taking stock of taxes

LLCs let sole proprietorships and partnerships have their cake and eat it, too: They get the same legal protection from liability as a corporation but don't have to pay corporate taxes or file all the forms required of a corporation. In fact, the IRS treats LLCs as partnerships or sole proprietorships unless they ask to be taxed as corporations by using Form 8832, "Entity Classification Election."

Reviewing reporting requirements

The issues of business formation and business reporting are essentially the same for a partnership and a sole proprietorship, whether or not the entity files as an LLC. To shield themselves from liability, many large legal and accounting firms file as LLCs rather than take the more formal route of incorporating. When LLCs seek outside funding, either by selling shares of ownership or by seeking loans, the IRS requires their financial reporting to be more formal. Some partnerships form as LLPs, or Limited Liability Partnerships. In an LLP, one partner is *not* responsible for the other partner's actions. In some countries, an LLP must have at least one general partner with unlimited liability.

Shielding Your Assets: S and C Corporations

Company owners seeking the greatest level of protection may choose to incorporate their businesses. The courts have clearly determined that corporations are separate legal entities, and their owners are protected from claims filed against the corporation's activities. An owner (shareholder) in a corporation can't get sued or face collections because of actions the corporation takes.

The veil of protection makes a powerful case in favor of incorporating. However, the obligations that come with incorporating are tremendous, and a corporation needs significant resources to pay for the required legal and accounting services. Many businesses don't incorporate and choose instead to stay unincorporated or to organize as an LLC to avoid these additional costs.

TIP

Before incorporating, a business must first form a board of directors, even if that means including spouses and children on the board. (Imagine what those family board meetings are like!)

Boards can be made up of both corporation owners and nonowners. Any board member who isn't an owner can be paid for his service on the board.

Before incorporating, a company must also divvy up ownership in the form of stock. Most small businesses don't trade their stock on an open exchange. Instead, they sell it privately among friends and investors.

Corporations are separate tax entities, so they must file tax returns and pay taxes or find ways to avoid them by using deductions. Two types of corporate structures exist:

- **S corporations:** These corporations have fewer than 100 shareholders and function like partnerships but give owners additional legal protection.
- **C corporations:** These corporations are separate legal entities formed for the purpose of operating a business. They're actually treated in the courts as individual entities, just like people. Incorporation allows owners to limit their liability from the corporation's actions. Owners must split their ownership by using shares of stock, which is a requirement specified as part of corporate law. As an investor, you're most likely to be a shareholder in a C corporation.

Paying taxes the corporate way

If a company organizes as an S corporation, it can avoid corporate taxation but still keep its legal protection. S corporations are essentially treated as partnerships for tax purposes, with profits and losses passed through to the shareholders, who then report the income or loss on their personal tax returns.

The biggest disadvantage of the S corporation is the way profits and losses are distributed. Although a partnership has a lot of flexibility in divvying up profits and losses among the partners, S corporations must divide them based on the amount of stock each shareholder owns. This structure can be a big problem if one of the owners has primarily given cash and bought stock while another owner is primarily responsible for day-to-day business operations. Because the owner responsible for operations didn't purchase stock, he isn't eligible for the profits unless he receives stock ownership as part of his contract with the company.

TECHNICAL STUFF

Only relatively small businesses can avoid taxation as a corporation. After a corporation has more than 100 shareholders, it loses its status as an S corporation. In addition, only U.S. residents can hold S corporation stock. Nonresident aliens (that is, citizens of another country) and nonhuman entities (such as other corporations or partnerships) don't qualify as owners. However, some tax-exempt organizations — including pension plans, profit-sharing plans, and stock bonus plans — *can* be shareholders in an S corporation.

One big disadvantage of the C corporation is that its profits are taxed twice — once through the corporate entity and once as dividends paid to its owners. C corporation owners can get profits only through dividends, but they can pay themselves a salary.

REMEMBER

Unlike S corporations, partnerships, and sole proprietorships, which pass any profits and losses to their owners, who then report them on their personal income tax forms, C corporations must file their own tax forms and pay taxes on any profits.

PAYING THE HIGH PRICE OF INCORPORATION

C corporations must pay the following tax rates:

Taxable Income	C Corporation Tax Rate
$0–$50,000	15%
$50,001–$75,000	25%
$75,001–$100,000	34%
$100,001–$335,000	39%
$335,001–$10,000,000	34%
$10,000,001–$15,000,000	35%
$15,000,001–$18,333,333	38%
Over $18,333,333	35%

Although you may think that C corporation tax rates look higher than individual tax rates, in reality, many corporations avoid taxes completely by taking advantage of loopholes and deductions in the tax code. Most major corporations have an entire tax department whose sole responsibility is to find ways to avoid taxation.

Getting familiar with reporting requirements

A company must meet several requirements to keep its corporate veil of protection in place. For example, corporations must hold board meetings, and the minutes from those meetings detail the actions the company must take to prove it's operating as a corporation. The actions that must be shown in the minutes include:

- Establishment of banking associations and any changes to those arrangements
- Loans from either shareholders or third parties
- The sale or redemption of stock shares
- The payment of dividends
- Authorization of salaries or bonuses for officers and key executives (Yep, those multimillion-dollar bonuses you've been hearing about as major corporate scandals must be voted on in board meetings. The actual list of salaries doesn't have to be in the minutes but can be included as an attachment.)
- Any purchases, sales, or leases of corporate assets
- The purchase of another company
- Any merger with another company
- Changes to the Articles of Incorporation or bylaws
- Election of corporate officers and directors

REMEMBER

These corporate minutes are official records of the company, and the IRS, state taxing authorities, and courts can review them. If a company and its owners are sued and the company wants to invoke the veil of corporate protection, it must have these board minutes in place to prove that it operated as a corporation.

If a C corporation's ownership is kept among family and friends, it can be flexible about its reporting requirements. However, many C corporations have outside investors and creditors who require formal financial reporting that meets GAAP standards (for more on this topic, see Chapter 18). Also, most C corporations must have their financial reports audited. I talk more about the auditing process in Chapter 18.

- Looking at the private side of business
- Checking out the public world of corporations
- Seeing what happens when a company decides to go public

Chapter 3

Public or Private: How Company Structure Affects the Books

Not every company wants to be under public scrutiny. Although some firms operate in the public arena by selling shares to the general public on the open market, others prefer to keep ownership within a closed circle of friends or investors. When company owners contemplate whether to keep their business private or to take it public, they're making a decision that can permanently change the company's direction.

In this chapter, I explain the differences between public and private companies, the advantages and disadvantages of each, and how the decision about whether to go public or stay private impacts a company's financial reporting requirements. I also describe the process involved when company owners decide to take their business public.

Investigating Private Companies

Private companies don't sell stock to the general public, so they don't have to report to the government (except for filing their tax returns, of course) or answer to the public. No matter how big or small these companies are, they can operate behind closed doors.

A private company gives owners the freedom to make choices for the firm without having to worry about outside investors' opinions. Of course, to maintain that freedom, the company must be able to raise the funds necessary for the business to grow — through either profits, debt funding, or investments from family and friends.

REAL WORLD EXAMPLE

KEEPING IT IN THE FAMILY

Mars, one of the world's largest private companies, makes some of your favorite candies — 3 Musketeers, M&M's, and Snickers. Mars has never gone public, which means it has never sold its shares of stock to the general public. The company is still owned and operated by the family that founded it.

Frank and Ethel Mars, who made candy in the kitchen of their Tacoma, Washington, home, started Mars in 1911. Their first worldwide success was the Milky Way bar, which became known as the Mars bar in Europe in the 1920s.

Today Mars is a $30 billion business with operations in more than 56 countries and sales of its products in over 100 countries. Mars isn't just making candy anymore, either. It also manufactures Whiskas and Pedigree pet food, Uncle Ben's rice products, vending systems, electronics for automated payment systems, and information technology related to its manufacturing operations. The family is still in control of all these businesses and makes the decisions about which businesses to add to its portfolio.

One of Mars's five key principles that shape its business is "Freedom." The company's statement about the importance of freedom clearly describes why the family decided to stay private:

Mars is one of the world's largest privately owned corporations. This private ownership is a deliberate choice. Many other companies began as Mars did, but as they grew larger and required new sources of funds, they sold stocks or incurred restrictive debt to fuel their business. To extend their growth, they exchanged a portion of their freedom. We believe growth and prosperity can be achieved another way.

Checking out the benefits

Private companies maintain absolute control over business operations. With absolute control, owners don't have to worry about what the public thinks of its operations, nor do they have to worry about the quarterly race to meet the numbers to satisfy Wall Street's profit watch. The company's owners are the only ones who worry about profit levels and whether the company is meeting its goals, which they can do in the privacy of a boardroom. Further advantages of private ownership include

- **Confidentiality:** Private companies can keep their records under wraps, unlike public companies, which must file quarterly financial statements with the Securities and Exchange Commission (SEC) and various state agencies. Competitors can take advantage of the information that public companies disclose, whereas private companies can leave their competitors guessing and even hide a short-term problem.

  Owners of private companies also like the secrecy they can keep about their personal net worth. Although public companies must disclose the number of shares their officers, directors, and major shareholders hold, private companies have no obligation to release these ownership details.

- **Flexibility:** In private companies, family members can easily decide how much to pay one another, whether to allow private loans to one another, and whether to award lucrative fringe benefits or other financial incentives, all without having to worry about shareholder scrutiny. Public companies must answer to their shareholders for any bonuses or other incentives they give to top executives. Private-company owners can take out whatever money they want without worrying about the best interests of outside investors, such as shareholders. Any disagreements the owners have about how they disburse their assets remain behind closed doors.

- **Greater financial freedom:** Private companies can carefully select how to raise money for the business and with whom to make financial arrangements. After public companies offer their stock in the public markets, they have no control over who buys their shares and becomes a future owner.

  REMEMBER

  If a private company receives funding from experienced investors, it doesn't face the same scrutiny that a public company does. Publicly disclosed financial statements are required only when stock is sold to the general public, not when shares are traded privately among a small group of investors.

Defining disadvantages

The biggest disadvantage a private company faces is its limited ability to raise large sums of cash. Because a private company doesn't sell stock or offer bonds to the general public, it spends a lot more time than a public company does finding investors or creditors who are willing to risk their funds. And many investors don't want to invest in a company that's controlled by a small group of people and that lacks the oversight of public scrutiny.

If a private company needs cash, it must perform one or more of the following tasks:

- Arrange for a loan with a financial institution
- Sell additional shares of stock to existing owners
- Ask for help from an *angel,* a private investor willing to help a small business get started with some upfront cash
- Get funds from a *venture capitalist,* someone who invests in start-up businesses, providing the necessary cash in exchange for some portion of ownership

These options for raising money may present a problem for a private company because

- A company's borrowing capability is limited and based on how much capital the owners have invested in the company. A financial institution requires that a certain portion of the capital needed to operate the business — sometimes as much as 50 percent — come from the owners. Just as when you want to borrow money to buy a home, the bank requires you to put up some cash before it loans you the rest. The same is true for companies that want a business loan. I talk more about this topic and how to calculate debt-to-equity ratios in Chapter 12.
- Persuading outside investors to put up a significant amount of cash if the owners want to maintain control of the business is no easy feat. Often major outside investors seek a greater role in company operations by acquiring a significant share of the ownership and asking for several seats on the board of directors.
- Finding the right investment partner can be difficult. When private-company owners seek outside investors, they must ensure that the potential investors have the same vision and goals for the business that they do.

REMEMBER

Another major disadvantage that a private company faces is that the owners' net worth is likely tied almost completely to the value of the company. If a business fails, the owners may lose everything and may even be left with a huge debt. If owners take their company public, however, they can sell some of their stock and diversify their portfolios, thereby reducing their portfolios' risk.

Figuring out reporting

Reporting requirements for a private company vary based on its agreements with stakeholders. Outside investors in a private company usually establish reporting requirements as part of the agreement to invest funds in the business. A private company circulates its reports among its closed group of stakeholders — executives, managers, creditors, and investors — and doesn't have to share them with the public.

A private company must file financial reports with the SEC when it has more than 500 common shareholders and $10 million in assets, as set by the Securities and Exchange Act of 1934. Congress passed this act so that private companies that reach the size of public companies and acquire a certain mass of outside ownership have the same reporting obligations as public companies. (See the nearby sidebar "Private or Publix?" for an example of this type of company.)

TECHNICAL STUFF

When a private company's stock ownership and assets exceed the limits set by the Securities and Exchange Act of 1934, the company must file a Form 10, which includes a description of the business and its officers, similar to an initial public offering (also known as an IPO, which is the first public sale of a company's stock). After the company files Form 10, the SEC requires it to file quarterly and annual reports.

REAL WORLD EXAMPLE

PRIVATE OR PUBLIX?

Publix Super Markets is a private company owned by more than 101,000 shareholders. You can think of it as a semipublic company. However, until Publix actually decides to sell stock on a public exchange — if it ever does — it's classified as a private company. Publix makes its stock available during designated public offerings that are open only to its employees and nonemployee members of its board of directors. It also offers employees a stock ownership plan, which has more than 139,000 participants. So even though Publix stock isn't sold on a stock exchange, Publix must file public financial reports with the SEC.

In some cases, private companies buy back stock from their current shareholders to keep the number of individuals who own stock under the 500 limit. But generally, when a company deals with the financial expenses of publicly reporting its earnings and can no longer keep its veil of secrecy, the pressure builds to go public and gain greater access to the funds needed to grow even larger.

Understanding Public Companies

A company that offers shares of stock on the open market is a *public company.* Public company owners don't make decisions based solely on their preferences — they must always consider the opinions of the business's outside investors.

Before a company goes public, it must meet certain criteria. Generally, investment bankers (who are actually responsible for selling the stock) require that a private company generate at least $10 million to $20 million in annual sales, with profits of about $1 million.

(Exceptions to this rule exist, however, and some smaller companies do go public.) Before going public, company owners must ask themselves the following questions:

- Can my firm maintain a high growth rate to attract investors?
- Does enough public awareness of my company and its products or services exist to make a successful public offering?
- Is my business operating in a hot industry that will help attract investors?
- Can my company perform as well as, and preferably better than, its competition?
- Can my firm afford the ongoing cost of financial auditing requirements (which can be as high as $2 million a year for a small company)?

If company owners are confident in their answers to these questions, they may want to take their business public. But they need to keep in mind the advantages and disadvantages of going public, which is a long, expensive process that takes months and sometimes even years.

REMEMBER

Companies don't take themselves public alone — they hire investment bankers to steer the process to completion. Investment bankers usually get multimillion-dollar fees or commissions for taking a company public. I talk more about the process in the upcoming section "Entering a Whole New World: How a Company Goes from Private to Public."

Examining the perks

If a company goes public, its primary benefit is that it gains access to additional capital (more cash), which can be critical if it's a high-growth business that needs money to take advantage of its growth potential. A secondary benefit is that company owners can become millionaires, or even billionaires, overnight if the initial public offering (IPO) is successful.

Being a public company has a number of other benefits:

- **New corporate cash:** At some point, a growing company usually maxes out its ability to borrow funds, and it must find people willing to invest in the business. Selling stock to the general public can be a great way for a company to raise cash without being obligated to pay interest on the money.
- **Owner diversification:** People who start a new business typically put a good chunk of their assets into starting the business and then reinvest most of the profits in the business in order to grow the company. Frequently, founders have a large share of their assets tied up in the company. Selling shares publicly allows owners to take out some of their investment and diversify their holdings in other investments, which reduces the risks to their personal portfolios.

REAL WORLD EXAMPLE

GOING PUBLIC, LOSING JOBS

Public company founders who don't keep their investors happy can find themselves out on the street and no longer involved in the company they started. Steve Jobs and Steve Wozniak, who started Apple Computer, found out the hard way that selling stock on the public market can ultimately take the company away from the founders.

Jobs and Wozniak became multimillionaires after Apple Computer went public, but shareholders ousted them from their leadership roles in a management shake-up in 1984. Wozniak decided to leave Apple soon after the shake-up. Apple's new CEO announced that he couldn't find a role for Jobs in the company's operations in 1985.

Interestingly, Jobs ended up as the head of Apple again in 1998, when the shareholders turned to him to rescue the company from failure. He engineered a comeback for Apple before his death in 2011.

- **Increased liquidity:** *Liquidity* is a company's ability to quickly turn an asset into cash (if it isn't already cash). People who own shares in a closely held private company may have a lot of assets but little chance to actually turn those assets into cash. Selling privately owned shares of stock is very difficult. Going public gives the stock a set market value and creates more potential buyers for the stock.
- **Company value:** Company owners benefit by knowing their firm's worth for a number of reasons. If one of the key owners dies, state and federal inheritance tax appraisers must set the company's value for estate tax purposes. Many times, these values are set too high for private companies, which can cause all kinds of problems for other owners and family members. Going public sets an absolute value for the shares held by all company shareholders and prevents problems with valuation. Also, businesses that want to offer shares of stock to their employees as incentives find that recruiting with this incentive is much easier when the stock is sold on the open market.

Looking at the negative side

Regardless of the many advantages of being a public company, a great many disadvantages also exist:

- **Costs:** Paying the costs of providing audited financial statements that meet the requirements of the SEC or state agencies can be very expensive — sometimes as high as $2 million annually. (I discuss the audit process in greater detail in Chapter 18.) Investor relations can also add significant costs in employee time, printing, and mailing expenses.
- **Control:** As stock sells on the open market, more shareholders enter the picture, giving each one the right to vote on key company decisions. The original owners and closed circle of investors no longer have absolute control of the company.
- **Disclosure:** A private company can hide difficulties it may be having, but a public company must report its problems, exposing any weaknesses to competitors, who can access detailed information about the company's operations by getting copies of the required financial reports. In addition, the net worth of a public company's owners is widely known because they must disclose their stock holdings as part of these reports.
- **Cash control:** In a private company, owners can decide their own salary and benefits, as well as the salary and benefits of any family member or friend involved in running the business. In a public company, the board of directors

must approve and report any major cash withdrawals, whether for salary or loans, to shareholders.

- **Lack of liquidity:** When a company goes public, a constant flow of buyers for the stock isn't guaranteed. For a stock to be liquid, a shareholder must be able to convert that stock to cash. Small companies that don't have wide distribution of their stock can be hard to sell on the open market. The market price may even be lower than the actual value of the firm's assets because of a lack of competition for shares of the stock. When not enough competition exists, shareholders have a hard time selling the stock and converting it to cash, making the investment nonliquid.

WARNING

A failed IPO or a failure to live up to shareholders' expectations can change what may have been a good business for the founders into a bankrupt entity. Although founders may be willing to ride out the losses for a while, shareholders rarely are. Many IPOs that raised millions before the Internet stock crash in 2000 are now defunct companies.

Filing and more filing: Government and shareholder reports

Public companies must file an unending stream of reports with the SEC. They must file financial reports quarterly as well as annually. They also must file reports after specific events, such as bankruptcy or the sale of a company division.

Quarterly reports

Each quarter, public companies must file audited financial statements on Form 10Q, in addition to information about the company's market risk, controls and procedures, legal proceedings, and defaults on payments.

Yearly report

Each year, public companies must file an annual report with audited financial statements and information about

- **Company history:** How the company was started, who started it, and how it grew to its current level of operations
- **Organizational structure:** How the company is organized, who the key executives are, and who reports to whom

» **Equity holdings:** A list of the major shareholders and a summary of all outstanding stock

» **Subsidiaries:** Other businesses that the company owns wholly or partially

» **Employee stock purchase and savings plans:** Plans that allow employees to own stock by purchasing it or participating in a savings plan

» **Incorporation:** Information about where the company is incorporated

» **Legal proceedings:** Information about any ongoing legal matters that may be material to the company

» **Changes or disagreements with accountants:** Information about financial disclosures, controls and procedures, executive compensation, and accounting fees and services

REMEMBER

In addition to the regular reports, public companies must file an 8-K, a form for reporting any major events that can impact the company's financial position. A major event may be the acquisition of another company, the sale of a company or division, bankruptcy, the resignation of directors, or a change in the fiscal year. A public company must report any event that falls under this requirement on the 8-K to the SEC within four days of the event's occurrence. I discuss the rules for SEC Form 8-K in greater detail in Chapter 19.

The rules of the Sarbanes-Oxley Act

All the scandals about public companies that emerged in the early 2000s have made this entire reporting process riskier and more costly for company owners. In 2002, Congress passed a bill called the Sarbanes-Oxley Act to try to correct some of the problems in financial reporting. This bill passed as details emerged about how corporate officials from companies like Enron, MCI, and Tyco hid information from the SEC.

New SEC rules issued after the Sarbanes-Oxley Act passed require CEOs and CFOs to certify financial and other information contained in their quarterly and annual reports. They must certify that

» They've established, maintained, and regularly evaluated effective disclosure controls and procedures.

» They've made disclosures to the auditors and audit committee of the board of directors about internal controls.

» They've included information in the quarterly and annual reports about their evaluation of the controls in place, as well as about any significant changes in their internal controls or any other factors that could significantly affect controls after the initial evaluation.

WARNING

If a CEO or CFO certifies this information and that information later proves to be false, he or she can end up facing criminal charges. Since the passage of the Sarbanes-Oxley Act, companies have delayed releasing financial reports if the CEO or CFO has any questions rather than risk charges. You'll probably hear more about delays in reporting as CEOs and CFOs become more reluctant to sign off on financial reports that may have questionable information. Shareholders often panic when they hear about a delay, and stock prices drop.

The Sarbanes-Oxley Act has added significant costs to the entire process of completing financial reports, affecting the following components:

» **Documentation:** Companies must document and develop policies and procedures relating to their internal controls over financial reporting. Although an outside accounting firm can assist with the documentation process, managers must be actively involved in the process of assessing internal controls — they can't delegate this responsibility to an external firm.

» **Audit fees:** Independent audit firms now look a lot more closely at financial statements and internal controls in place over financial reporting, and the SEC's Public Company Accounting Oversight Board (PCAOB) now regulates the accounting profession. The PCAOB inspects accounting firms to be sure they're in compliance with the Sarbanes-Oxley Act and SEC rules.

» **Legal fees:** Because companies need lawyers to help them comply with the new provisions of the Sarbanes-Oxley Act, their legal expenses are increasing.

» **Information technology:** Complying with the Sarbanes-Oxley Act requires both hardware and software upgrades to meet the internal control requirements and the speedier reporting requirements.

» **Boards of directors:** Most companies must restructure their board of directors and audit committees to meet the Sarbanes-Oxley Act's requirements, ensuring that independent board members control key audit decisions. The structure and operation of nominating and compensation committees must eliminate even the appearance of conflicts of interest. Companies must make provisions to give shareholders direct input in corporate governance decisions. Businesses also must provide additional education to board members to be sure they understand their responsibilities to shareholders.

BEARING THE BURDEN AND EXPENSE OF SARBANES-OXLEY

Many major corporations already had the internal controls in place and produced the documentation that the Sarbanes-Oxley Act required. Smaller companies were hit harder with these new requirements. The SEC's only concession for smaller companies was *when* they must be in compliance with the new rules on internal controls: All small businesses had to be in compliance by November 2004.

The rules imposed by Sarbanes-Oxley were such a significant burden on small companies that some of them decided to buy out shareholders and make the companies private again, or merge with larger companies, or even liquidate.

When a private company thinks about going public, it must consider whether the process is worth the costs. With the new Sarbanes-Oxley rules in place, a small company pays close to $3 million in legal, accounting, and other costs of being public. Before Sarbanes-Oxley, these costs totaled closer to $2 million. Large corporations budget more than $7 million to cover the costs of being a public company nowadays.

Entering a Whole New World: How a Company Goes from Private to Public

So the owners of a company have finally decided to sell the company's stock publicly. Now what? In this section, I describe the role of an investment banker in helping a company sell its stock. I also explain the process of making a public offering.

Teaming up with an investment banker

The first step after a company decides to go public is to choose who will handle the sales and which market to sell the stock on. Few firms have the capacity to approach the public stock markets on their own. Instead, they hire an investment banker to help them through the complicated process of going public. A well-known investment banker can lend credibility to a little-known small company, which makes selling the stock easier.

Investment bankers help a company in the following ways:

- **They prepare the required SEC documents and register the new stock offering with the SEC.** These documents must include information about the company (its products, services, and markets) and its officers and directors. Additionally, they must include information about the risks the firm faces, how the business plans to use the money raised, any outstanding legal problems, holdings of company insiders, and, of course, audited financial statements.
- **They price the stock so it's attractive to potential investors.** If the stock is priced too high, the offering could fall flat on its face, with few shares sold. If the stock is priced too low, the company could miss out on potential cash that investors, who buy IPO shares, can get as a windfall from quickly turning around and selling the stock at a profit.
- **They negotiate the price at which the stock is offered to the general public and the guarantees they give to the company owners for selling the stock.** An investment banker can give an *underwriting guarantee,* which guarantees the amount of money that will be raised. In this scenario, the banker buys the stock from the company and then resells it to the public. Usually, an investment banker puts together a syndicate of investment bankers who help find buyers for the stock.

  Another method that's sometimes used is called a *best efforts agreement.* In this scenario, the investment banker tries to sell the stock but doesn't guarantee the number of shares that will sell.
- **They decide which stock exchange to list the stock on.** The New York Stock Exchange (NYSE) has the highest level of requirements. If a company wants to list on this exchange, it must have a pretax income of at least $10 million over the last three years and 2,200 or more shareholders. The NASDAQ has lower requirements. Companies can also sell stock over the counter, which means the stock isn't listed on any exchange, so selling the stock both as an IPO and after the IPO is much harder.

Making a public offering

After the company and the investment banker agree to work together and set the terms for the public offering, as well as the commission structure (how the investment banker gets paid), the banker prepares the registration statement to be filed with the SEC.

After the registration is filed, the SEC imposes a "cooling-off period" to give itself time to investigate the offering and to make sure the documents disclose all necessary information. The length of the cooling-off period depends on how complete the documents are and whether the SEC asks for additional information. During the cooling-off period, the underwriter produces the *red herring,* which is an initial prospectus that includes the information in the SEC registration without the stock price or effective date.

After the underwriter completes the red herring, the company and the investment bankers do *road shows* — presentations held around the country to introduce the business to major institutional investors and start building interest in the pending IPO. A company can't transact sales until the SEC approves the registration information, but it can start generating excitement and getting feedback about the IPO at these meetings.

When the SEC finishes its investigation and approves the offering, the company can set an *effective date*, or the date of the stock offering. The company and investment bankers then sit down and establish a final stock price. Although they discuss the stock price in initial conversations, they can't set the final price until they know the actual effective date. Market conditions can change significantly from the time the company first talks with investment bankers and the date when the stock is finally offered publicly. Sometimes the company and investment banker decide to withdraw or delay an IPO if a market crisis creates a bad climate for introducing a new stock or if the road shows don't identify enough interested major investors.

After the stock price is set, the stock is sold to the public. The company gets the proceeds minus any commissions it pays to the investment bankers.

» Understanding the two main accounting methods

» Deciphering debits and credits

» Examining the Chart of Accounts

» Looking at the different types of profit

Chapter 4
Digging into Accounting Basics

Ah, the language of financial accounting — debits, credits, double-entry accounting! Just reading the words makes your heart beat faster, doesn't it? The language and practices of accountants can get the best of anyone, but there's a method to the madness. Figuring out that method is a crucial first step to understanding financial reports.

In this chapter, I help you understand the logic behind the baffling and unique world of financial accounting. And you don't even need a pocket protector!

Making Sense of Accounting Methods

Officially, two types of accounting methods dictate how a company records its transactions in its financial books: cash-basis accounting and accrual accounting. The key difference between the two types is how the company records cash coming into and going out of the business.

Within that simple difference lies a lot of room for error — or manipulation. In fact, many of the major corporations involved in financial scandals have gotten into trouble because they played games with the nuts and bolts of their accounting method. I talk more about those games in Chapter 23.

Cash-basis accounting

In *cash-basis accounting,* companies record expenses in financial accounts when the cash is actually laid out, and they book revenue when they actually hold the cash in their hot little hands — or, more likely, in a bank account. For example, if a painter completes a project on December 30, 2012, but doesn't get paid for it until the owner inspects it on January 10, 2013, the painter reports those cash earnings on his 2013 tax report. In cash-basis accounting, cash earnings include checks, credit card receipts, and any other form of revenue from customers.

REMEMBER

Smaller companies that haven't formally incorporated and most sole proprietors use cash-basis accounting because the system is easier for them to use on their own, meaning that they don't have to hire a large accounting staff.

Accrual accounting

If a company uses *accrual accounting,* it records revenue when the actual transaction is completed (such as the completion of work specified in a contract agreement between the company and its customer), not when it receives the cash. In other words, the company records revenue when it earns it, even if the customer hasn't paid yet. So the painter who finishes a job in 2012 but doesn't get the cash for that job until 2013 still reports the income on his 2012 taxes. He enters the income into the books when the job is completed.

Companies handle expenses in the same way. A company records any expenses when they're incurred, even if it hasn't yet paid for the supplies. For example, when a carpenter buys lumber for a job, he may likely do so on account and not actually lay out the cash for the lumber until a month or so later, when he gets the bill.

REMEMBER

All incorporated companies must use accrual accounting according to the *generally accepted accounting principles* (GAAP) because revenues are matched to expenses in the same month they occur. If you're reading a corporation's financial reports, what you see is based on accrual accounting.

Why method matters

The accounting method a business uses can have a major impact on the total revenue it reports, as well as on the expenses it subtracts from the revenue to get the bottom line. Here's how:

» **Cash-basis accounting:** Expenses and revenues aren't carefully matched on a month-to-month basis. The company doesn't recognize expenses until it actually pays the money, even if it incurs the expenses in previous months.

Likewise, the business doesn't recognize the revenues it earned in previous months until it actually receives the cash. However, cash-basis accounting excels in tracking the actual cash available, as well as the cash going in and out of the business.

- **Accrual accounting:** Expenses and revenue are matched, giving a company a better idea of how much it's spending to operate each month and how much profit it's making. The company records (or accrues) expenses in the month incurred, even if it doesn't pay out the cash until the next month. Likewise, the company records revenues in the month it completes the project or ships the product, even if the company hasn't yet received the cash from the customer.

The way a company records payment of payroll taxes, for example, differs with these two methods. In accrual accounting, each month the company sets aside the amount it expects to pay toward its quarterly tax bills for employee taxes using an *accrual* (a paper transaction in which no money changes hands). The entry goes into a *tax liability account* (an account for tracking tax payments that the company has made or must still make). If the company incurs $1,000 of tax liabilities in March, it enters that amount in the tax liability account even if it hasn't yet paid out the cash. That way, the expense is matched to the month in which it's incurred.

In cash accounting, the company doesn't record the liability until it actually pays the government the cash. Although it incurs tax expenses each month, a company using cash accounting shows a higher profit during two months every quarter, and possibly even shows a loss in the third month when the taxes are paid.

To see how these two methods can result in totally different financial statements, imagine that a carpenter contracts a job with a total cost to the customer of $2,000. The carpenter's expected expenses for the supplies, labor, and other necessities are $1,200, so his expected profit is $800. He contracts the work on December 23, 2012, and completes the job on December 31, 2012, but he isn't paid until January 3, 2013. The contractor takes no cash up front and instead agrees to be paid in full upon completion.

If he uses the cash-basis accounting method, then because no cash changes hands, he doesn't have to report any revenues from this transaction in 2012. But say he lays out the cash for his expenses in 2012. In this case, his bottom line is $1,200 less, with no revenue to offset it, and his net profit (the amount of money his company earns, minus expenses) for the business in 2012 is lower. This scenario may not necessarily be bad if he's trying to reduce his tax hit for 2012.

TIP

If you're a small business owner looking to manage your tax bill and you use cash-basis accounting, you can ask vendors to hold payments until the beginning of the next year, to reduce your net income and thereby lower your tax payments for the year.

INCENTIVES AND THE BOTTOM LINE

To improve the bottom line, many companies offer their salespeople different kinds of incentives at the end of a month, quarter, or year. The more the salespeople sell, the more income the company records, allowing it to report stronger earnings for that period.

You've probably seen this concept in action if you've ever made a major purchase, such as a car, at the end of the month. You probably found that you could be much more aggressive with your negotiations if the salesperson hadn't met quota or was competing to win a sales contest.

If a company gets really aggressive with its end-of-period revenue-booking practices, it can inflate its actual earnings, especially if salespeople allow customers to sign orders with the promise that they can cancel their orders early in the next month or accounting period. Some companies have gotten into trouble by recording sales on products that weren't yet shipped in order to make a quarterly or monthly goal.

If the same carpenter uses accrual accounting, his bottom line is different. In this case, he books his expenses when they're actually incurred. He also records the income when he completes the job on December 31, 2012, even though he doesn't get the cash payment until 2013. He increases his net income with this job — and also his tax hit. Chapter 7 covers the ins and outs of reporting income on the income statement.

Understanding Debits and Credits

You probably think of the word *debit* as a reduction in your cash. Most nonaccountants see debits only when they're taken out of their banking account. Credits likely have a more positive connotation in your mind. You see them most frequently when you've returned an item and your account is credited.

WARNING

Forget everything you *think* you know about debits and credits! You're going to have to erase these assumptions from your mind to understand *double-entry accounting*, which is the basis of most accounting done in the business world.

Both cash-basis and accrual accounting use this method, in which a credit may be added to or subtracted from an account, depending on the type of account. The same is true with debits; sometimes they add to an account, and sometimes they subtract from an account.

Double-entry accounting

When you buy something, you do two things: You get something new (say, a chair) and you have to give up something to get it (most likely, cash or your credit line). Companies that use double-entry accounting show both sides of every transaction in their books, and those sides must be equal.

REMEMBER

Probably at least 95 percent of businesses in the U.S. use double-entry accounting, whether they use the cash-basis or accrual accounting method. It's the only way a business can be certain that it has considered both sides of every transaction.

For example, if a company buys office supplies with cash, the value of the office supplies account increases, while the value of the cash account decreases. If the company purchases $100 in office supplies, here's how it records the transaction on its books:

Account	Debit	Credit
Office supplies	$100	
Cash		$100

In this case, the debit increases the value of the *Office supplies* account and decreases the value of the *Cash* account. Both accounts are *asset accounts,* which means both accounts represent things the company owns that are shown on the balance sheet. (The *balance sheet* is the financial statement that gives you a snapshot of the assets, liabilities, and shareholders' equity as of a particular date. I cover balance sheets in greater detail in Chapter 6.)

The assets are balanced or offset by the *liabilities* (claims made against the company's assets by creditors, such as loans) and the *equity* (claims made against the company's assets, such as shares of stock held by shareholders). Double-entry accounting seeks to balance these assets and claims. In fact, the balance sheet of a company is developed using this formula:

Assets = Liabilities + Owner's equity

Profit and loss statements

In addition to establishing accounts to develop the balance sheet and make entries in the double-entry accounting system, companies must set up accounts that they use to develop the *income statement* (also known as the *profit and loss statement,* or *P&L*), which shows a company's revenue and expenses over a set period of time. (See Chapter 7 for more on revenue and expenses.) The double-entry accounting method impacts not only the way assets and liabilities (balance sheet accounts) are entered, but also the way revenue and expenses (income statement accounts) are entered.

The effect of debits and credits on sales

If you're a sales manager tracking how your department is doing for the year, you want to be able to decipher debits and credits. If you think you've found an error, your ability to read reports and understand the impact of debits and credits is critical. For example, anytime you think the income statement doesn't accurately reflect your department's success, you have to dig into the debits and credits to be sure your sales are being booked correctly. You also need to be aware of the other accounts — especially revenue and expense accounts — that are used to book transactions that impact your department.

A common entry that impacts both the balance sheet and the income statement is one that keeps track of the amount of cash customers pay to buy the company's product. If the customers pay $100, here's how the entry looks:

Account	Debit	Credit
Cash	$100	
Sales revenue		$100

In this case, both the *Cash* account and the *Sales revenue* account increase. One increases using a debit, and the other increases using a credit. Yikes — I know, accounting can be so confusing! Whether an account increases or decreases from a debit or a credit depends on the type of account it is. See Table 4-1 to find out when debits and credits increase or decrease an account.

TIP

Make a copy of Table 4-1, and tack it up where you review your department's accounts until you become familiar with the differences.

TABLE 4-1 **Effect of Debits and Credits**

Account	Debits	Credits
Assets	Increases	Decreases
Liabilities	Decreases	Increases
Income	Decreases	Increases
Expenses	Increases	Decreases

Depreciation and amortization

REMEMBER

Depreciation and amortization are accounting methods you use to track the use of an asset and record its value as it ages. Tangible assets (assets you can touch or hold in your hand, like cars or inventory) are *depreciated* (reduced in value by a certain percentage each year to show that the company is using up the tangible asset). Intangible assets (like intellectual property or patents) are *amortized* (reduced in value by a certain percentage each year to show that the company is using up the intangible asset).

For example, each vehicle a company owns loses value throughout the normal course of business every year. Cars and trucks are usually estimated to have five years of useful life, which means the number of years the vehicle will be of use to the company.

Suppose a company pays $30,000 for a car. To calculate its depreciation on a five-year schedule, divide $30,000 by 5 to get $6,000 in depreciation. Each of the five years this car is in service, the company records a depreciation expense of $6,000.

When the company makes the initial purchase of the vehicle using a loan, it records the purchase this way:

Account	Debit	Credit
2008 ABC company car	$30,000	
Loans payable — Vehicles		$30,000

In this transaction, both the debit and the credit increase the accounts affected. The debit recording the car purchase increases the total of the assets in the vehicle account, and the credit recording the new loan also increases the total of the loans payable for cars.

The company records its depreciation expenses for the car at the end of each year this way:

Account	Debit	Credit
Depreciation expense	$6,000	
Accumulated depreciation — Vehicles		$6,000

In this case, the debit increases the expense for depreciation. The credit increases the amount accumulated for depreciation. The line item *Accumulated depreciation — Vehicles* is listed directly below the asset *Vehicles* on the balance sheet and is shown as a negative number to be subtracted from the value of the *Vehicles* assets. This way of presenting the information on the balance sheet helps the financial report reader quickly see how old an asset is and how much value and useful life it has. Some financial reports only show the net value of an asset with deprecation already subtracted. In those cases the financial report reader may need to find the detail in the Notes to the Financial Statement.

A similar process, *amortization*, is used for intangible assets, such as patents. Just as with depreciation, a company must write down the value of a patent as it nears expiration. Amortization expenses appear on the income statement, and the balance sheet shows the value of the asset. The line item *Patent* is shown first on the balance sheet, with another line item called *Accumulated amortization* below it. The *Accumulated amortization* line shows how much has been written down against the asset in the current year and any past years. The financial report reader thus has a way to quickly calculate how much value is left in a company's patents.

Checking Out the Chart of Accounts

A company groups the accounts it uses to develop the financial statements in the *Chart of Accounts*, which is a listing of all open accounts that the accounting department can use to record transactions, according to the role of the accounts in the statements. All businesses have a Chart of Accounts, even if it's so small that they don't even realize they do and have never formally gone about designing it.

The Chart of Accounts for a business sort of builds itself as the company buys and sells assets for its use and records revenue earned and expenses incurred in its day-to-day operations.

THE GRANDDADDY OF BOOKKEEPING

Every transaction a company makes during the year eventually finds its way into the general ledger. Although companies often use the *general ledger* just for a summary of what happens in each of their accounts, some companies include details about specific transactions in their subledgers. For example, accounts receivable is likely summarized in the general ledger by just using the end-of-month totals for outstanding customer accounts. The actual detail of the transactions that take place during the month involving accounts receivable are in an accounts receivable subledger. In addition, accounting records show details for each customer, including what the customers bought and how much they still owe.

If you work for a company and have responsibility for its transactions, you'll have a copy of the Chart of Accounts so that you know which account you want to use for each transaction. If you're a financial report reader with no internal company responsibilities, you won't get to see this Chart of Accounts — but you still need to understand what goes into these different accounts to understand what you're seeing in the financial statements.

Each account in a Chart of Accounts is assigned a number. This clearly defined structure helps accountants move from job to job and still quickly get a handle on the Chart of Accounts. Also, because most companies use computerized accounting, the software is developed with these numerical definitions. Some companies make up an alphabetical listing of their Chart of Accounts with numbers in parentheses to make finding accounts easier for managers who are unfamiliar with the structure.

The accounts in the Chart of Accounts appear in the following order:

- Balance sheet asset accounts (usually in the number range of 1,000 to 1,999)
- Liability accounts (with numbers ranging from 2,000 to 2,999)
- Equity accounts (3,000 to 3,999)
- Income statement accounts/revenue accounts (4,000 to 4,999)
- Expense accounts (5,000 to 6,999)

In the old days, these accounts were recorded on paper, and finding a specific transaction on the dozens or even hundreds of pages was a nightmare. Today, because most companies use computerized accounting, you can easily design a report to find most types of transactions electronically by grouping them according to account type, customer, salesperson, product, or almost any other configuration that helps you decipher the entries.

To help you become familiar with the types of accounts in the Chart of Accounts and the types of transactions in those accounts, I review the most common accounts in this section in the order in which you're most likely to read them in a financial report. I assign the accounts numbers that computer programs most commonly generate, but you may find that your company uses a different numbering system.

Asset accounts

Asset accounts come first in the Chart of Accounts, with the most current accounts (ones that the company will use in less than 12 months) listed before the long-term accounts (ones that the company will use in more than 12 months).

Tangible assets

Assets that you can hold in your hand are *tangible assets*, and they include current assets and long-term assets. *Current assets* are assets that the company will use up in the next 12 months. The following are examples of current-asset accounts:

- **Cash in checking:** This account is always the first one listed. Businesses use this account most often. They deposit their cash received as revenue and their cash paid out to cover bills and debt.
- **Cash in savings:** This account is where firms keep cash they don't need for daily operations. It usually earns interest until the company decides how it wants to use this surplus cash.
- **Cash on hand:** This account tracks the actual cash the company keeps at its business locations. Cash on hand includes money in the cash registers, as well as petty cash. Most companies have several different cash-on-hand accounts. For example, a store may have its own account for tracking cash in the registers, and each department may have its own petty cash account. How these accounts are structured depends on the company and the security controls it has in place to manage the cash on hand. Companies always leave plenty of room for additions in this account category.
- **Accounts receivable:** In this account, businesses record transactions in which customers bought products on store or company credit. Only companies that use the accrual method of accounting need this account.
- **Inventory:** This account tracks the cost of products the company has available for sale, whether it purchases the products from other companies or produces them in-house. Businesses adjust this account periodically throughout the year to reflect the changes in inventory affected by sales or other factors, such as breakage or theft. Although some firms use a computerized inventory system that adjusts the account almost instantaneously, others adjust the account only at the end of an accounting period.

Long-term assets are assets that a company will hold for more than 12 months. The following are common long-term asset accounts:

- **Land:** This account records any purchases of land as a company asset. Companies list land separately because it doesn't depreciate in value like the building or buildings sitting on it do.
- **Buildings:** This account lists the value of any buildings the company owns. This value is always a positive number.
- **Accumulated depreciation:** This account tracks the depreciation of company-owned buildings. Each year, the firm deducts a portion of the building's value

based on the building's costs and the number of years the building will have a productive life.

- **Leasehold improvements:** This account tracks improvements to buildings that the company leases rather than buys. In most cases, when a company leases retail or warehouse space, it must pay the costs of improving the property for its unique business use. These improvements are also depreciated, so the company uses a companion depreciation account called *Accumulated depreciation — Leasehold improvements.*
- **Vehicles:** This account tracks the cars, trucks, and other vehicles that a business owns. The initial value added to this account is the value of the vehicles when put into service. Vehicles are also depreciated, and the depreciation account is *Accumulated depreciation — Vehicles.*
- **Furniture and Fixtures:** This account tracks all the desks, chairs, and other fixtures a company buys for its offices, warehouses, and retail stores. Yes, these items, too, are depreciated, and the depreciation account is named *Accumulated depreciation — Furniture and fixtures.*
- **Equipment:** This account tracks any equipment a company purchases that's expected to have a useful life of more than one year. This equipment includes computers, copiers, cash registers, and any other equipment needs. The depreciation account is *Accumulated depreciation — Equipment.*

Intangible assets

Companies also hold intangible assets, which have value but are often difficult to measure. The following are the most common intangible assets in the Chart of Accounts:

- **Goodwill:** A company needs this account only when it has bought another company. Frequently, a business that purchases another business pays more than the actual value of its assets minus its liabilities. The premium paid, which may account for factors such as customer loyalty, an exceptional workforce, and a great location, is listed on the books as goodwill.
- **Intellectual property:** This category includes copyrights, patents, and written work or products for which the company has been granted exclusive rights. For example, the government grants patents to a company or individual that invents a new product or process. These assets are amortized, which is similar to depreciation, because intellectual property has a limited lifespan. The amortization account is *Accumulated amortization — Intellectual property.*

  REMEMBER

  Having exclusive rights to a product allows a company to hold off competition, which can mean a lot of extra profits. Patented products can often command a much higher price than products that aren't patented.

Liability accounts

Money a company owes to creditors, vendors, suppliers, contractors, employees, government entities, and anyone else who provides products or services to the company is called a *liability*.

Current liabilities

Current liabilities include money owed in the next 12 months. The following accounts record current liability transactions:

- **Accounts payable:** This account includes all the payments to suppliers, vendors, contractors, and consultants that are due in less than one year. Most of the payments made on these accounts are for invoices due in less than two months.
- **Sales tax collected:** This account tracks taxes collected for the state, local, or federal government on merchandise the company has sold. Firms record daily transactions in this account as they collect cash and make payments (usually monthly) to government agencies.
- **Accrued payroll taxes:** This account includes any taxes that the company must pay to the state or federal government, based on taxes withheld from employees' checks. These payments are usually made monthly or quarterly.
- **Credit card payable:** This account tracks the payments to corporate credit cards. Some companies use these accounts as management tools for tracking employee activities and set them up by employee name, department name, or whatever method the company finds useful for monitoring credit card use.

Long-term liabilities

Long-term liabilities include money due beyond the next 12 months. Companies use the following accounts to record long-term liability transactions:

- **Loans payable:** This account tracks debts, such as mortgages or loans on vehicles, that are incurred for longer than one year.
- **Bonds payable:** This account tracks corporate bonds that have been issued for a term longer than one year. Bonds are a type of debt sold on the market that must be repaid in full with interest.

Equity accounts

Equity accounts reflect the portion of the assets that isn't subject to liabilities and is therefore owned by a company's shareholders. If the company isn't incorporated, the ownership of the partners or sole proprietors is represented in this part of the balance sheet in an account called *Owner's equity* or *Shareholders' equity.* The following is a list of the most common equity accounts:

- **Common stock:** This account reflects the value of the outstanding shares of common stock. Each share of common stock represents a portion of ownership, and this portion is calculated by multiplying the number of outstanding shares by the value of each share. Even companies that haven't sold stock in the public marketplace, but have incorporated, list shareholders on the incorporation documents and list the value of their shares on the balance sheet. Each common stock shareholder has a vote in the company's operations.
- **Preferred stock:** This account reflects the value of outstanding shares of preferred stock, which falls somewhere between bonds and shares of stock. Although a company has no obligation to repay the preferred shareholders for their investment, it does promise these shareholders dividends. If the company can't pay the dividends for some reason, they're accrued for payment in later years. Any unpaid preferred stock dividends must be paid before a company pays dividends to common stock shareholders. Preferred shareholders don't vote in the firm's operations. If the business is liquidated, preferred shareholders receive their share of the assets before common shareholders.
- **Retained Earnings:** This account tracks the profits or losses for a company each year. These numbers reflect earnings retained instead of being paid out as dividends to shareholders. They show a company's long-term success or failure.

Revenue accounts

At the top of every income statement is the revenue the company brings in. This revenue is offset by any costs directly related to it. The top section of the income statement includes sales, cost of goods sold, and gross margin. Below this section, and before the profit and loss section, are the expenses. In this section, I review the key accounts in the Chart of Accounts that make up the income statement (see Chapter 7).

Revenue

A company records all sales of products or services in revenue accounts. The following accounts record revenue transactions:

- **Sales of goods or services:** This account tracks the company's revenues for the sale of its products or services.
- **Sales discounts:** This account tracks any discounts the company offers to increase its sales. If a company is heavily discounting its products, either it

may be competing intensely or interest in the product may be falling. A company outsider probably doesn't see these numbers, but if you're reading the reports prepared for internal management, this account gives you a view of how discounting is used.

- **Sales returns and allowances:** This account tracks problem sales from unhappy customers. A large number here may reflect customer dissatisfaction, which could be the result of a quality-control problem. A company outsider probably doesn't see these numbers, but internal management financial reports show this information. A dramatic increase in this number is usually a red flag for company management.

Cost of goods sold

A company tracks the costs directly related to the sale of goods or services in cost of goods sold accounts. The details usually appear only on internally distributed income statements and aren't distributed to company outsiders. Cost of goods sold is usually shown as a single line item, but it includes the transactions from all these accounts:

- **Purchases:** This account tracks the cost of merchandise a company buys. A manufacturing company has an extensive tracking system for its cost of goods that includes accounts for items like raw materials, components, and labor to produce the final product.
- **Purchase discounts:** This account tracks any cost savings a company is able to negotiate because of accelerated payment plans or volume buying. For example, if a vendor offers a 2 percent discount when a customer pays an invoice within 10 days rather than the normal 30 days, the vendor tracks this cost saving in purchase discounts.
- **Purchase returns and allowances:** This account tracks any transactions involving the return of any damaged or defective products to the manufacturer or vendor.
- **Freight charges:** This account tracks the costs of shipping the goods sold.

Expense accounts

Any costs not directly related to generating revenue are considered *expenses*. Expenses fall into four categories: operating, interest, depreciation or amortization, and taxes. A large company can have hundreds of expense accounts, so I don't name each one. Instead, I give you a broad overview of the types of expense accounts that fall into each of these categories:

» **Operating expenses:** The largest share of expense accounts falls under the umbrella of operating expenses, which include advertising, dues and subscriptions, equipment rental, store rental, insurance, legal and accounting fees, meals, entertainment, salaries, office expenses, postage, repairs and maintenance, supplies, travel, telephone, utilities, vehicle expenses, and just about anything else that goes into the cost of operating a business and isn't directly related to selling a company's products.

» **Interest expenses:** Interest paid on a company's debt is reflected in the accounts for interest expenses — credit cards, loans, bonds, or any other type of debt the company may carry.

» **Depreciation and amortization expenses:** I discuss how depreciation is calculated in "Depreciation and amortization," earlier in this chapter. The process for amortization is similar. The depreciation and amortization accounts track the amount written off each year for any type of asset, and the income statement shows expenses related to depreciation and amortization in each individual year.

» **Taxes:** A company pays numerous types of taxes. Sales taxes aren't listed in the expense area because they're paid by customers and accrued as a liability until paid. Taxes withheld from employee paychecks are also accrued as a liability and aren't listed as an expense.

REMEMBER

The types of taxes that *are* expenses for a company include the employer's half of Social Security and Medicare taxes, unemployment taxes and other related payroll taxes that vary depending on state, and corporate taxes, if the company has incorporated. Businesses that aren't incorporated don't have to pay taxes on income. Instead, the owners report that income on their personal tax returns. I talk more about taxes and company structure in Chapter 3.

Differentiating Profit Types

A company doesn't actually make different kinds of profits, but it has different ways to track a profit and compare its results with similar companies. The three key profit types are gross profit, operating profit, and net profit. In Chapter 11, I discuss how these profit types can test a company's viability.

Gross profit

The *gross profit* reflects the revenue earned minus any direct costs of generating that revenue, such as costs related to the purchase or production of goods before any expenses, including operating, taxes, interest, depreciation, and amortization.

The gross profit isn't actually part of the Chart of Accounts. You calculate the number for the income statement to show the profit a company makes before expenses.

Operating profit

The *operating profit* is the next profit figure you see on the income statement. This number measures a company's earning power from its ongoing operations. The operating profit is calculated by subtracting operating expenses from gross profit. Some companies include depreciation and amortization expenses in this calculation, calling this line item *EBIT*, or *earnings before interest and taxes.*

TECHNICAL STUFF

Others add an additional line called *EBITDA*, or *earnings before interest, taxes, depreciation, and amortization.* Accountants started using EBITDA in the 1980s because it gave analysts a number they could use to compare profitability among companies and eliminated the effects of financing and accounting.

Interest is a financial decision. A company has the choice to finance new product development or other major projects by selling bonds, taking loans, or issuing stock. If the company chooses to raise money using bonds or loans, it has to pay interest. Money raised by issuing stock doesn't have interest costs. I talk more about this difference and the impact on a company's profits in Chapter 11.

Believe it or not, taxes are also an accounting game. Most corporations report different tax numbers on their financial statements than they pay to the government because of various tax write-offs they're able to use to reduce their tax bill.

REMEMBER

Companies don't actually pay out cash for depreciation and amortization expenses. Instead, depreciation and amortization are an accounting requirement that comes into play when determining the value of assets.

Net profit

Net profit is the bottom line after all costs, expenses, interest, taxes, depreciation, and amortization have been deducted. Net profit reflects how much money a company makes. If the company isn't incorporated, it can pay out the profit to shareholders or company owners, or it can reinvest the money in growing itself. Firms add reinvested money to the retained earnings account on the balance sheet.

2 Checking Out the Big Show: Annual Reports

IN THIS PART . . .

Discover the parts of an annual report and look at how to summarize financial information.

Check out assets, liabilities, and equity, and see how to review and examine them to keep things in balance.

Understand how to use income statements to determine whether a company has made a profit.

Look at statements of cash flows to determine whether the company has enough cash to operate.

Read behind the numbers and scour financial reports for red flags.

Understand consolidated financial statements and look at ways companies buy other companies.

» Getting acquainted with the parts of the annual report

» Looking at the three most important documents

» Summing up the financial information

Chapter 5

Exploring the Anatomy of an Annual Report

No doubt the financial statements are the meat of any annual report, but lots of trimmings make up an annual report, and you need to be able to read and understand them. Although companies must follow set rules for how they format the key financial statements, how they present the rest of the report is left to their creativity.

Some companies spend millions of dollars putting on a glossy show with color pictures throughout the report. Others put out a plain-vanilla, black-and-white version without pictures. Still, the major components of an annual report are standard, although the order in which companies present them may vary.

REMEMBER

When you see a fat, glossy annual report from a company, you can be certain that you'll find a lot of fluff in it and probably a lot of spin about all the good things the company accomplished. No matter how fancy or plain the annual report is, as a careful reader, you need to focus on four key parts, listed in order:

- **Auditors' report:** A statement by the auditors regarding the findings of their audit of the company's books
- **Financial statements:** The balance sheet, income statement, and statement of cash flows

» **Notes to the financial statements:** Additional information on the data in the financial statements

» **Management's discussion and analysis:** Management's perspective regarding the company's results

In this chapter, I explain why these four parts of an annual report are so critical. I also define the other parts of an annual report and their purposes.

Everything but the Numbers

Most people think of numbers when they hear the words *annual report,* but any savvy investor can find a lot more useful information in the report than just numbers. Some parts of the report are fluff pieces written for public consumption, but others can give you great insight into the company's prospects, as well as suggest some areas of management concern. You just need to be a detective: Read between the lines, and read the fine print.

Debunking the letter to shareholders

What would an annual report be if not an opportunity for the head honchos to tout their company's fabulousness? Near the front of most annual reports, you find a letter to the shareholders from the chief executive officer (CEO) and the chairman of the board; other key executives may have signed their names, too.

WARNING

Don't put too much stock in this letter, no matter how appealing it looks and how exciting its message is. Few CEOs actually write the letter to shareholders; the company's public relations department usually carefully designs the letter to highlight the positive aspects of the company's year. Negative results, when mentioned at all, are typically hidden in the middle of a paragraph somewhere in the middle of the letter.

In these letters, you usually find information about the key business activities for the year, such as a general statement about the company's financial condition, performance summaries of key divisions or subsidiaries that were the shining stars, and the company's major prospects.

REMEMBER

Don't let these letters fool you. They *will* focus on the positive news and try to minimize the bad news. Do read the company's optimistic view, but don't depend on this letter to make a decision about whether to invest in the company. You can find more definitive information in other parts of the report to help you make investment decisions.

TRANSLATING THE LANGUAGE OF LETTERS TO SHAREHOLDERS

Maintaining a long and proud tradition, letters to shareholders present companies in the best possible light using a positive spin to hide whatever trouble may lie under the surface. A careless reader may feel reassured by the everything's-hunky-dory tone, but a few often-used niceties may tip off careful readers that things aren't necessarily what they seem.

- A company frequently uses *challenging* when it's facing significant difficulties selling its product or service.
- *Restructuring* means something isn't working. Find out what that something is and how much the company is spending to fix the problem.
- Sometimes letters to shareholders gloss over mistakes by using phrases like "corrective actions are being taken." Look for details about both the cause and the plan for corrective actions in the notes to the financial statements or the management's discussion and analysis.
- If you come across the term *difficulties*, look for details on those difficulties highlighted in the management's discussion and analysis or notes to the financial statements.

The best place to find full details on these issues is in the notes to the financial statements or the management's discussion and analysis. For more on these sections, go to "Getting the skinny from management" and "Reading the notes," later in this chapter.

Making sense of the corporate message

After the letter to shareholders, but before the juicy information, you usually find more rah-rah text in the form of a summary of the company's key achievements throughout the year. Like the president's letter, these pages present more of the type of message the corporation wants to portray, which may or may not give you the true picture. Few companies include much information about negative results in this section. Often chock-full of glossy, colorful images, this section is pure public relations fluff that focuses on the year's top performance highlights.

WARNING

Although you may enjoy the pictures, don't count on the info printed around them to help you make any decisions about the company. Even if a company doesn't use pretty color pictures, this section usually includes bold graphics and lots of headlines that focus on the successes. Don't expect to find any warning signs in this image-setting section.

Although this section is basically advertising, it may give you a good overview of what the company does and the key parts of its operations. The firm generally presents its key divisions or units, highlights the top products within these divisions, and gives a brief summary of the financial results of the top divisions. In addition, you usually find some discussion of market share and position in the market of the company's key products or services.

Meeting the people in charge

Want to find out who's running the place? After the corporate message, one or two pages list the members of the board of directors and sometimes a brief bio of each member. You also find a listing of top executives or managers and their responsibilities. If you want to complain to someone at the top, this is where you can find out where to send your letters!

But seriously, reviewing the backgrounds of the company's leaders can help you get an idea of the experience these leaders bring to the company. If they don't impress you, it may be a good sign that you should walk away from the investment.

Finding basic shareholder information

At the end of the key financial statements, you usually find a *statement of shareholders' equity,* which is a summary of changes to shareholders' equity over the past three years. The key parts of this statement for current-year results are in the equity section of the balance sheet (one of the key financial statements that I talk about in greater detail in Chapter 6).

This information is good to know because you can get an overview of changes to shareholders' equity over the past three years, but you don't need this information to analyze a company's prospects. When I show you how to analyze results by using information about shareholders' equity, I use numbers that you can find on the balance sheet.

Getting the skinny from management

The management's discussion and analysis (MD&A) section is one of the most important sections of an annual report. The MD&A may not be the most fun section to look at, but in it you find the key discussions about what went smoothly over the year and what went wrong.

REMEMBER

Read the MD&A section carefully. It has a lot of the meat-and-potatoes information that gives you details about how the company's doing.

The Securities and Exchange Commission (SEC) monitors the MD&A section closely to make sure that companies present all critical information about current operations, capital, and liquidity. Management must also include forward-looking statements about known market and economic trends that may impact the company's liquidity and material events, as well as uncertainties that may cause reported information to not necessarily reflect future operating results or future financial conditions. For example, if a company manufactures its products in a country that's facing political upheaval or labor strife, those conditions may impact the company's ability to continue manufacturing its products at the same low cost. The company must report this information, indicating how this situation may impact its future earning potential.

The SEC pays special attention to a number of key factors that the MD&A is supposed to cover:

- **Revenue recognition:** In a retail store, recognizing revenue can be a relatively straightforward process: A customer buys a product off the shelves, and the revenue is *recognized* — that is, recorded in the company's books. But matters aren't that cut-and-dried in many complex corporate deals. For example, in the computer and hardware industries, revenue recognition can be complex because purchase contracts frequently include multiple parts, such as software, hardware, services, and training. When a company actually recognizes the revenue for each of these parts can vary, depending on the terms of a contract.

  REMEMBER

  When reading financial reports for a particular industry, reviewing how management describes its revenue-recognition process compared to similar companies in the same industry is important.

- **Restructuring charges:** When a company restructures a portion of itself — which can include shutting down factories, disbanding a major division, or enacting other major changes related to how the company operates — management discusses the impact this had on the company (or may have in the future). This portion of the report explains costs for employee severance, facility shutdowns, and other expenses related to restructuring.

- **Impairments to assets:** The SEC expects companies to report any losses to assets in a timely manner. If an asset is damaged or destroyed, or for any reason loses value, companies must report that loss to shareholders. Look for information about the loss of value to assets in the MD&A. Also look for information about the depreciation or amortization of these assets (see Chapter 4 for more details on depreciation and amortization).

- **Pension plans:** Accounting for pension plans includes many assumptions, such as the amount of interest or other gains the company expects to make on the assets it holds in its pension plans and the expenses the company anticipates paying out when employees retire. If the company has a pension plan for its employees, you'll find a discussion about how the company finances this plan and whether it expects to have difficulty meeting its plan's requirements.

- **Environmental and product liabilities:** All companies face some liability for products that fail to operate as expected or products that may cause damage to an individual or property. In some industries — such as oil, gas, and chemicals — an error can cause considerable environmental damage. You've probably heard stories about a chemical spill destroying a local stream or drinking water supply, or an oil spill wiping out an area's entire ecological system. In the MD&A section, the company must acknowledge the liabilities it faces and the way it prepares financially for the possibility of taking a loss after paying the liability. The company must estimate its potential losses and disclose the amount of money it has set aside or the insurance it has to protect against such losses.
- **Stock-based compensation:** To attract and keep top executives, many companies offer *stock incentives* (such as shares of stock as bonuses) as part of an employee compensation package. This part of the annual report must mention details of any stock-based compensation. Many recent scandals have included disclosures of unusually lavish stock-based compensation programs for top executives. Keep a watchful eye (or ear) out for discussion of bonuses or other employee compensation that involves giving employees shares of stock or selling employees' shares of stock below the market value.
- **Allowance for doubtful accounts:** Any company that offers credit to customers will encounter some nonpayers in the group. Management must discuss what it allows for loss on accounts that aren't paid and whether this allowance increased or decreased from the previous year. An increase in the allowance for doubtful accounts may indicate a problem with collections or be a sign of significant problems in the industry as a whole.

TIP

The discussion in this section of the annual report can get technical. If you don't understand what you read, you can always make a call to the investor relations department to ask for clarification. Whenever you're considering a major investment in a company's stock, be certain that you understand the key points in the MD&A. Any time you find the information beyond your comprehension, don't hesitate to research further and ask a lot of questions before investing in the stock.

In the MD&A, managers focus on three key areas: company operations, capital resources, and liquidity.

Company operations

Management commentary on this topic focuses on the income the company's operations generate and the expenses related to them. To get an idea of how well the company may perform in the future, look for the following:

- Discussion about whether sales increased or decreased
- Details on how well the company's various product lines performed
- Explanations of economic or market conditions that may have impacted the company's performance

The MD&A section also discusses these areas:

- **Distribution systems:** How products are distributed.
- **Product improvements:** Changes to products that improve their performance or appearance.
- **Manufacturing capacity:** The number of manufacturing plants and their production capability. The MD&A also mentions the percentage of the company's manufacturing capacity that it's using. For example, if the firm uses only 50 percent of its manufacturing capacity, it may have a lot of extra resources that are idle. If the company is using 100 percent of its manufacturing capacity, it may have maxed out its resources and may need to expand.
- **Research and development projects:** The research or development the business is doing to develop new products or improve current products.

The manager also comments on key profit results and how they may differ from the previous year's projections.

Management as a whole?

Also look for cost information related to product manufacturing or purchase. Cost-control problems may mean that future results won't be as good as the current year's, especially if management mentions that the cost of raw materials isn't stable.

Look for statements about interest expenses, major competition, inflation, or other factors that may impact the success of future operations.

Capital resources

A company's *capital resources* are its assets and its ability to fund its operations for the long term. In addition to a statement that the company is in a strong financial position, you'll find discussions on these topics:

- Acquisitions or major expansion plans
- Any major capital expenses carried out over the past year or planned in future years

- Company debt
- Plans the company may have for taking on new debt
- Other key points about the company's cash flow

Liquidity

A company's *liquidity* is its cash position and its ability to pay its bills on a short-term or day-to-day basis. I cover how to analyze liquidity in Chapters 12, 15, and 16.

Getting guarantees from management

Management has been required to include a section called "Corporate Responsibility for Financial Reports" or "Management's Responsibility for Financial Reports" since the financial reporting scandals of the late 1990s and early 2000s. When the Sarbanes-Oxley Act of 2002 passed Congress, this guarantee became more critical.

Today the chief executive officer (CEO) and chief financial officer (CFO) must prepare a statement to accompany the audit report to certify that, "based on such officer's knowledge, the financial statements, and other financial information included in the report, fairly present in all material respects the financial condition and results of operations of the issuer as of, and for, the periods presented in the report," according to Section 302 of the Act.

Executives were asked to provide these letters in the past, but this new requirement must include a certified statement, signed and notarized for public view, indicating that management takes full responsibility and can be held legally accountable for what's in the financial reports.

Executives can now be held personally responsible for their actions and may face up to a five-year prison term, fines, and other disciplinary action. They may also face civil and criminal litigation, and the SEC may bar them from serving as a corporate officer or director.

CEOs and CFOs have responded to this new requirement by looking for ways to shield their money and property from shareholder lawsuits and federal prosecution. The key question not yet answered is whether we will actually see this enforced and whether it will protect investors and the public from the corporate scandals we have seen in the past.

Bringing the auditors' answers to light

Any publicly traded company must provide financial reports that outside auditors have examined. (I talk more about the audit process in Chapter 18.) You usually find the *auditors' report* (a letter from the auditors to the company's board of directors and shareholders) either before the financial information or immediately following it.

REMEMBER

Before you read the financial statements or the notes to the financial statements, be sure that you've read the auditors' report. You read the auditors' report first to find out whether the auditor raised any red flags about the company's financial results. But you don't find the answers to these questions in the auditors' report. To find the details, you need to read the MD&A, the financial statements, and the notes to the financial statements. But if you haven't read the auditors' report first, you may overlook some critical details.

To lend credibility to management's assurances, companies call in independent auditors from an outside accounting firm to audit their internal controls and financial statements. Auditors don't check every transaction, so their reports don't give you 100 percent assurance that the financial statements don't include misstatements about the company's assets and liabilities. Auditors don't endorse the company's financial position or give indications about whether the company is a good investment.

Most standard auditors' reports include these three paragraphs:

- **Introductory paragraph:** Here you find information about the time period the audit covers and who's responsible for the financial statements. In most cases, this paragraph states that management is responsible for the financial statements and that the auditors only express an opinion about the financial statements based on their audit. Essentially, this is a "protect your fanny" paragraph in which the auditors attempt to limit their responsibility for possible inaccuracies.
- **Scope paragraph:** In this paragraph, the auditors describe how they carried out the audit, including a statement that they used *generally accepted audit standards.* These standards require that auditors plan and prepare their audit to be reasonably sure that the financial statements are free of material misstatements. A *material misstatement* is an error that significantly impacts the company's financial position, such as reporting revenue before it's actually earned.
- **Opinion paragraph:** Here the auditors state their opinion of the financial statements. If the auditors don't find any problems with the statements, they simply say that these statements are prepared "in conformity with generally accepted accounting principles" (or GAAP). For more on GAAP, see Chapter 2.

When an auditors' report follows the outline I describe here, it's called a *standard auditors' report.* And because no qualifiers (or red flags) limit the auditors' opinions, it's also an *unqualified audit report.*

If the auditors find a problem, the report is a *nonstandard auditors' report.* In a nonstandard report, auditors must explain their opinions in a *qualified audit report* — in other words, they qualify their opinions and note problem areas. (I discuss possible problems auditors may encounter later in this section.) A nonstandard auditors' report and a standard auditors' report have the same structure; the only difference is that the nonstandard report includes information about the problems the auditors found.

REMEMBER

When you see a nonstandard auditors' report, be sure that you find a discussion of the problems in the MD&A and in the notes to the financial statements. Also, when reading the MD&A, be certain that you understand how management is handling the problems the auditors noted and how these problems may impact the company's long-term financial prospects before you invest your hard-earned dollars. (Call the investor relations department to ask for clarification, if you need to.) If you've already invested, look carefully at the issues to be sure you want to continue holding your stock in the company.

A nonstandard auditors' report may include paragraphs that discuss problems the auditors found, such as the following:

- **Work performed by a different auditor:** In many cases, this isn't a major problem. Maybe a different auditor handled the audit in previous years or audited a subsidiary of a newly acquired company.

  But whenever a company changes auditors, you need to know why it made the change, and you need to research the issue. You probably won't find the reason for the change in the annual report, so you may have to research the change in news reports or analysts' reports. Because changing auditors can negatively impact a firm's stock price, companies are usually very careful about doing so. Wall Street typically gets concerned whenever a change of auditors occurs because it can be a sign of a major accounting problem that hasn't surfaced yet.

- **Accounting policy changes:** If a company decides to change its accounting policies or how it applies an accounting method, the auditors must note the change in a nonstandard auditors' report. These changes may not indicate a problem, and if the auditors agree that the company had a good reason for making the change, you most likely have no reason for concern. For example, if the company changed how it reported an asset because the SEC required that change, then it's a good reason for making the change.

  If the auditors disagree with the company's decision to change accounting methods, they question the change and provide a *qualified opinion* (which

I discuss later in this section) in the nonstandard auditors' report. If their report indicates a change in accounting policy, be sure to look in the notes portion of the annual report for the full explanation of the change and how it may impact the financial statements. When companies change an accounting policy or method, the change impacts your ability to compare the previous year's results to the current year's.

- **Material uncertainties:** If the auditors find an area of uncertainty, it's impossible for management or the auditors to determine the potential financial consequences of an event. Uncertainties may include debt-agreement violations, damages the company must pay if it loses a pending lawsuit, or the loss of a major customer or market share. If the auditors believe that these material uncertainties may impact future earnings, they include a paragraph about the uncertainty and give a qualified opinion.

  If a loss is probable and the auditors can estimate it, the financial statements usually reflect this loss, and the auditors give an unqualified opinion. So in reality, the impact of a known loss can be a greater problem than a possible loss with unknown consequences. The company and the auditors have a responsibility to make you aware of the uncertainty so that you can factor it into any decisions you make about your potential dealings with or investment in the company.

- **Going-concern problems:** If the auditors have substantial doubt that the company has the ability to stay in business, they indicate that the company has a *going-concern problem.* Problems that can lead to this type of paragraph in the auditors' report include ongoing losses, capital deficiencies, or a significant contract dispute. If you see a statement by the auditors that the company has a going-concern problem, it's a major red flag and a good indication that you don't want to invest in this company.

- **Specific disclosures:** Sometimes auditors indicate concerns about a specific financial matter but still give the company a nonqualified opinion.

  Many times the auditor believes that these are matters the public needs to know about but aren't signs of a serious problem. For example, if the company is doing business with another company that has officers involved in both firms, the auditor may note this issue in a special paragraph. The notes to the financial statements explain any specific disclosure in greater detail.

- **Qualified opinions:** Any time the auditors issue a nonstandard report, they also issue a qualified opinion in the final paragraph of the report. A qualified opinion isn't always cause for alarm, but it does mean that you need to do additional research to make sure you understand the qualification. Sometimes a qualified opinion simply indicates that the auditors didn't have sufficient information available at the time of the audit to determine whether the issue raised will have a significant financial impact on the company. Look in the notes to the financial statements or the MD&A for any explanation of the matter that caused the auditors to issue a qualified opinion.

Presenting the Financial Picture

The main course of any annual report is the financial statements. In this part, you find out what the company owns, what the company owes, how much revenue it took in, what expenses it paid out, and how much profit it made or how much it lost. I cover each of the following statements in great detail throughout the book, so I mention them briefly here and indicate in which chapters you can find additional information.

REMEMBER

When looking at a company's financial results, make sure that you're comparing periods of similar length or a similar collection of months.

For example, a retail store usually has much better results in the last quarter of the year (from October to December) because of the holiday season than it does in the first quarter (from January to March). Comparing these two quarters doesn't make sense when you're trying to determine how well a business is doing. To judge a retail company's growth prospects, compare the fourth quarter of one year with the fourth quarter of another year. I talk more about income statements in Chapter 7 and tell you how to analyze these statements in Part 3.

- **Balance sheet:** Also known as the *statement of financial position,* this document gives a snapshot of a company's assets and liabilities at a specific point in time. I discuss all the parts of the balance sheet in Chapter 6, and I talk about analyzing the financial reports in Part 3.
- **Income statement:** Also known as the *profit and loss statement* or *P&L statement,* this document reviews a company's operations over a specific amount of time. This period can last for one month, one quarter, six months, one year, or any other period indicated at the top of the statement. I discuss the income statement in Chapter 7 and how to analyze the statement in Part 3.
- **Statement of cash flows:** This document discusses the actual flow of cash into and out of the company. The statement has three sections focusing on changes to cash status from operations, from investing, and from financing. Like the income statement, the statement of cash flows reflects results over a specific period of time. I discuss this statement in greater detail in Chapter 8, and I talk about cash-flow analysis in Chapter 13.

Summarizing the Financial Data

Knowing that most people won't spend the time to read all the way through the annual report, many companies summarize their numbers in various ways. The two most common ways to summarize are to highlight the financial data presented in the financial statements and to summarize some key information in the notes to the financial statements. But beware: Most summaries highlight the good news and skip over the bad.

Finding the highlights

The highlights to the financial data summarize the financial results for the year being reported. Typically, this summary is called the *financial highlights,* but companies can be creative because this section isn't a required part of the report. And because the highlights aren't required, they're not always presented according to GAAP rules, so don't count on their accuracy. You usually find the financial highlights at the front of the annual report, after the letter from the CEO and chairman of the board. Some companies include them inside the annual report's back cover.

WARNING

You frequently find financial highlights at the front of the annual report, designed in a graphically pleasing way. Most companies show either a 10-year or 11-year summary that doesn't include much detail but allows you to see the firm's growth trends. Although this type of summary can be a good historical overview, don't count on it. Instead, do your own research of the company's financial history to be sure that you're aware of both the good and the bad news. Remember that even outstanding companies have some bad years that they want to gloss over.

Reading the notes

The notes to the financial statements is the section where you find any warts on a company's financial record. The notes are a required part of the annual report, and they give you the details behind the numbers presented in the financial statements. Companies like to hide their problems in the notes; in fact, most companies even print this part of the annual report in smaller type.

Most of the details in the notes discuss the impact that the following business aspects may have on the company's future financial health:

- Accounting methods used
- Changes to accounting methods
- Key financial commitments that can impact current and future operations
- Lease obligations
- Pension and retirement benefits

If any red flags pop up in a company's annual report, this part is where you can find the financial details and explanations. The auditors' report probably highlights any potential problems and red flags that you want to search for in the notes. You may also find problems mentioned in the MD&A section, but the notes section probably covers the full explanations for these problems in greater detail.

REMEMBER

Don't get turned off by the visually unpleasing presentation. The notes to the financial statements is one of the most critical parts of the annual report. I cover the importance of the notes in more detail in Chapter 9.

» **Defining assets, liabilities, and equity**

» **Exploring the basics of balance sheets**

» **Reviewing assets**

» **Understanding liabilities**

» **Examining equity**

Chapter **6**

Balancing Assets against Liabilities and Equity

Picture a tightrope walker carefully making her way across a tightrope. Now imagine that she's carrying plates of equal weight on both sides of a wobbling rod. What would happen if one of those plates were heavier than the other? You don't have to understand squat about physics to know that it isn't gonna be a pretty sight.

Just as a tightrope walker must be in balance, so must a company's financial position. If the assets aren't equal to the claims against those assets, then that company's financial position isn't in balance, and everything topples over. In this chapter, I introduce you to the balance sheet, which gives the financial report reader a snapshot of a company's financial position.

Understanding the Balance Equation

A company keeps track of its financial balance on a *balance sheet*, which is a summary of the company's financial standing at a particular point in time. To understand balance sheets, you first have to understand the following terms, which typically appear on a balance sheet:

- **Assets:** Anything the company owns, from cash, to inventory, to the paper it prints the reports on
- **Liabilities:** Debts the company owes
- **Equity:** Claims made by the company's owners, such as shares of stock

The assets a company owns are equal to the claims against that company, by either debtors (liability) or owners (equity). The claims side must equal the assets side for the balance sheet to stay in balance. The parts always balance according to this formula:

Assets = Liabilities + Equity

REMEMBER

As a company and its assets grow, its liabilities and equities grow in similar proportion. For example, whenever a company buys a major asset, such as a building, it has to either use another asset to pay for the building or use a combination of assets and liabilities (such as bonds or a mortgage) or equity (owner's money or outstanding shares of stock).

Introducing the Balance Sheet

Trying to read a balance sheet without having a grasp of its parts is a little like trying to translate a language you've never spoken — you may recognize the letters, but the words don't mean much. Unlike a foreign language, however, a balance sheet is pretty easy to get a fix on as soon as you figure out a few basics.

Digging into dates

The first parts to notice when looking at the financial statements are the dates indicated at the top of the statements. You need to know what date or period of time the financial statements cover. This information is particularly critical when you start comparing results among companies. You don't want to compare the 2012 results of one firm with the 2011 results of another. Economic conditions certainly vary, and the comparison doesn't give you an accurate view of how well the companies competed in similar economic conditions.

WHEN A YEAR IS MORE THAN A YEAR

REAL WORLD EXAMPLE

Things can get confusing if a company picks a certain point in time instead of an actual date for its fiscal year. For example, a company can decide to end its fiscal year on the last Friday of a particular month, which means its fiscal year is sometimes 52 weeks and sometimes 53 weeks. If a firm chooses a point in time instead of a year-end or month-end date, you usually find an explanation in the notes to the financial statements about how it handles its 52- and 53-week years, which can get convoluted.

For example, Darden Restaurants explained its 52- and 53-week years when it released its 2009 annual report like this:

"We operate on a 52/53 week fiscal year, which ends on the last Sunday in May. Fiscal 2009 consisted of 53 weeks of operation. Fiscal 2008 and 2007 each consisted of 52 weeks of operation."

Looking at this paragraph, you can see the complications of a fiscal year ending on a set period in time instead of one that ends on the last day of a month. The quarter with the extra week is 17 weeks. Comparing a 16-week quarter with a 17-week quarter can be misleading because an extra week of sales certainly looks better.

On a balance sheet, the date at the top is written after "As of," meaning that the balance sheet reports a company's financial status on that particular day. A balance sheet differs from other kinds of financial statements, such as the income statement or statement of cash flows, which show information for a period of time such as a year, a quarter, or a month. I discuss income statements in Chapter 7 and statements of cash flows in Chapter 8.

If a company's balance sheet states "As of December 31, 2012," the company is most likely operating on the calendar year. Not all firms end their business year at the end of the calendar year, however. Many companies operate on a fiscal year instead, which means they pick a 12-month period that more accurately reflects their business cycles. For example, most retail companies end their fiscal year on January 31. The best time of year for major retail sales is during the holiday season and post-holiday season, so stores close the books after those periods end.

To show you how economic conditions can make comparing the balance sheets of two companies difficult during two different fiscal years, consider an example surrounding the terrorist attacks on September 11, 2001.

If one company's fiscal year runs from September 1 to August 31 and another's runs from January 1 to December 31, the results may be very different. The company that reports from September 1, 2000, to August 31, 2001, wasn't impacted by that devastating event on its 2000/2001 financial reports. Its holiday season sales from October 2000 to December 2000 are likely much different from those of the company that reports from January 1, 2001, to December 31, 2001, because those results include sales after September 11, when the economy slowed considerably. However, the first company's balance sheet for September 1, 2001, to August 31, 2002, shows the full impact of the attacks on its financial position.

Nailing down the numbers

As you start reading the financial reports of large corporations, you see that they don't use large numbers to show billion-dollar results (1,000,000,000) or carry off an amount to the last possible cent, such as 1,123,456,789.99. Imagine how difficult reading such detailed financial statements would be!

At the top of a balance sheet or any other financial report, you see a statement indicating that the numbers are in millions, thousands, or however the company decides to round the numbers. For example, if a billion-dollar company indicates that numbers are in millions, you see 1 billion represented as 1,000 and 35 million as 35. The 1,123,456,789.99 figure would appear as 1,123.

REMEMBER

Rounding off numbers makes a report easier on the eye, but be sure you know how companies are rounding their numbers before you start comparing financial statements among them. This issue is particularly crucial when you compare a large company with a smaller one. The large company may round to millions, whereas the smaller company may round to thousands.

Figuring out format

Balance sheets come in three different styles: the account format, the report format, and the financial position format. I show you a sample of each format in the following figures, using simple numbers to give you an idea of what you can expect to see. Of course, real balance sheets have much larger and more complex numbers.

Account format

The *account format* is a horizontal presentation of the numbers, as Figure 6-1 shows.

Current assets	$300	Current liabilities	$200
Long-term assets	$150	Long-term liabilities	$100
Other assets	$ 50	Total liabilities	$300
		Shareholders' equity	$200
Total assets	$500	Total liabilities/equity	$500

FIGURE 6-1: The account format.

A balanced sheet shows total assets equal to total liabilities/equity.

Report format

The *report format* is a vertical presentation of the numbers. You can check it out in Figure 6-2.

Current assets	$300
Long-term assets	$150
Other assets	$ 50
Total assets	$500
Current liabilities	$200
Long-term liabilities	$100
Total liabilities	$300
Shareholders' equity	$200
Total liabilities/equity	$500

FIGURE 6-2: The report format.

Financial position format

Companies in the U.S. rarely use the *financial position format*, although it is common internationally, especially in Europe. The key difference between this format and the other two is that it has two lines that don't appear on the account and report formats:

- **Working capital:** This line indicates the current assets the company has available to pay bills. You find the working capital by subtracting the current assets from the current liabilities.
- **Net assets:** This line shows what's left for the company's owners after all liabilities have been subtracted from total assets.

Figure 6-3 shows you what the financial position format looks like. (Keep in mind that *noncurrent assets* are long-term assets as well as assets that aren't current but also aren't long term, such as stock ownership in another company.)

TIP

As investing becomes more globalized, you may start comparing U.S. companies with foreign companies. Or perhaps you are considering buying stock directly in European or other foreign companies. You need to become more familiar with the financial position format if you want to read reports from foreign companies. I take a closer look at regulations for foreign company reporting in Chapter 20.

Current assets	$300
Less: current liabilities	$200
Working capital	$100
Plus: noncurrent assets	$200
Total assets less current liabilities	$300
Less: long-term liabilities	$100
Net assets	$200

FIGURE 6-3: The financial position format.

Ogling Assets

Anything a company owns is considered an asset. Assets can include something as basic as cash or as massive as a factory. A company must have assets to operate the business. The asset side of a balance sheet gives you a summary of what the company owns.

Current assets

Anything a company owns that it can convert to cash in less than a year is a current asset. Without these funds, the company wouldn't be able to pay its bills and would have to close its doors. Cash, of course, is an important component of this part of the balance sheet, but a company uses other assets during the year to pay the bills.

Cash

For companies, cash is basically the same as what you carry around in your pocket or keep in your checking and savings accounts. Keeping track of the money is a lot more complex for companies, however, because they usually keep it in many different locations. Every multimillion-dollar corporation has numerous locations, and every location needs cash.

Even in a *centralized accounting system*, in which all bills are paid in the same place and all money is collected and put in the bank at the same time, a company keeps cash in more than one location. Keeping most of the money in the bank and having a little cash on hand for incidental expenses doesn't work for most companies.

For example, retail outlets and banks need to keep cash in every cash register or under the control of every teller to be able to transact business with their customers. Yet a company must have a way of tracking its cash and knowing exactly how much it has at the end of every day (and sometimes several times a day, for high-volume businesses). The cash drawer must be counted out, and the person counting out the draw must show that the amount of cash matches up with the total that the day's transactions indicate should be there.

If a company has a number of locations, each location likely needs a bank to deposit receipts and get cash as needed. So a large corporation has a maze of bank accounts, cash registers, petty cash, and other places where cash is kept daily. At the end of every day, each company location calculates the cash total and reports it to the centralized accounting area.

REMEMBER

The amount of cash that you see on the balance sheet is the amount of cash found at all company locations on the particular day for which the balance sheet was created.

Managing cash is one of the hardest jobs because cash can so easily disappear if proper internal controls aren't in place. Internal controls for monitoring cash are usually among the strictest in any company. If this subject interests you, you can find out more about it in any basic accounting book, such as *Accounting For Dummies*, 5th Edition, by John A. Tracy (published by Wiley).

Accounts receivable

Any company that allows its customers to buy on credit has an accounts receivable line on its balance sheet. *Accounts receivable* is a collection of individual customer accounts listing money that customers owe the company for products or services they've already received.

A company must carefully monitor not only whether a customer pays, but also how quickly she pays. If a customer makes her payments later and later, the company must determine whether to allow her to get additional credit or to block further purchases. Although the sales may look good, a nonpaying customer hurts a company because she's taking out — and failing to pay for — inventory that another customer could've bought. Too many nonpaying or late-paying customers can severely hurt a company's cash-flow position, which means the firm may not have the cash it needs to pay the bills.

TIP

Comparing a company's accounts receivable line over a number of years gives you a good idea of how well the company is doing collecting late-paying customers' accounts. Although you may see a company report positive sales numbers and a major increase in sales, if the accounts-receivable number is also rising rapidly, the business may be having trouble collecting the money on those accounts. I show you how to analyze accounts receivable in Chapter 16.

Marketable securities

Marketable securities are a type of liquid asset, meaning they can easily be converted to cash. They include holdings such as stocks, bonds, and other securities that are bought and sold daily.

Securities that a company buys primarily as a place to hold on to assets until the company decides how to use the money for its operations or growth are considered *trading securities.* Marketable securities held as current assets fit in this category. A company must report these assets at their fair value based on the market value of the stock or bond on the day the company prepares its financial report.

A firm must report any *unrealized losses or gains* — changes in the value of a holding that it hasn't sold — on marketable securities on its balance sheet to show the impact of those losses or gains on the company's earnings. The amount you find on the balance sheet is the *net marketable value*, the book value of the securities adjusted for any gains or losses that haven't been realized.

REMEMBER

The balance sheet is the show for general consumption, but the notes to the financial statements are where you find the small print that most people don't read. You find lots of juicy details in the notes that you don't want to miss. I talk more about the notes and their importance in Chapter 9.

Inventory

Any products a company holds ready for sale are considered *inventory.* The inventory on the balance sheet is valued at the cost to the company, not at the price the company hopes to sell the product for. Companies can pick from among five different methods to track inventory, and the method they choose can significantly impact the bottom line. Following are the different inventory tracking systems:

- **First in, first out (FIFO):** This system assumes that the oldest goods are sold first, and it's used when a company is concerned about spoilage or obsolescence. Food stores use FIFO because items that sit on the shelves too long spoil. Computer firms use it because their products quickly become outdated, and they need to sell the older products first. Assuming that older goods cost less than newer goods, FIFO makes the bottom line look better because the lowest cost is assigned to the goods sold, increasing the net profit from sales.
- **Last in, first out (LIFO):** This system assumes that the newest inventory is sold first. Companies with products that don't spoil or become obsolete can use this system. The bottom line can be significantly affected if the cost of goods to be sold is continually rising. The most expensive goods that come in last are assumed to be the first sold. LIFO increases the cost of goods figured, which, in turn, lowers the net income from sales and decreases a company's tax liability because its profits are lower after the higher costs are subtracted.

Hardware stores that sell hammers, nails, screws, and other items that have been the same for years and won't spoil are good candidates for LIFO.

- **Average costing:** This system reflects the cost of inventory most accurately and gives a company a good view of its inventory's cost trends. As the company receives each new shipment of inventory, it calculates an average cost for each product by adding in the new inventory. If the firm frequently faces inventory prices that go up and down, average costing can help level out the peaks and valleys of inventory costs throughout the year. Because the price of gasoline rises and falls almost every day, gas stations usually use this type of system.
- **Specific identification:** This system tracks the actual cost of each individual piece of inventory. Companies that sell big-ticket items or items with differing accessories or upgrades (such as cars) commonly use this system. For example, each car that comes onto the lot has a different set of features, so the price of each car differs.
- **Lower of cost or market (LCM):** This system sets the value of inventory based on which is lower — the actual cost of the products on hand or the current market value. Companies that sell products with market values that fluctuate significantly use this system. For instance, a brokerage house that sells marketable securities may use this system.

TIP

You usually find some information on the type of inventory system a company uses in the notes to the financial statements. Any significant detail about inventory costs appears in the notes section or in the management's discussion and analysis section.

REMEMBER

After a company chooses a type of inventory system, it must use that system for the rest of its corporate life unless it files special explanations with its tax returns to explain the reasons for changing systems. Because the way companies track inventory costs can have a significant impact on the net income and the amount of taxes due, the IRS closely monitors any changes in inventory tracking methods.

Long-term assets

Assets that a company plans to hold for more than one year belong in the long-term assets section of the balance sheet. Long-term assets include land and buildings; capitalized leases; leasehold improvements; machinery and equipment; furniture and fixtures; tools, dies, and molds; intangible assets; and others. This section of the balance sheet shows you the assets that a company has to build its products and sell its goods.

Land and buildings

Companies list any buildings they own on the balance sheet's *land and buildings* line. Companies must depreciate (show that the asset is gradually being used up by deducting a portion of its value) the value of their buildings each year, but the land portion of ownership isn't depreciated.

Many people believe that depreciating the value of a building actually results in undervaluing a company's assets. The IRS allows 39 years for depreciation of a building; after that time, the building is considered valueless. That fact may be true in many cases, such as with factories that need to be updated to current-day production methods, but a well-maintained office building usually lasts longer. A company that has owned a building for 20 or more years may, in fact, show the value of that building depreciated below its market value.

Real estate over the past 20 years has appreciated (gone up in value) greatly in most areas of the country. So a building's value may actually increase because of market appreciation. You can't figure out this appreciation by looking at the financial reports, though. You have to find research reports written by analysts or the financial press to determine the true value of these assets.

Sometimes you see an indication that a company holds *hidden assets* — they're hidden from your view when you read the financial reports because you have no idea what the true marketable value of the buildings and land may be. For example, an office building that a company purchased for $390,000 and held for 20 years may have a marketable value of $1 million if it were sold today but has been depreciated to $190,000 over the past 20 years.

Capitalized leases

Whenever a company takes possession of or constructs a building by using a lease agreement that contains an option to purchase that property at some point in the future, you see a line item on the balance sheet called *capitalized leases.* It means that, at some point in the future, the company may likely own the property and then can add the property's value to its total assets owned. You can usually find a full explanation of the lease agreement in the notes to the financial statements.

Leasehold improvements

Companies track improvements to property they lease and don't own in the *leasehold improvements account* on the balance sheet. These items are depreciated because the improvements will likely lose value as they age.

Machinery and equipment

Companies track and summarize all machinery and equipment used in their facilities or by their employees in the *machinery and equipment accounts* on the balance sheet. These assets depreciate just like buildings, but for shorter periods of time, depending on the company's estimate of their useful life.

Furniture and fixtures

Some companies have a line item for *furniture and fixtures*, whereas others group these items in machinery and equipment or other assets. You're more likely to find furniture and fixture line items on the balance sheet of major retail chains that hold significant furniture and fixture assets in their retail outlets than on the balance sheet for manufacturing companies that don't have retail outlets.

Tools, dies, and molds

You find *tools, dies, and molds* on the balance sheet of manufacturing companies, but not on the balance sheet of businesses that don't manufacture their own products. Tools, dies, and molds that are unique and are developed specifically by or for a company can have significant value. This value is amortized, which is similar to the depreciation of other tangible assets. I discuss depreciation and amortization in Chapter 4.

Intangible assets

Any assets that aren't physical — such as patents, copyrights, trademarks, and goodwill — are considered *intangible assets*. Patents, copyrights, and trademarks are actually registered with the government, and a company holds exclusive rights to these items. If another company wants to use something that's patented, copyrighted, or trademarked, it must pay a fee to use that asset.

Patents give companies the right to dominate the market for a particular product. For example, pharmaceutical companies can be the sole source for a drug that's still under patent. Copyrights also give companies exclusive rights for sale. Copyrighted books can be printed only by the publisher or individual who owns that copyright, or by someone who has bought the rights from the copyright owner.

Goodwill is a different type of asset, reflecting the value of a company's locations, customer base, or consumer loyalty, for example. Firms essentially purchase goodwill when they buy another company for a price that's higher than the value of the company's tangible assets or market value. The premium that's paid for the company is kept in an account called *Goodwill* that's shown on the balance sheet.

Other assets

Other assets is a catchall line item for items that don't fit into one of the balance sheet's other asset categories. The items shown in this category vary by company; some firms group both tangible and intangible assets here.

Other companies may put unconsolidated subsidiaries or affiliates in this category. Whenever a company owns less than a controlling share of another company (less than 50 percent) but more than 20 percent, it must list the ownership as an *unconsolidated subsidiary* (a subsidiary that's partially but not fully owned) or an *affiliate* (a company that's associated with the corporation but not fully owned). I talk more about consolidation and affiliation in Chapter 10.

Ownership of less than 20 percent of another company's stock is tracked as a marketable security (see the section "Marketable securities," earlier in this chapter). Long before a firm reaches even the 20 percent mark, you usually find discussion of its buying habits in the financial press or in analysts' reports. Talk of a possible merger or acquisition often begins when a company reaches the 20 percent mark.

You usually don't find more than a line item that totals all unconsolidated subsidiaries or affiliates. Sometimes the notes to the financial statements or the management's discussion and analysis sections mention more detail, but you often can't tell by reading the financial reports and looking at this category what other businesses the company owns. You have to read the financial press or analyst reports to find out the details.

Accumulated depreciation

On a balance sheet, you may see numerous line items that start with accumulated depreciation. These line items appear under the type of asset whose value is being depreciated or shown as a total at the bottom of long-term assets. *Accumulated depreciation* is the total amount depreciated against tangible assets over the life span of the assets shown on the balance sheet. I explain depreciation in greater detail in Chapter 4.

Although some companies show accumulated depreciation under each of the long-term assets, it's becoming common for companies to total accumulated depreciation at the bottom of the balance sheet's long-term assets section. This method of reporting makes it harder for you to determine the actual age of the assets because depreciation isn't indicated by each type of asset. You have no idea which assets have depreciated the most — in other words, which ones are the oldest.

TIP

The age of machinery and factories can be a significant factor in trying to determine a company's future cost and growth prospects. A firm with mostly aging plants needs to spend more money on repair or replacement than a company that has mostly new facilities. Look for discussion of this in the management's discussion and analysis or the notes to the financial statements. If you don't find this information there, you have to dig deeper by reading analyst reports or reports in the financial press. For example, the toy companies Mattel and Hasbro both show their property, plant, and equipment on one line in the balance sheet, but you find a complete breakdown in the notes to the financial statements.

Looking at Liabilities

Companies must spend money to conduct their day-to-day operations. Whenever a company makes a commitment to spend money on credit, be it short-term credit using a credit card or long-term credit using a mortgage, that commitment becomes a debt or liability.

Current liabilities

Current liabilities are any obligations that a company must pay during the next 12 months. These include short-term borrowings, the current portion of long-term debt, accounts payable, and accrued liabilities. If a company can't pay these bills, it may go into bankruptcy or out of business.

Short-term borrowings

Short-term borrowings are usually lines of credit a company takes to manage cash flow. A company borrowing this way isn't much different from you using a credit card or personal loan to pay bills until your next paycheck. As you know, these types of loans usually carry the highest interest-rate charges, so if a firm can't repay them quickly, it converts the debt to something longer term with lower interest rates.

WARNING

This type of liability should be a relatively low number on the balance sheet, compared with other liabilities. A number that isn't low may be a sign of trouble, indicating that the company is having difficulty securing long-term debt or meeting its cash obligations.

Current portion of long-term debt

This line item of the balance sheet shows payments due on long-term debt during the current fiscal year. The long-term liabilities section reflects any portion of the debt that a company owes beyond the current 12 months.

Accounts payable

Companies list money they owe to others for products, services, supplies, and other short-term needs (invoices due in less than 12 months) in *accounts payable.* They record payments due to vendors, suppliers, contractors, and other companies they do business with.

Accrued liabilities

Liabilities that a company has accrued but hasn't yet paid at the time it prepares the balance sheet are totaled in *accrued liabilities.* For example, companies include income taxes, royalties, advertising, payroll, management incentives, and employee taxes they haven't yet paid in this line item. Sometimes a firm breaks out items individually, like income taxes payable, without using a catchall line item called accrued liabilities. When you look in the notes, you see more details about the types of financial obligations included and the total of each type of liability.

Long-term liabilities

Any money a business must pay out for more than 12 months in the future is considered a long-term liability. Long-term liabilities don't throw a company into bankruptcy, but if they become too large, the company may have trouble paying its bills in the future.

Many companies keep the long-term liabilities section short and sweet, and group almost everything under one lump sum, such as long-term debt. *Long-term debt* includes mortgages on buildings, loans on machinery or equipment, or bonds the company needs to repay at some point in the future. Other companies break out the type of debt, showing mortgages payable, loans payable, and bonds payable.

For example, both Hasbro and Mattel take the short-and-sweet route, giving the financial report reader little detail on the balance sheet. Instead, a reader must dig through the notes and management's discussion and analysis to find more details about the liabilities.

REMEMBER

You can find more details about what a company actually groups in the other liability category in the notes to the financial statements. (Guess you're getting used to that phrase!)

Navigating the Equity Maze

The final piece of the balancing equation is equity. All companies are owned by somebody, and the claims that owners have against the assets the company owns are called *equity*. In a small company, the equity owners are individuals or partners. In a corporation, the equity owners are shareholders.

Stock

Stock represents a portion of ownership in a company. Each share of stock has a certain value, based on the price placed on the stock when it's originally sold to investors. The current market value of the stock doesn't affect this price; any increase in the stock's value after its initial offering to the public isn't reflected here. The market gains or losses are actually taken by the shareholders, not the company, when the stock is bought and sold on the market.

Some companies issue two types of stock:

- **Common stock:** These shareholders own a portion of the company and have a vote on issues. If the board decides to pay *dividends* (a certain portion per share it pays to common shareholders from profits), common shareholders get their portion of those dividends as long as the preferred shareholders have been paid in full.
- **Preferred stock:** These shareholders own stock that's actually somewhere in between common stock and a *bond* (a long-term liability to be paid back over a number of years). Although they don't get back the principal they pay for the stock, as a bondholder does, these shareholders have first dibs on any dividends.

  Preferred shareholders are guaranteed a certain dividend each year. If a company doesn't pay dividends for some reason, it accrues these dividends for future years and pays them when it has enough money. A company must pay preferred shareholders their accrued dividends before it pays any money to common shareholders. The disadvantage for preferred shareholders is that they have no voting rights in the company.

You may also find Treasury stock in the equity section of the balance sheet. This is stock that the company has bought back from shareholders. Many companies did that between 2008 and 2013, so look for that on balance sheets. When a company buys back stock, it means less shares on the market. With fewer shares available for purchase on the open market, stock prices tend to rise.

If a firm goes bankrupt, the bondholders hold first claim on any money remaining after the company pays the employees and *secured debtors* (debtors who've loaned money based on specific assets, such as a mortgage on a building). The preferred shareholders are next in line; the common shareholders are at the bottom of the heap and are frequently left with valueless stock.

Retained earnings

Each year, companies make a choice to either pay out their net profit to their shareholders or retain all or some of the profit for reinvesting in the company. Any profit a company doesn't pay to shareholders over the years accumulates in an account called *retained earnings.*

Capital

You don't find this line item on a corporation's financial statement, but you'll likely find it on the balance sheet of a small company that isn't publicly owned. *Capital* is the money that the company's founders initially invested.

If you don't see this line item on the balance sheet of a small, privately owned company, the owners likely didn't invest their own capital to get started, or they already took out their initial capital when the company began to earn money.

Drawing

Drawing is another line item you don't see on a corporation's financial statement. Only unincorporated businesses have a drawing account. This line item tracks money that the owners take out from the yearly profits of a business. After a company is incorporated, owners can take money as salary or dividends, but not on a drawing account.

» Getting acquainted with the income statement

» Considering different types of revenue

» Determining a company's expenses

» Analyzing a company's finances using profits and losses

» Figuring out earnings per share

Chapter 7

Using the Income Statement

Every business person needs to know how well his business has done over the past month, quarter, or year. Without that information, he has no idea where his business has come from and where it may go next. Even a small business that has no obligation to report to the public is sure to do income statements on at least a quarterly or (more likely) monthly basis to find out whether the business made a profit or took a loss.

REMEMBER

The income statement you see in public financial statements is likely very different from the one you see if you work for the company. The primary difference is the detail in certain line items.

In this chapter, I review the detail that goes into an income statement, but don't be surprised if some of the detail never shows up in the financial reports you get as a company outsider. Much of the detail is considered confidential and doesn't go to people outside the company. I include this detailed information in this chapter so you know what's behind the numbers you do see. If you're a company insider, this additional information can help you understand the internal reports you receive.

Introducing the Income Statement

The *income statement* is where you find out whether a company made a profit or took a loss. You also find information about the company's revenues, its sales levels, the costs it incurred to make those sales, and the expenses it paid to operate the business. These are the key parts of the statement:

- **Sales or revenues:** How much money the business took in from its sales to customers.
- **Cost of goods sold:** What it cost the company to produce or purchase the goods it sold.
- **Expenses:** How much the company spent on advertising, administration, rent, salaries, and everything else that's involved in operating a business to support the sales process.
- **Net income or loss:** The bottom line that tells you whether the company made a profit or operated at a loss.

TECHNICAL STUFF

The income statement is one of the three reports the Securities and Exchange Commission (SEC) and the Financial Accounting Standards Board (FASB) require; I describe their roles in the preparation of financial statements in Chapters 18 and 19. In fact, the FASB specifies that the income statement provide a report of comprehensive income, which means the report must reflect any changes to a company's equity during a given period of time that are caused by transactions, events, or other circumstances involving transactions with nonowner sources. In simpler terms, this statement must reflect any changes in equity that aren't raised by investments from owners or distributed to owners.

When looking at an income statement, you can expect to find a report of either

- **Excess of revenues over expenses:** This report means the company earned a profit.
- **Excess of expenses over revenues:** This report means the company faced a loss.

Because the income statement shows profits and losses, some people like to call it the profit and loss statement (or P&L), but that isn't actually one of its official names. In addition to "statement of income," the income statement has a number of official names that you may find in a financial report:

- Statement of operations
- Statement of earnings
- Statement of operating results

Digging into dates

Income statements reflect an *operating period*, which means that they show results for a specific length of time. At the top of an income statement, you see the phrase "Years Ended" or "Fiscal Years Ended" and the month the period ended for an annual financial statement. You may also see "Quarters Ended" or "Months Ended" for reports based on shorter periods of time. Companies are required to show at least three periods of data on their income statements, so if you're looking at a statement for 2012, you also find columns for 2011 and 2010.

TIP

Many people believe you need to analyze at least five years' worth of data if you're thinking about investing in a company. You can easily get hold of this data by ordering a two-year-old annual report along with the current one. You can also find most annual and quarterly reports online at a company's website or by visiting the SEC's Edgar website (`www.sec.gov/edgar.shtml`), which posts all financial reports filed with the SEC. Because each report must have three years' worth of data, a 2012 report shows data for 2011 and 2010, too. And a 2009 report shows 2008 and 2007 data also. So you actually have six years' worth of data with these reports: 2012, 2011, 2010, 2009, 2008, and 2007.

Figuring out format

Not all income statements look alike. Basically, companies can choose to use one of two formats for the income statement: the single-step or the multistep.

Both formats give you the same bottom-line information. The key difference between them is whether they summarize that information to make analyzing it easier. The single-step format is easier to produce, but the multistep format gives you a number of subtotals throughout the statement that make analyzing a company's results easier. Most public corporations use the multistep format, but many smaller companies that don't have to report to the general public use the single-step format.

Single-step format

The *single-step format* groups all data into two categories: revenue and expenses. Revenue includes income from sales, interest income, and gains from sales of equipment. It also includes income that a company raises from its regular operations or from one-time transactions, such as from the sale of a building. Expenses include all the costs that are involved in bringing in the revenue.

The single-step format (see Figure 7-1) gets its name because you perform only one step to figure out a company's net income — you subtract the expenses from the revenue.

Revenues	
Sales	$1,000
Interest income	200
Total Revenue	**$1,200**
Expenses	
Cost of goods sold	$ 500
Depreciation	50
Advertising	50
Salaries and wages	100
Insurance	50
Research and development	100
Supplies	50
Interest expense	50
Income taxes	50
Total Expenses	**$1,000**
Net Income	**$ 200**

FIGURE 7-1: The single-step format.

Multistep format

The *multistep format* divides the income statement into several sections and gives the reader some critical subtotals that make analyzing the data much easier and quicker. Even though the single-step and multistep income statements include the same revenue and expense information, they group the information differently. The key difference is that the multistep format has the following four profit lines:

- **Gross profit:** This line reflects the profit generated from sales minus the cost of the goods sold.
- **Income from operations:** This line reflects the operating income the company earned after subtracting all its operating expenses.
- **Income before taxes:** This line reflects all income earned — which can include gains on equipment sales, interest revenue, and other revenue not generated by sales — before subtracting taxes or interest expenses.
- **Net income (or Net loss):** This line reflects the bottom line — whether the company made a profit.

Many companies add even more profit lines, like earnings before interest, taxes, depreciation, and amortization, known as EBITDA for short (see the section "EBITDA," later in this chapter).

Some companies that have discontinued operations include that information in the line item for continuing operations. But it's better for the financial report reader if that information is on a separate line; otherwise, the reader doesn't know what the actual profit or loss is from continuing operations. I delve a bit deeper into these various profit lines in "Sorting Out the Profit and Loss Types," later in this chapter.

Figure 7-2 shows the multistep format, using the same items as in the single-step format example (refer to Figure 7-1).

Revenues	
Sales	$1000
Cost of goods sold	$ 500
Gross Profits	**$ 500**
Operating Expenses	
Advertising	50
Salaries and wages	100
Insurance	50
Research and development	100
Supplies	50
Operating Income	**$ 150**
Other Income	
Interest income	200
Other Expenses	
Interest expense	50
Depreciation	50
Income before Taxes	**$ 250**
Income taxes	50
Net Income	**$ 200**

FIGURE 7-2: The multistep format.

Delving into the Tricky Business of Revenues

You may think that figuring out when to count something as revenue is a relatively simple procedure. Well, forget that. Revenue acknowledgment is one of the most complex issues on the income statement. In fact, you may have noticed that, with the recent corporation scandals, the most common reason companies have gotten into trouble has to do with the issue of misstated revenues.

In this section, I define revenue and explain the three line items that make up the revenue portion of the income statement: sales, cost of goods sold, and gross profit.

Defining revenue

When a company recognizes something as revenue, it doesn't always mean that cash changed hands, nor does it always mean that a product was even delivered. Accrual accounting leaves room for deciding when a company actually records revenue. A company recognizes revenue when it earns it and recognizes expenses when it incurs them, without regard to whether cash changes hands. You can find out more about accounting basics in Chapter 4.

WARNING

Because accrual accounting doesn't require that a company actually have the cash in hand to count something as revenue, senior managers can play games to make the bottom line look the way they want it to look by either counting or not counting income. Sometimes they acknowledge more income than they should to improve the financial reports; other times they reduce income to reduce the tax bite. I talk more about these shenanigans in Chapter 23.

When a company wants to count something as revenue, several factors can make that decision rather muddy, leaving questions about whether a particular sale should be counted:

- **If the seller and buyer haven't agreed on the final price for the merchandise and service, the seller can't count the revenue collected.**

  For example, when a company is in the middle of negotiating a contract for a sale of a major item such as a car or appliance, it can't include that sale as revenue until the final price has been set and a contract obligating the buyer is in place.

- **If the buyer doesn't pay for the merchandise until the company resells it to a retail outlet (which may be the case for a company that works with a distributor) or to the customer, the company can't count the revenue until the sale to the customer is final.**

  For example, publishers frequently allow bookstores to return unsold books within a certain amount of time. If there's a good chance that some portion of the product may be returned unsold, companies must take this into account when reporting revenues. For instance, a publisher uses historical data to estimate what percentage of books will be returned and adjusts sales downward to reflect those likely returns.

- **If the buyer and seller are related, revenue isn't acknowledged in the same way.**

  No, I'm not talking about kissing cousins here. I'm talking about when the buyer is the parent company or subsidiary of the seller. In that case, companies must handle the transaction as an internal transfer of assets.

- **If the buyer isn't obligated to pay for the merchandise because it's stolen or physically destroyed before it's delivered or sold, the company can't acknowledge the revenue until the merchandise is actually sold.**

  For example, a toy company works with a distributor or other middleman to get its toys into retail stores. If the middleman doesn't have to pay for those toys until they're delivered or sold to retailers, the manufacturer can't count the toys it shipped to the middleman as revenue until the middleman completes the sale.

- **If the seller is obligated to provide significant services to the buyer or aid in reselling the product, the seller can't count the sale of that product as revenue until the sale is actually completed with the final customer.**

  For example, many manufacturers of technical products offer installation or follow-up services for a new product as part of the sales promotion. If those services are a significant part of the final sale, the manufacturer can't count that sale as revenue until the installation or service has been completed with the customer. Items shipped for sale to local retailers under these conditions aren't considered sold, so they can't be counted as revenue.

Adjusting sales

Not all products sell for their list price. Companies frequently use discounts, returns, or allowances to reduce the prices of products or services. Whenever a firm sells a product at a discount, it needs to keep track of those discounts, as well as its returns and allowances. It's the only way the company can truly analyze how much money it's making on the sale of its products and how accurately it's pricing the products to sell in the marketplace.

REMEMBER

If a company must offer too many discounts, it's usually a sign of a weak or very competitive market. If a company has a lot of returns, it may be a sign of a quality-control problem or a sign that the product isn't living up to customers' expectations. The sales adjustments I talk about here help a company track and analyze its sales and recognize any negative trends.

As a financial report reader, you don't see the specifics about discounts in the income statement, but you may find some mention of significant discounting in the notes to the financial statements. Here are the most common types of adjustments companies make to their sales:

- **Volume discounts:** To get more items in the marketplace, manufacturers offer major retailers *volume discounts,* which means these retailers agree to buy a large number of a manufacturer's product so they can save a certain percentage of money off the price. One of the reasons you get such good prices at discount sellers like Wal-Mart and Target is that they buy products from the manufacturer at greatly discounted prices. Because they purchase for thousands of stores, they can buy a large number of goods at one time. Volume discounts reduce the revenue of the company that gives them.
- **Returns:** *Returns* are arrangements between the buyer and seller that allow the buyer to return goods for a number of reasons. I'm sure you've returned goods that you didn't like, that didn't fit, or that possibly didn't even work. Returns are subtracted from a company's revenue.
- **Allowances:** Gift cards and other accounts that a customer pays for up front without taking merchandise are types of *allowances.* Allowances are actually liabilities for a store because the customer hasn't yet selected the merchandise and the sale isn't complete. Revenues are collected up front, but at some point in the future, merchandise will be taken off the shelves and the company won't receive additional cash.

REMEMBER

Most companies don't show you the details of their discounts, returns, and allowances, but they do track them and adjust their revenue accordingly. When you see a *net sales* or *net revenue* figure (the company's sales minus any adjustments) at the top of an income statement, the company has already adjusted the figure for these items.

Internally, managers see the details of these adjustments in the sales area of the income statement so that they can track trends for discounts, returns, and allowances. Tracking such trends is an important aspect of the managerial process. If a manager notices that any of these line items show a dramatic increase, she needs to investigate the reason for the increase. For example, an increase in discounts may mean that the company has to consistently offer its products for less money, which then may mean that the market is softening and fewer customers are buying fewer products. A dramatic increase in returns may mean that the products the business is selling have a defect that needs to be corrected.

Considering cost of goods sold

Like the *Sales* line item, the *Cost of goods sold* (what it costs to manufacture or purchase the goods being sold) line item has many different pieces that make up its calculation on the income sheet. You don't see the details for this line item unless you're a company manager. Few firms report the details of their cost of goods sold to the general public.

Items that make up the cost of goods sold vary depending on whether a company manufactures the goods in-house or purchases them. If the company manufactures them in-house, you track the costs all the way from the point of raw materials and include the labor involved in building the product. If the company purchases its goods, it tracks the purchases of the goods as they're made.

In fact, a manufacturing firm tracks several levels of inventory, including

- **Raw materials:** The materials used for manufacturing
- **Work-in-process inventory:** Products in the process of being constructed
- **Finished-goods inventory:** Products ready for sale

Sometimes tracking begins from the time the raw materials are purchased, with adjustments based on discounts, returns, or allowances given. Companies also add to the income statement's cost of goods sold section freight charges and any other costs involved directly in acquiring goods to be sold.

When a company finally sells the product, it becomes a *Cost of goods sold* line item. Managing costs during the production phase is critical for all manufacturing companies. Managers in this type of business receive regular reports that include the cost details. Trends that show dramatically increasing costs certainly must be investigated as quickly as possible because the company must consider a price change to maintain its profit margin.

TIP

Even if a company is only a service company, it likely has costs for the services it provides. In this case, the line item may be called *Cost of services sold* instead of *Cost of goods sold*. You may even see a line item called *Cost of goods or services sold* if a company gets revenue from the sale of both goods and services.

Gauging gross profit

The *Gross profit* line item in the income statement's revenue section is simply a calculation of net revenue or net sales minus the cost of goods sold. Basically, this number shows the difference between what a company pays for its inventory and the price at which it sells this inventory. This summary number tells you how much profit the company makes selling its products before deducting the expenses of its operation. If the company shows no profit or not enough profit here, it's not worth being in business.

Managers, investors, and other interested parties closely watch the trend of a company's gross profit because it indicates the effectiveness of the company's purchasing and pricing policies. Analysts frequently use this number not only to gauge how well a company manages its product costs internally, but also to gauge how well the firm manages its product costs compared with other companies in the same business.

If profit is too low, a company can do one of two things: find a way to increase sales revenue or find a way to reduce the cost of the goods it's selling.

To increase sales revenue, the company can raise or lower prices to increase the amount of money it's bringing in. Raising the prices of its product brings in more revenue if the same number of items is sold, but it may bring in less revenue if the price hike turns away customers and fewer items are sold.

Lowering prices to bring in more revenue may sound strange to you, but if a company determines that a price is too high and is discouraging buyers, doing so may increase its volume of sales and, therefore, its gross margin. This scenario is especially true if the company has a lot of *fixed costs* (such as manufacturing facilities, equipment, and labor) that it isn't using to full capacity. The firm can use its manufacturing facilities more effectively and efficiently if it has the capability to produce more product without a significant increase in the *variable costs* (such as raw materials or other factors, like overtime).

A company can also consider using cost-control possibilities for manufacturing or purchasing if its gross profit is too low. The company may find a more efficient way to make the product, or it may negotiate a better contract for raw materials to reduce those costs. If the company purchases finished products for sale, it may be able to negotiate better contract terms to reduce its purchasing costs.

Acknowledging Expenses

Expenses include the items a company must pay for to operate the business that aren't directly related to the sale and production of specific products. Expenses differ from the cost of goods sold, which can be directly traced to the actual sale of a product. Even when a company is making a sizable gross profit, if management doesn't carefully watch the expenses, the gross profit can quickly turn into a net loss.

REMEMBER

Expenses make up the second of the two main parts of the income statement; revenues make up the first part.

Advertising and promotion, administration, and research and development are all examples of expenses. Although many of these expenses impact the ability of a company to sell its products, they aren't direct costs of the sales process for individual items. The following are details about the key items that fit into the expenses part of the income statement:

- **Advertising and promotion:** For many companies, one of the largest expenses is advertising and promotion. Advertising includes TV and radio ads, print ads, and billboard ads. Promotions include product giveaways (hats, T-shirts, pens with the company logo on it, and so on) or name identification on a sports stadium. If a company helps promote a charitable event and has its name on T-shirts or billboards as part of the event, it must include these expenses in the *Advertising and promotion expense* line item.
- **Other selling administration expenses:** This category is a catchall for any selling expenses, including salespeople's and sales managers' salaries, commissions, bonuses, and other compensation expenses. The costs of sales offices and any expenses related to those offices also fall into this category.
- **Other operating expenses:** If a company includes line-item detail in its financial reports, you usually find that detail in the notes to the financial statements. All operating expenses that aren't directly connected to the sale of products fall into the category of other operating expenses, including these expenses:
  - **General office needs:** Administrative salaries and expenses for administrative offices, supplies, machinery, and anything else needed to run the general operations of a company are reported in general office needs. Expenses for human resources, management, accounting, and security also fall into this category.
  - **Royalties:** Any *royalties* (payments made for the use of property) paid to individuals or other companies fall under this umbrella. Companies most commonly pay royalties for the use of patents or copyrights that another

company or individual owns. Companies also pay royalties when they buy the rights to extract natural resources from another person's property.

- **Research and product development:** This line item includes any costs for developing new products. Most likely, you find details about research and product development in the notes to the financial statements or in the managers' discussion and analysis. Any company that makes new products has research and development costs because if it isn't always looking for ways to improve its product or introduce new products, it's at risk of losing out to a competitor.

» **Interest expenses:** This line item shows expenses paid for interest on long- or short-term debt. You usually find some explanation for the interest expenses in the notes to the financial statements.

» **Interest income:** If a company receives interest income for any of its holdings, you see it in this line item. This category includes notes or bonds that the company holds, such as marketable securities, or interest paid by another company to which it loaned short-term cash.

» **Depreciation and amortization expenses:** Depreciation on buildings, machinery, or other items, as well as amortization on intangible items, fall into this line item. You have to look in the notes to the financial statements to find more details on depreciation and amortization. To discover how these expenses are calculated, see Chapter 4.

» **Insurance expenses:** In addition to insurance expenses for items such as theft, fire, and other losses, companies usually carry life insurance on their top executives and errors and omissions insurance for their top executives and board members. *Errors and omissions insurance* protects executives and board members from being sued personally for any errors or omissions related to their work for the company or as part of their responsibility on the company's board.

» **Taxes:** All corporations have to pay income taxes. In the taxes category, you find the amount the company actually paid in taxes. Many companies and their investors complain that corporate income is taxed twice — once directly as a corporation and a second time on the dividends that the shareholders receive. In reality, many corporations can use so many tax write-offs that their tax bill is zero or near zero.

» **Other expenses:** Any expenses that don't fit into one of the earlier line items in this list fall into this category. What goes into this category varies among companies, depending on what each company chooses to show on an individual line item and what it groups in other expenses. However, a firm doesn't include expenses relating to operating activities in this category; those expenses go on the line item for other operating expenses. Companies separate operating expenses from nonoperating expenses.

Sorting Out the Profit and Loss Types

When you hear earnings or profits reports on the news, most of the time, the reporters are discussing the net profit, net income, or net loss. For readers of financial statements, that bottom-line number doesn't tell the entire story of how a company is doing. Relying solely on the bottom-line number is like reading the last few pages of a novel and thinking that you understand the entire story. All you really know is the end, not how the characters got to that ending.

Because companies have so many different charges or expenses unique to their operations, different profit lines are used for different types of analysis. I cover the types of analysis in Part III, but in this section, I review what each of these profit types includes or doesn't include. For example, gross profit is the best number to use to analyze how well a company is managing its sales and the costs of producing those sales, but gross profit gives you no idea how well the company is managing the rest of its expenses.

Using operating profits, which show you how much money a company made after considering all costs and expenses for operating, you can analyze how efficiently the company is managing its operating activities, but you don't get enough detail to analyze product costs.

EBITDA

A commonly used measure to compare companies is *earnings before interest, taxes, depreciation, and amortization*, also known as EBITDA. With this number, analysts and investors can compare profitability among companies or industries because it eliminates the effects of the companies' activities to raise cash outside their operating activities, such as by selling stock or bonds. EBITDA also eliminates any accounting decisions that may impact the bottom line, such as the companies' policies relating to depreciation methods.

TIP

Investors reading the financial report can use this line item to focus on the profitability of each company's operations. If a company does include this line item, it appears at the bottom of the expenses section but before line items listing interest, taxes, depreciation, and amortization.

How a firm chooses to raise money can greatly impact its bottom line. Selling equity has no annual costs if dividends aren't paid. Borrowing money means interest costs must be paid every year, so a company will have ongoing required expenses.

EBITDA gives financial report readers a quick view of how well a company is doing without considering its financial and accounting decisions. This number became popular in the 1980s, when leveraged buyouts were common. A *leveraged buyout* takes place when an individual or company buys a controlling interest (which means more than 50 percent) in a company, primarily using debt (up to 70 percent or more of the purchase price). This fad left many businesses in danger of not earning enough from operations to pay their huge debt load.

Today EBITDA is frequently touted by technology companies or other high-growth companies with large expenses for machinery and other equipment. In these situations, the companies like to discuss their earnings before the huge write-offs for depreciation, which can make the bottom line look pretty small. Be aware that a company can use EBITDA as an accounting gimmick to make earnings sound better to the general public or to investors who don't take the time to read the fine print in the annual report.

TIP

Firms can get pretty creative when it comes to their income statement groupings. If you don't understand a line item, be sure to look for explanations in the notes to the financial statements. If you can't find an explanation there, call investor relations and ask questions.

Nonoperating income or expense

If a company earns income from a source that isn't part of its normal revenue-generating activities, it usually lists this income on the income statement as *nonoperating income*. Items commonly listed here include the sale of a building, manufacturing facility, or company division. Other types of nonoperating income include interest from notes receivable and marketable securities, dividends from investments in other companies' stock, and rent revenue (if the business subleases some of its facilities).

Companies also group one-time expenses in the nonoperating section of the income statement. For example, the severance and other costs of closing a division or factory appear in this area, or, in some cases, the statement has a separate section on discontinuing operations. Other types of expenses include casualty losses from theft, vandalism, or fire; loss from the sale or abandonment of property, plant, or equipment; and loss from employee or supplier strikes.

You usually find explanations for income or expenses from nonoperating activities in the notes to the financial statements. Companies need to separate these nonoperating activities; otherwise, investors, analysts, and other interested parties can't gauge how well a company is doing with its core operating activities. The *Core operating activities* line item is where you find a company's continuing income. If those core activities aren't raising enough income, the firm may be on the road to significant financial difficulties.

A major gain may make the bottom line look great, but it can send the wrong signal to outsiders, who may then expect similar earnings results the next year. If the company doesn't repeat the results the following year, Wall Street will surely hammer its stock. A major one-time loss also needs special explanation so that Wall Street doesn't downgrade the stock unnecessarily if the one-time nonoperating loss won't be repeated in future years.

REMEMBER

Whether a gain or a loss, separating nonoperating income from operating income and expenses helps avoid sending the wrong signal to analysts and investors about a company's future earnings and growth potential.

Net profit or loss

REMEMBER

The bottom line of any income statement is net profit or loss. This number means little if you don't understand the other line items that make up the income statement. Few investors and analysts look solely at net profit or loss to make a major decision about whether a company is a good investment.

Calculating Earnings per Share

In addition to net income, the other number you hear almost as often about a company's earnings results is earnings per share. *Earnings per share* is the amount of net income the company makes per share of stock available on the market. For example, if you own 100 shares of stock in ABC Company and it earns $1 per share, $100 of those earnings are yours unless the company decides to reinvest the earnings for future growth. In reality, a company rarely pays out 100 percent of its earnings; it usually pays out a small fraction of those earnings.

TIP

You find the calculation for earnings per share on the income statement after net income, or in a separate statement called the statement of shareholders' equity. The calculation for earnings per share is relatively simple: You divide the net earnings or net income (which you find on the income statement) by the number of outstanding shares (which you can find on the balance sheet).

Basically, earnings per share shows you how much money each shareholder made for each of her shares. In reality, this money doesn't get paid back to the shareholder. Instead, most is reinvested in future operations of the company. The net income or loss is added to the retained earnings number on the balance sheet.

Any dividends declared per share appear on the income statement under the earnings per share information. You find the amount of dividends paid on the statement of cash flows, which I talk about in Chapter 8. The company's board of directors declares dividends either quarterly or annually.

At the bottom of an income statement, you see two numbers:

- The *basic earnings per share* is a calculation based on the number of shares outstanding at the time the income statement is developed.
- The *diluted earnings per share* includes other potential shares that may eventually be outstanding. This category includes shares designated for items like stock options (options companies give to employees to buy shares of stock at a set price, usually lower than the market price), *warrants* (shares of stock companies promise to bondholders or preferred shareholders for additional shares of stock at a set price, usually below the stock's market value), and *convertibles* (shares of stock companies promise to a lender who owns bonds that are convertible to stock).

These numbers give you an idea of how much a company earns per share. You can use them to analyze the company's profitability, which I show you how to do in Chapter 11.

» Exploring the statement of cash flows

» Understanding operating activities

» Getting a grip on investments

» Figuring out the financing section

» Looking at other line items

» Finding net cash from all company activities

Chapter 8
The Statement of Cash Flows

Cash is a company's lifeblood. If a company expects to manage its assets and liabilities and to pay its obligations, it has to know the amount of cash flowing into and out of the business, which isn't always easy to figure out when using accrual accounting. (You can find out more about accrual accounting in Chapter 4.)

The reason accrual accounting makes it hard to figure out how much cash a company actually holds is that cash doesn't have to change hands for the company to record a transaction. The *statement of cash flows* is the financial statement that helps the financial report reader understand a company's cash position by adjusting for differences between cash and accruals. (See Chapter 4 for more information on cash and accruals.) This statement tracks the cash that flows into and out of a business during a specified period of time and lays out the sources of that cash. In this chapter, I explore the basic parts of the statement of cash flows.

Digging into the Statement of Cash Flows

Basically, a statement of cash flows gives the financial report reader a map of the cash receipts, cash payments, and changes in cash that a company holds, minus the expenses that arise from operating the company. In addition, the statement looks at money that flows into or out of the firm through investing and financing activities. As with the income statement (see Chapter 7), companies provide three years' worth of information on the statement of cash flows.

TIP

When reading the statement of cash flows, you need to be looking for answers to these three questions:

- Where did the company get the cash needed for operations during the period shown on the statement — from revenue generated, funds borrowed, or stock sold?
- What cash did the company actually spend during the period shown on the statement?
- What was the change in the cash balance during each of the years shown on the statement?

Knowing the answers to these questions helps you determine whether the company is thriving and has the cash needed to continue to grow its operations or the company appears to have a cash-flow problem and may be nearing a point of fiscal disaster. In this section, I show you how to use the statement of cash flows to find the answers to these questions.

The parts

Transactions shown on the statement of cash flows are grouped in three parts:

- **Operating activities:** This part includes revenue the company takes in through sales of its products or services and expenses the company pays out to carry out its operations.
- **Investing activities:** This part includes the purchase or sale of the company's investments and can include the purchase or sale of long-term assets, such as a building or a company division. Spending on *capital improvements* (upgrades to assets the company holds, such as the renovation of a building) also fits into this category, as does any buying or selling of short-term invested funds.

- **Financing activities:** This part involves raising cash through long-term debt or by issuing new stock. It also includes using cash to pay down debt or buy back stock. Companies include any dividends paid in this section.

REMEMBER

Operating activities is the most important section of the statement of cash flows. In reading this section, you can determine whether the company's operations are generating enough cash to keep the business viable. I discuss how to analyze this statement and make these determinations in Chapter 12.

The formats

Companies can choose between two different formats when preparing their statement of cash flows. Both arrive at the same total but provide different information to get there:

- **Direct method:** The Financial Accounting Standards Board (FASB; see Chapter 18) prefers the direct method, which groups major classes of cash receipts and cash payments. For example, cash collected from customers is grouped separately from cash received on interest-earning savings accounts or from dividends paid on stock the company owns. Major groups of cash payments include cash paid to buy inventory, cash disbursed to pay salaries, cash paid for taxes, and cash paid to cover interest on loans. Figure 8-1 shows you the direct method.
- **Indirect method:** Most companies (90 percent) use the indirect method, which focuses on the differences between net income and net cash flow from operations, and allows firms to reveal less than the direct method, leaving their competitors guessing. The indirect method is easier to prepare. Figure 8-2 shows you the indirect method.

REMEMBER

The direct and indirect methods differ only in the operating activities section of the report. The investing activities and financing activities sections are the same.

Cash flows from operating activities
Cash received from customers
Cash paid to suppliers and employees
Interest received
Interest paid, net of amounts capitalized
Income tax refund received
Income taxes paid
Other cash received (paid)
Net cash provided by (used in) operating activities

FIGURE 8-1: The direct method.

Cash flows from operating activities
Net income (loss)
Adjustments to reconcile net income (loss) to net cash provided by (used in) operating activities:
  Depreciation and amortization
  Provision for deferred taxes
  Decrease (increase) in accounts receivable
  Decrease (increase) in inventories
  Decrease (increase) in prepaid expenses
  Increase (decrease) in accounts payable
  Increase (decrease) in other current liabilities
  Exchange (gain) loss
  Net cash provided by (used in) operating activities

FIGURE 8-2: The indirect method.

Using the indirect method, you just need the information from two years' worth of balance sheets and income statements to make calculations. For example, you can calculate changes in accounts receivable, inventories, prepaid expenses, current assets, accounts payable, and current liabilities by comparing the totals shown on the balance sheet for the current year and the previous year. If a company shows $1.5 million in inventory in 2011 and $1 million in 2012, the change in inventory using the indirect method is shown easily: "Decrease in Inventory — $500,000." The statement of cash flows for the indirect method summarizes information already given in a different way, but it doesn't reveal any new information.

With the direct method, the company has to reveal the actual cash it receives from customers, the cash it pays to suppliers and employees, and the income tax refund it receives. Someone reading the balance sheet and income statement won't find these numbers in other parts of the financial report.

In addition to having to reveal details about the actual cash received or paid to customers, suppliers, employees, and the government, companies that use the direct method must prepare a schedule similar to one used in the indirect method for operating activities to meet FASB requirements. Essentially, companies save no time, must reveal more detail, and must still present the indirect method. Why bother? You can see why you'll most likely see the indirect method used in the vast majority of financial reports you read.

The investing activities and financing activities sections for both the direct and indirect methods look something like Figure 8-3 and Figure 8-4, both of which show the basic line items. Read on to find out what each of these line items includes. If you're interested in finding out about line items that make their way onto the statement only in special circumstances, see "Recognizing the Special Line Items," later in the chapter.

Cash flows from investing activities
Additions (sale) of property, plant, and equipment
Investments and acquisitions
Sales of investments
Other
Net cash utilized for investing activities

FIGURE 8-3: The investing activities section.

Cash flows from financing activities
Proceeds from borrowing
Net proceeds from repayments
Purchase or sale of common stock
Stock option transactions
Dividends paid
Net cash provided (utilized) by financing activities
Cash and short-term investments at beginning of the year
Cash and short-term investments at end of the year

FIGURE 8-4: The financing activities section.

Checking Out Operating Activities

The operating activities section is where you find a summary of how much cash flowed into and out of the company during the day-to-day operations of the business.

REMEMBER

Operating activities is the most important section of the statement of cash flows. If a company isn't generating enough cash from its operations, it isn't going to be in business long. Although new companies often don't generate a lot of cash in their early years, they can't survive that way for long before going bust.

FINDING OUT THE IMPORTANCE OF CASH THE HARD WAY

Dot.com babies certainly discovered the importance of cash on hand the hard way. Many newly minted dot.com companies raised millions of dollars in cash in the late 1990s and were able to stay in business for two or three years. But after these companies could no longer raise money from investors or borrow funds, the dot.com babies went bankrupt. Most dot.com companies died when the investor cash dried up in 2000 because they didn't generate enough money from their operations. In fact, more than 850 dot.com companies bit the dust between January 2000 and January 2002.

The primary purpose of the operating activities section is to adjust the net income by adding or subtracting entries that were made in order to abide by the rules of accrual accounting that don't actually require the use of cash. In this section, I describe several of the accounts in the operating activities section of the statement and explain how they're impacted by the changes required to revert accrual accounting entries to actual cash flow.

Depreciation

A company that buys a lot of new equipment or builds new facilities has high depreciation expenses that lower its net income. This fact is particularly true for many high-tech businesses that must always upgrade their equipment and facilities to keep up with their competitors.

The bottom line may not look good, but all those depreciation expenses don't represent the use of cash. In reality, no cash changes hands to pay depreciation expenses. These expenses are actually added back into the equation when you look at whether the company is generating enough cash from its operations because the company didn't actually lay out cash to pay for these expenses.

For example, if the company's net income is $200,000 for the year and its depreciation expenses are $50,000, the $50,000 is added back in to find the net cash from operations, which totals $250,000. Essentially, the firm is in better shape than it looked to be before the depreciation expenses because of this noncash transaction.

Inventory

Another adjustment on the statement of cash flows that usually adds cash to the mix is a decrease in inventory. If a company's inventory on hand is less in the current year than in the previous year, the company bought some of the inventory sold with cash in the previous year.

On the other hand, if the company's inventory increases from the previous year, then it spent more money on inventory in the current year, and it subtracts the difference from the net income to find its current cash holdings. For example, if inventory decreases by $10,000, the company adds that amount to net income on the statement of cash flows.

Accounts receivable

Accounts receivable is the summary of accounts of customers who buy their goods or services on direct credit from the company. Customers who buy their goods by using credit cards from banks or other financial institutions aren't included in accounts receivable. Payments by outside credit sources are instead counted as cash because the company receives cash from the bank or financial institution. The bank or financial institution collects from those customers, so the company that sells the good or service doesn't have to worry about collecting the cash.

When accounts receivable increase during the year, the company sells more products or services on credit than it collects in actual cash from customers. In this case, an increase in accounts receivable means a decrease in cash available.

The opposite is true if accounts receivable are lower during the current year than the previous year. In this case, the company collects more cash than it adds credit to customers' credit accounts. In this situation, a decrease in accounts receivable results in more cash received, which adds to the net income.

Accounts payable

Accounts payable is the summary of accounts of bills due that haven't yet been paid, which means the company must still lay out cash in a future accounting period to pay those bills.

When accounts payable increase, a company uses less cash to pay bills in the current year than it did in the previous one, so more cash is on hand. This has a positive effect on the cash situation. Expenses incurred are shown on the income statement, which means net income is lower. But in reality, the company hasn't yet laid out the cash to pay those expenses, so an increase is added to net income to find out how much cash is actually on hand.

Conversely, if accounts payable decrease, the company pays out more cash for this liability. A decrease in accounts payable means the company has less cash on hand, and it subtracts this number from net income.

The cash flow from activities section, summed up

To give you a taste of what all these line items look like in the statement of cash flows, see Table 8-1, where I roll together the information from the previous sections.

In Table 8-1, the company has $30,000 more in cash from operations than it reported on the income statement, so the company actually generated more cash than you may have thought if you just looked at net income.

TABLE 8-1 **Cash Flows from Operating Activities**

Line Item	Cash Received or Spent
Net income	$200,000
Depreciation	50,000
Increase in accounts receivable	(20,000)
Decrease in inventories	10,000
Decrease in accounts payable	(10,000)
Net cash provided by (used in) operating activities	$230,000

REAL WORLD EXAMPLE

If you compare the statements for the toy companies Mattel and Hasbro in 2012 (you can download them at `www.mattel.com` and `www.hasbro.com`), you can see that Mattel's net cash flow totaled $1,276 million after adjustments on $777 million net income, whereas Hasbro's net cash was $535 million on $336 million of net income. For Hasbro, depreciation and amortization adjustments added $100 million to the company's net cash position. Mattel added $157 million to its net cash with depreciation and amortization. Mattel increased accounts payable, accrued liabilities, and income taxes by $312 million to hold on to cash. Hasbro decreased its cash with a $22 million decrease in accrued liabilities and accounts payable. It also used $59 million in cash to pay for production costs.

Investigating Investing Activities

The investment activities section of the statement of cash flows, which looks at the purchase or sale of major new assets, is usually a drainer of cash. Consider what this section typically lists:

- Purchases of new buildings, land, and major equipment
- Mergers or acquisitions
- Major improvements to existing buildings
- Major upgrades to existing factories and equipment
- Purchases of new marketable securities, such as bonds or stock

The sale of buildings, land, major equipment, and marketable securities also appears in the investment activities section. When any of these major assets are sold, they're shown as cash generators rather than as cash drainers.

TIP

The primary reason to check out the investments section is to see how the company is managing its *capital expenditures* (money spent to buy or upgrade assets) and how much cash it's using for these expenditures. If the company shows large investments in this area, be sure to look for explanations in the management's discussion and analysis and the notes to the financial statements (see Chapter 9) to get more details about the reasons for the expenditures.

If you believe that the firm is making the right choices to grow the business and improve profits, investing in its stock may be worthwhile. If the company is making most of its capital expenditures to keep old factories operating as long as possible, that may be a sign that it isn't keeping up with new technology.

TIP

Compare companies in the same industry to see what type of expenditures each lists in investment activities and the explanations for those expenditures in the notes to the financial statements. Comparing a company with one of its peers helps you determine whether the company is budgeting its capital expenditures wisely.

REAL WORLD EXAMPLE

In comparing the statements of Hasbro and Mattel, you can see that Mattel spent more on purchases of tools, dies, molds, property, plant, and equipment. Mattel's spending totaled more than $219 million, whereas Hasbro spent about $112 million.

Understanding Financing Activities

Companies can't always raise all the cash they need from their day-to-day operations. Financing activities are another means of generating cash. Any cash raised through activities that don't include day-to-day operations appears in the financing section of the statement of cash flows.

Issuing stock

When a company first sells its shares of stock, it shows the money it raises in the financing section of the statement of cash flows. The first time a company sells shares of stock to the general public, this sale is called an *initial public offering* (IPO; see Chapter 3 for more information). Whenever a company decides to sell additional shares to raise capital, all additional sales of stock are called *secondary public offerings.*

Usually, when companies decide to do a secondary public offering, they do so to raise cash for a specific project or group of projects that they can't fund by ongoing operations. The financial department must determine whether it wants to raise funds for these new projects by borrowing money (new debt) or by issuing stock (new equity). If the company already has a great deal of debt and finds that borrowing more is difficult, it may try to sell additional shares to cover the shortfall. I talk more about debt versus equity in Chapter 12.

Buying back stock

Sometimes you see a line item in the financing section indicating that a company has bought back its stock. Most often, companies that announce a stock buyback are trying to accomplish one of two goals:

- Increase the market price of their stock. (If companies buy back their stock, fewer shares remain on the market, thus raising the value of shares still available for purchase.)
- Meet internal obligations regarding employee stock options, which guarantee employees the opportunity to buy shares of stock at a price that's usually below the price outsiders must pay for the stock.

Sometimes a company buys back stock with the intention of going private (see Chapter 3). In this case, company executives and the board of directors decide that they no longer want to operate under the watchful eyes of investors and the government. Instead, they prefer to operate under a veil of privacy and not to have to worry about satisfying so many company outsiders. I discuss the advantages and disadvantages of staying private in Chapter 3.

For many firms, an announcement that they're buying back stock is an indication that they're doing well financially and that the executives believe in their company's growth prospects for the future. Because buybacks reduce the number of outstanding shares, a company can make its per-share numbers look better even though a fundamental change hasn't occurred in the business's operations.

TIP

If you see a big jump in earnings per share, look for an indication of stock buyback in the financing activities section of the statement of cash flows.

Paying dividends

Whenever a company pays dividends, it shows the amount paid to shareholders in the financing activities section. Companies aren't required to pay dividends each year, but they rarely stop paying dividends after the shareholders have gotten used to their dividend checks.

WARNING

If a company retrenches on its decision to pay dividends, the market price of the stock is sure to tumble. The company's decision not to pay dividends after paying them in the previous quarter or previous year usually indicates that it's having problems, and it raises a huge red flag on Wall Street.

Incurring new debt

When a company borrows money for the long term, this new debt also appears in the financing activities section. This type of new debt includes the issuance of bonds, notes, or other forms of long-term financing, such as a mortgage on a building.

TIP

When you read the statement of cash flows and see that the company has taken on new debt, be sure to look for explanations in the management's discussion and analysis and the notes to the financial statements about how the company is using this debt (see Chapter 9).

Paying off debt

Debt payoff is usually a good sign, often indicating that the company is doing well. However, it may also be an indication that the company is simply rolling over existing debt into another type of debt instrument.

TIP

If you see that the company paid off one debt and took on another debt that costs about the same amount of money, it likely indicates that the firm simply refinanced the original debt. Ideally, that refinancing involves lowering the company's interest expenses. Look for a full explanation of the debt payoff in the notes to the financial statements.

REAL WORLD EXAMPLE

If you compare the financing activities of Mattel and Hasbro, you see that Mattel paid off long-term debt, bought back stock, and paid dividends to deplete its cash holdings. Hasbro also paid dividends and purchased common stock, but it raised cash by taking on short-term borrowings and collecting cash from stock option transactions. Mattel used $410 million of its cash for its financing activities, while Hasbro used $219 million.

When you look at the financing activities on a statement of cash flows for younger companies, you usually see financing activities that raise capital. Their statements include funds borrowed or stock issued to raise cash. Older, more established companies begin paying off their debt and buying back stock when they've generated enough cash from operations.

Recognizing the Special Line Items

Sometimes you see line items on the statement of cash flows that appear unique to a specific company. Businesses use these line items in special circumstances, such as the discontinuation of operations. Companies that have international operations use a line item that relates to exchanging cash among different countries, which is called *foreign exchange.*

Discontinued operations

If a company *discontinues operations* (stops the activities of a part of its business), you usually see a special line item on the statement of cash flows that shows whether the discontinued operations have increased or decreased the amount of cash the company takes in or distributes. Sometimes discontinued operations increase cash because the firm no longer has to pay the salaries and other costs related to that operation.

Other times, discontinued operations can be a one-time hit to profits because the company has to make significant severance payments to laid-off employees and has to continue paying manufacturing and other fixed costs related to those operations. For example, if a company leases space for the discontinued operations, it's contractually obligated to continue paying for that space until the contract is up or the company finds someone to sublease the space.

Foreign currency exchange

Whenever a company has global operations, it's certain to have some costs related to moving currency from one country to another. The U.S. dollar, as well as currencies from other countries, experiences changes in currency exchange rates — sometimes 100 times a day or more.

REAL WORLD EXAMPLE

Each time the dollar exchange rate between two countries changes, moving currency between those countries can result in a loss or a gain. Any losses or gains related to foreign currency exchanges appear on a special line item on the statement of cash flows called *Effect of currency exchange rate changes on cash.* Both Mattel and Hasbro show the effects of currency exchange on their statements in 2007 — Hasbro's net cash decreased by $1 million, and Mattel's increased by $2 million.

Adding It All Up

This is the big one, the highlight, the bottom line: *Cash and short-term investments at end of year*. This number shows you how much cash or cash equivalents a company has on hand for continuing operations the next year.

Cash equivalents are any holdings that the company can easily change to cash, such as cash, cash in checking and savings accounts, certificates of deposit that are redeemable in less than 90 days, money-market funds, and stocks sold on the major exchanges that can be easily converted to cash.

The top line of the statement starts with net income. Adjustments are made to show the impact on cash from operations, investing activities, and financing. These adjustments convert that net income figure to actual cash available for continuing operations. Remember that this is the cash on hand that the company can use to continue its activities the next year.

REAL WORLD EXAMPLE

If you look at the statement of cash flows for Mattel and Hasbro, you can see that Mattel had about $1,336 million on hand at the end of December 2012 on net earnings of $777 million. Hasbro had about $850 million in cash and cash equivalents at the end of December 2012 on net earnings of $336 million. Mattel's cash on hand was down slightly from 2011, while Hasbro increased its cash holdings.

In Part 3, I delve more deeply into how the cash results of these two companies differ. I also show you how you can use the figures on the statement of cash flows and other statements in the financial reports to analyze the results and make judgments about a company's financial position.

» Describing the notes and their importance

» Understanding the fine print of accounting methods

» Finding out about financial commitments

» Getting acquainted with mergers and acquisitions

» Reading notes about pensions and retirement

» Detailing segmented businesses and significant events

» Keeping an eye out for red flags

Chapter 9

Scouring the Notes to the Financial Statements

Would you ever sign an important contract without reading the fine print first? I didn't think so. Remember this philosophy when you read financial statements because the corporate world certainly doesn't escape the cliché about sweeping ashes under the rug. Hiding problems in the notes to the financial statements is a common practice for companies in trouble.

In this chapter, I explain the role of the notes as part of the financial statements, I discuss the most common issues addressed in the notes, and I point out some key warning signs that raise a red flag if you see them mentioned in the notes. And to help you become a note-reading expert, I refer to the financial reports of Hasbro and Mattel (both toy companies) throughout the chapter. (You can view their complete annual reports at `www.hasbro.com` and `www.mattel.com`.)

TIP

When searching for a company's financial reports on its website, first find the corporation information section. Within that section, you find the investor-relations section, which contains links to the company's annual and quarterly reports.

Deciphering the Small Print

Figuring out how to read and understand the small print of the notes to the financial statements can be a daunting task. Most times, companies present these notes in the least visually appealing way and deliberately fill them with accounting jargon so they're hard for the general public to understand. By making these notes so difficult to decipher, companies fulfill their obligations to the Securities and Exchange Commission (SEC) to give the required financial report to the reader, but at the same time, they make it hard for the reader to actually understand the information presented.

But don't give up. These notes contain a lot of important information that you need to know, including accounting methods used, red flags about a company's finances, and any legal entanglements that may threaten the company's future. I point out the key sections of the notes to the financial statements and what types of information to pluck out of these sections.

The first indication of the notes to the financial statements appears at the bottom of the financial statements. You see an indication that the accompanying notes are an integral part of the statement. In the same small print, you find the actual notes on numerous pages after the financial statements.

REMEMBER

The information on the financial statement is just a listing of numbers. To really analyze how well a company is doing financially, you need to understand what the numbers mean and what decisions the company made to get the numbers. Sometimes a line item refers you to a specific note, but most times, you see only a general reference to the notes at the bottom of the statement.

The notes have no specific format, but you're likely to find at least one note regarding several key issues in every company's financial report. Read on to find out what these key issues are.

Accounting Policies Note: Laying out the Rules of the Road

The first note in almost every company's financial report gives you the ammunition you need to understand the accounting policies used to develop the financial statements. This note explains the accounting rules the company used to develop its numbers. The note is usually called the "Summary of significant accounting policies." Issues discussed in this note include:

- **Asset types:** The types of things the company owns. (See Chapters 4 and 6 for more information on assets.)
- **Method of valuation:** How the company values its assets. (See Chapters 4 and 6 for more information on valuation.)
- **Methods of depreciation and amortization:** The methods the firm uses to show the use of its assets. (See Chapters 4 and 6 for more information on depreciation and amortization.)
- **How revenue and expenses are recognized:** How the company records the money it takes in from sales and the money it pays out to cover its expenses. (See Chapters 4 and 7 for more information on revenue and expenses.)
- **Pensions:** The obligations the business has to its current and future retirees.
- **Risk management:** What the company does to minimize its risk.
- **Stock-based compensation:** Employee incentive plans involving stock ownership.
- **Income taxes:** The company's income tax obligations and the amount the company paid in taxes.

REMEMBER

Carefully read the summary of significant accounting policies. If you don't understand a policy, research it further so you can make a judgment about how this policy may impact the company's financial position. You can either research the issue yourself on the Internet or call the company's investor relations office to ask questions. Also, compare policies among the companies you're analyzing. You want to see whether the differences in the ways companies handle the valuation of assets or the recognition of revenues and expenses make it more difficult for you to analyze and compare the results.

For example, if companies use different methods to value their inventory, this can have a major impact on net income. I explain the impact of inventory valuation on net income in Chapter 15. Many times, you don't actually have enough details to make apples-to-apples comparisons of two firms that use different accounting policies, but you need to be aware that the policies differ as you analyze the companies' financial results, and be alert to the fact that you may be comparing apples to oranges.

Depreciation

One significant difference in accounting policies that can affect the bottom line is the amount of time a company allows for the depreciation of assets. One company may use a 15- to 25-year time frame, and another may use a 10- to 40-year span. The time frame used for depreciation directly impacts the value of the assets, which is recorded on the line item of the balance sheet called *Cost less accumulated depreciation.* A faster depreciation method reduces the value of these assets more quickly.

Depreciation expenses are also deducted from general revenue. A company that writes off its buildings quickly — say, in 25 years rather than up to 40 years — has higher depreciation expenses and lower net income than a company that takes longer to write off its buildings. I discuss how depreciation works in greater detail in Chapter 4.

Revenue

You can find some noteworthy differences between companies by reading the revenue recognition section of the summary of significant accounting policies. Differences regarding the timing of revenue recognition can impact the total revenues reported. For example, one company may recognize revenue when a product ships to the customer. Another company may recognize revenue when the customer receives the product. If products are shipped at the end of the month, a company that includes shipped products may include the revenue in that month, but a company that recognizes revenue only when products are received may not include the revenue until the next month.

Other revenue-recognition differences to pay attention to include the following:

- **Sales price:** Some companies sell products with a fixed sales price, but others indicate that prices aren't fixed and are determined between the company and the customer.
- **Collectibility:** Some companies may indicate that whether they report income depends on whether all the revenue is likely to be collected. Successful collection can depend on the business environment, a customer's financial condition, historical collection experience, accounts receivable aging, and customer disputes. If collectibility is uncertain, the revenue isn't reported. I talk more about accounts receivable collections and how to analyze them in Chapter 16.

Expenses

Expenses differ widely among companies. As you read this part of the accounting policies note, be sure to notice the types of expenses the company chooses to highlight. Sometimes the differences between companies can give you insight into how the companies operate. Here are two key areas where you may see differences in how a company reports expenses:

- **Product development:** Some companies develop all their products in-house, whereas others pay royalties to inventors, designers, and others to develop and market new products. In-house product development is reported as research and development expenses.

  If the company develops new products primarily by using outside sources, these expenses are in a line item for royalty expenses.

- **Advertising:** Some companies indicate that all advertising is expensed at the time the advertising is printed or aired. Others may write off advertising over a longer period of time. Companies that depend on catalog sales typically spread out their ad expenses over several months or even a year if they can prove that sales continued to come in during that longer period of time.

TIP

As you compare two firms' financial reports, look for both the similarities and differences in their accounting policies. You may need to make some assumptions regarding the financial statements, to compare apples to apples when trying to decide which company is the better investment. For example, if the companies depreciate assets differently, you must remember that their asset valuations aren't the same, nor are their depreciation expenses (based on the same assumptions).

REAL WORLD EXAMPLE

Sometimes you find a special note when a significant event impacts company operations. Such an event did occur for Mattel, and it's reflected in a special note entitled "Note 4 — Product Recalls and Withdrawals." During 2007, Mattel had several major recalls because of defective products manufactured in China. In response to these recalls, Mattel wrote:

> As a result of third quarter 2007 recalls, Mattel intentionally slowed down its shipments out of Asia while it conducted extensive product testing in the third quarter 2007. Also, export licenses at several manufacturing facilities in China were temporarily suspended in September 2007 while safety procedures were reviewed, but all licenses were in place on December 31, 2007. Mattel's ability to import products into certain countries was also temporarily impacted by product recalls as certain countries and regulatory authorities reviewed Mattel's safety procedures; however, these import and export issues were largely resolved early in the fourth quarter of 2007 and did not have a significant financial impact on Mattel's 2007 results.

Although Mattel states the recalls didn't have a significant impact on its bottom line, costs to straighten out this mess legally and administratively totaled $42 million, according to Note 4. Product recalls cost the company another $68.4 million. Luckily for Mattel, the company was able to put a fix in place before its key fourth-quarter sales period during the holiday season. Otherwise, some popular Mattel toys may not have been available for Christmas and Chanukah shoppers. But that $110.4 ($42 + $68.4) million equaled about 18 percent of Mattel's net income of about $600 million, which, to me, seems like a significant impact.

Figuring out Financial Borrowings and Other Commitments

How a company manages its debt is critical to its short- and long-term profitability. You can find out a lot about a company's financial management by reading the notes related to financial commitments.

You always find at least one note about the financial borrowings and other commitments that impact the short- and long-term financial health of the company.

REAL WORLD EXAMPLE

Mattel has one note that summarizes everything under one umbrella called "Seasonal financing and long-term debt." Hasbro splits this note into two. One is called "Financing arrangements," for the short-term borrowings and other special arrangements, and the second is called "Long-term debt."

REMEMBER

No matter how a company structures its notes related to financial borrowings and other commitments, as you read the notes, break the information into two piles: long-term borrowings and short-term borrowings. The *long-term borrowings* involve financial obligations of more than one year, and the *short-term borrowings* involve obligations due within the 12-month period being discussed in the financial report.

Long-term obligations

For accounting purposes on the financial statements, only two types of debt are recognized: current debt and long-term debt. *Current debt* is due over the next 12 months, and *long-term debt* includes debt that a company must pay during any period beyond the next 12 months. Both medium- and long-term notes or bonds fall into the long-term debt category. *Medium-term notes or bonds* are debt that a company borrows for two to ten years. *Long-term notes or bonds* include all debt borrowed for more than ten years.

In the discussion of long-term financial debts, you find two key charts. One chart shows the terms of the borrowings, and the other shows the amount of cash that the company must pay toward this debt for each of the next five years and beyond.

REAL WORLD EXAMPLE

Table 9-1 shows Mattel's long-term debt.

If a company is managing its debt well, it frequently looks for opportunities to lower its interest expenses. Because interest rates have dropped considerably, when you see interest rates on these charts that are significantly higher than interest rates available in the current market environment, you need to wonder whether the company is doing a good job of managing its debt.

TABLE 9-1 Mattel's Long-term Debt

Long-term Debt	As of Year End 2012 (in Thousands)	As of Year End 2011 (in Thousands)
Medium-term notes (6.5% to 6.51%, weighted average 6.53%) due from November 2013	$50.000	$100.000
Senior notes (fixed rate) due March 2013 (5.625%)	$350,000	$350,000
Senior notes (fixed rate) due October 2020 and October 2040 (4.35% to 6.2%)	$500,000	$500,000
Senior notes due (fixed rate) November 2016 and November 2041 (4.35% to 6.2%)	$600,000	$600,000
Less: Current portion (to be paid in 2008)	($400,000)	($50,000)
Total long-term debt	$1,100,000	$1,500,000

REAL WORLD EXAMPLE

Table 9-2 shows Hasbro's long-term debt information.

I take a closer look at this issue and how it impacts the companies' liquidity in Chapter 12. I also show you how potential lenders analyze a company's borrowing habits.

Short-term debt

Short-term debt can have a greater impact than long-term debt on a company's earnings each year, as well as on the amount of cash available for operations. The reason is that companies must pay short-term debt over the next 12 months, whereas for long-term debt, they must pay only interest and some of the principal in the next 12 months.

TABLE 9-2 **Hasbro's Long-term Debt (Carrying Cost)**

Long-term Debt	As of Year End 2012 (in Thousands)	As of Year End 2011 (in Thousands)
6.35% notes due 2040	$500,000	$500,000
6.125% notes due 2014	$436,526	$440,977
6.60% debentures due 2028	$109,895	$109,875
6.3% notes due 2017	$350,00	$350,00
Total notes due	$1,396,421	$1,400,872

The type of short-term debt you see on a firm's balance sheet varies greatly, depending on the type of business. Companies whose sales are seasonal may carry a lot more short-term debt to get themselves through the slow times than companies that have a consistent cash flow from sales throughout the year.

Seasonal companies carry large lines of credit to help them buy or produce their products during the off-season times so they can have enough product to sell during the high season. For example, a company that sells toys sells most of its product during the Christmas or other peak toy-selling seasons; during the other times of the year, it has very low sales. So Mattel and Hasbro — both toy companies with significant seasonal financing needs — maintain large lines of credit to be ready for Christmas and peak toy-selling seasons.

Another way that firms raise cash if they don't have enough on hand is to sell their accounts receivable (credit extended to customers). A company can sell the receivables to a bank or other financial institution and quickly get cash for immediate needs instead of waiting for the customers to pay. I talk more about accounts receivable management in Chapter 16.

TIP

Be sure to look for a statement in the financial obligations notes that indicates how the company is meeting its cash needs and whether it's having any difficulty meeting those needs. Some companies use "financial obligations" in the title of the note; others may have one note on short-term debt obligations and another on long-term debt obligations.

Lease obligations

Instead of purchasing plants, equipment, and facilities, many companies choose to lease them. You usually find at least one note to the financial statements that spells out a company's lease obligations. Many analysts consider lease obligations to be just another type of debt financing that doesn't have to be shown on the balance sheet. Whether the lease is shown on the balance sheet or in the notes depends on the type of lease:

- **Capital leases:** These leases provide ownership at no cost or at a greatly reduced cost at the end of the lease. This type of lease appears as a long-term debt obligation on the balance sheet.
- **Operating leases:** These leases offer no ownership provisions or provisions that require a considerable amount of cash to purchase the leased item. This type of lease is mentioned in the notes to the financial statements but doesn't appear on the balance sheet as debt.

Companies that must constantly update certain types of equipment to avoid obsolescence use operating leases rather than capital leases. At the end of the lease period, the companies return the equipment and replace it by leasing new, updated equipment. Operating leases have the lowest monthly payments.

TIP

When reading the notes, be sure to look for an explanation of the types of leases the company has and what percentage of its fixed assets are under operating leases. Some high-tech companies have larger obligations in operating-lease payments than they do in long-term liabilities. When calculating *debt ratios* (ratios that show the proportion of debt versus the type of asset or equity being considered; I show you how to calculate debt ratios in Chapter 12), many analysts use at least two-thirds, and sometimes the entire amount, of these hidden operating-lease costs in their debt-measurement calculations to judge a company's liquidity.

REMEMBER

When you see operating leases that total close to 50 percent of a firm's net fixed assets or that exceed the total of its long-term liabilities, be sure to use at least two-thirds of the obligations, if not all the payments, in your debt-measurement calculations. The fact that these obligations are only mentioned in the notes to the financial statements doesn't negate their potential role in creating future cash problems for the company.

Mergers and Acquisitions: Finding Noteworthy Information

Sometimes one company decides to buy another. Other times, two companies decide to merge into one.

If a company acquires another company or merges during the year the annual report covers, a note to the financial statements is dedicated to the financial implications of that transaction. In this note, you see information about

- The market value of the company purchased
- The amount paid for the company
- Any exchange of stock involved in the transaction
- The transaction's impact on the bottom line

When a company acquires another company, it frequently pays more for that acquisition than for the total value of the purchased company's assets. The additional money spent to buy the firm falls into the line item called *Goodwill.* Goodwill includes added value for customer base, brand name, locations, customer loyalty, and intangible factors that increase a business's value. If a company has goodwill built over the years from previous mergers or acquisitions, you see that indicated on the balance sheet as an asset. I discuss goodwill in greater detail in Chapter 4.

WARNING

In an acquisition, the acquired company's net income is added to the parent company's bottom line. This addition occurs even if the closing of the sale takes place at the end of the year. Many times, this addition can inflate the bottom line and make the net income look better than it actually will be when the companies are fully merged. Be sure to look closely at the impact any mergers, acquisitions, or even sales of parts of an acquired company have on net income.

WARNING

A merger or acquisition may positively impact the bottom line for a year or two, and then the company's performance drops dramatically as it sorts out various issues regarding overlapping operations and staff. Many times, the announcement of a merger or acquisition generates excitement, causing stock prices to skyrocket temporarily before dropping back to a more realistic value. Don't get caught up in the short-term euphoria of a merger or acquisition when you're considering the purchase of stocks. Read the details in the notes to the financial statements to find out more about the true impacts of the merger or acquisition transaction.

Pondering Pension and Retirement Benefits

You may not think of pension and other retirement benefits as types of debt, but they are. In fact, for most companies that offer pension benefits, the amount of money they owe their employees is higher than the amount they owe to bondholders and banks. Some companies offer both pensions (which are an obligation to pay retirees a certain amount for the rest of their lives after they leave the company) and other retirement benefits (which include contributions to retirement savings plans such as 401(k)s or profit-sharing plans).

When looking at the note about pensions and other retirement benefits, find out which type of plan the company offers:

- **Defined benefit plan:** The company promises a retirement benefit to each of its employees and is obligated to pay that benefit. This type of plan includes traditional retirement plans, in which employees get a set monthly or annual benefit from the company after retirement.

  Defined benefit plans carry obligations for the firm for as long as an employee lives — and sometimes for as long as both the employee and his spouse live. Determining how much that benefit will cost in the future is based on assumptions regarding how much return the company expects from its retirement portfolios and how long its employees and their spouses will live after retirement. As people live longer, pension obligations become much greater for companies that offer defined benefit plans. Many companies are phasing out this type of retirement benefit.
- **Defined contribution plan:** The employer and employee both make contributions to a retirement plan. A 401(k) is an example of a defined contribution plan. The company isn't required to pay any additional money to the employee after the employee retires and pulls her retirement funds from the company's plan, rolling the funds into individual retirement savings or an annuity option. An *annuity* is a type of insurance policy that guarantees a set payment based on terms set up at the time the annuity is purchased.

TECHNICAL STUFF

In the notes to the financial statements, you find a calculation of the expected pension expense, the funding position of the plan, and the expectations for the future obligations of that plan based on complicated assumptions figured by an *actuary* (a statistician who looks at life span and other risk factors to make assumptions about the company's long-term pension obligations). Insurance companies commonly use actuaries to determine costs for life, health, and other insurance products.

WARNING

In the pension and retirement benefits note, you find a chart that shows the annual payments the company is currently making to retirees. If you see these payments increasing more rapidly each year, it may be a sign of a long-term problem for the business. Companies need to provide a table that shows the current plan assets at fair value and projects their ability to meet pension obligations in the future.

REMEMBER

You need to compare certain figures that companies use in calculating their estimates for pension obligations. Companies in similar industries typically use similar assumptions. Numbers to watch include the

- **Discount rate:** The interest rate used to determine the present value of the projected benefit obligations
- **Rate of return on assets:** The long-term return the company expects to earn on the assets in the retirement investment portfolio
- **Rate of compensation increases:** The estimate the company makes related to salary increases and the impact those increases have on future pension obligations

Each of these rates requires assumptions about unknown future events involving the state of the economy, interest rates, investment returns, and employee life spans. A company can do no more than make an educated guess. To be sure that the company's guesses are reasonable, all you can do is check that it makes guesses that are similar to the guesses of other companies in the same industry. Also look for information in the notes about whether the company's retirement savings portfolio is sufficient to meet its expected current and future pension obligations. This information is usually shown in a chart as part of the note. If the company's retirement savings portfolio falls short, it may be a red flag for future cash-flow problems.

Breaking Down Business Breakdowns

Can you imagine what it takes to manage a multibillion-dollar company? Just reading the numbers can be a daunting task. Think about how many products are sent out to make that many sales and how many people are needed to keep the business afloat.

Most major firms deal with their massive size by splitting up the company into manageable segments. This division makes managing all aspects of the business — from product development, to product distribution, to customer satisfaction — easier.

These segments help the company more easily track the performance of each of its product lines. In the notes to the financial statements, you find at least one note related to these segment breakdowns. This note gives you details about how each of the company's segments is doing, as well as the product lines that fall under each segment.

You may also find some details about these areas:

- **Target markets:** These markets are the key market segments that the company targets, such as age group (teens, tots, adults), locations (north, south, east, west), or interest groups (sportsmen, hobbyists, and so on). Target markets are limited only by the creativity of the marketing team, which develops the groups of customers that it wants to win over.
- **The largest customers:** The company usually names the top customers that buy its products. For example, a manufacturer that sells a large portion of its products to major retailers such as Wal-Mart and Target usually gives some details about these relationships. If a small number of companies make up most of the customer base, this could be a sign of a problem in the future if one of the primary customers decides to stop using the company.
- **Manufacturing and other operational details:** The company gives you information about how it groups its product manufacturing and where its products are manufactured. If the firm manufactures its products internationally, look for indications about problems that may have occurred during the year related to those operations. Sometimes labor or political strife can have a great impact on a company's manufacturing operations. Also, weather conditions can greatly impact manufacturing conditions. For example, if the company's manufacturing for a certain product line is in Singapore, and Singapore experienced numerous damaging storms, the company may indicate that the problem occurred and that it had difficulty producing enough product for market.
- **Trade sanctions:** All companies that operate internationally must deal with trade laws, which differ in every country. Some countries impose high tariffs on products coming from outside their borders, to discourage importing. Sometimes countries impose sanctions on other countries for political actions they disagree with. For example, the U.S. doesn't allow trade with Cuba for political reasons, so a business that buys products from Cuba can't import into the U.S.

TIP

If a company faces specific marketing or manufacturing problems, you also find details about these problems in the note about segment breakdowns. Don't skip over this note!

How a company breaks down its management segments varies depending on the industry and management preferences. Some companies divide into regions based on geography; others designate segments based on product lines or customer target groups.

If a company operates internationally, you usually see the U.S. market segments separated from the non-U.S. segments, and sometimes you find the international portion broken into regions, such as Europe, Asia, or the Middle East.

You don't find any hard-and-fast rules about how to segment a business. How a company segments itself depends on how the company has operated historically or what management style the company's executives adopt.

Reviewing Significant Events

Each year, every company faces significant challenges. One year, a firm may find out that its customers are suing it for a defective product. Another year, a business may get notice from a state or local government that one of its manufacturing facilities is polluting the environment.

You may also find in the notes mention of significant events that aren't related to external forces, such as the decision to close a factory or combine two divisions.

You can look in a number of places in the notes for information on significant events. Sometimes an event has its own note, such as a note about the discontinuation of operations. Other times the event is just part of a note called "Commitments and Contingencies." Scan the notes to find significant events that impact the company's financial position. You're most likely to find significant events regarding topics such as the following:

REAL WORLD EXAMPLE

- **Lawsuits:** The company may explain any pending lawsuits (usually in the "Commitments and Contingencies" note), which can sometimes have a huge impact on the company's future. For example, Dow Corning, which is owned by Dow Chemical Corporation, is still suffering financially from lawsuits by women who face significant health problems from breast implants the company made. The breast implants first hit the market in 1962. Suits were filed against the company beginning in the 1990s, when the breast implants ruptured and caused health problems. Dow Corning ended up in bankruptcy trying to settle these lawsuits.

REAL WORLD EXAMPLE

- **Environmental concerns:** These concerns can become a significant event if the company is involved in a major environmental cleanup because of discharges from one of its plants. Cleanup can cost millions or even billions of dollars. For example, Exxon has paid more than $7 billion in reparations and fines for damages related to the *Valdez* oil spill in Alaska's Prince William Sound in 1989. BP has paid $4.5 billion in a settlement and may still be held liable for billions more, pending a civil trial, after its Deepwater Horizon oil rig exploded in the Gulf of Mexico in 2010.

- **Restructuring:** When a company decides to regroup its products, close down a plant, or make some other major change to the way it does business, this action is called *restructuring*. You usually find an individual note explaining the restructuring and how it will impact the company's income in the current year and future years.
- **Discontinued operations:** Sometimes a company decides not to restructure, but closes down an operation entirely. When this happens, you're likely to find a separate note on the financial impact of the discontinued operations, which likely includes the costs of closing down facilities and laying off or relocating employees.

Many times the information included in these notes discusses not only the financial impact of an event in the current year, but also any impact expected on financial performance in future years.

When a company discusses lawsuits and potential environmental liability cases in the notes, it commonly indicates that, in the opinion of management, the matter in question won't result in a material loss. Use your own judgment after reading the details that management provides. If you think the company may be facing bigger problems than it mentions, do your own research on the matter before investing in that company.

REMEMBER

A company facing a lawsuit isn't necessarily a matter of great concern. Given the litigious nature of society, most major corporations face lawsuits annually. But sometimes these suits do raise red flags.

Finding the Red Flags

As you probably know by now, companies love hiding their dirty laundry in the small print of the notes to the financial statements. As you read through the notes, keep an eye out for possible red flags.

WARNING

Whenever you see notes titled "Restructuring," "Discontinued operations," and "Accounting changes," look for red flags that may mean continuing expenses for a number of years. The company may detail the costs of any of these changes. Be sure to consider long-term financial impacts that may be a drain on the company's future earnings — which may mean stock prices will suffer.

WARNING

Also be on the lookout for potential lawsuits that may result in huge settlements. If you see that a lawsuit has been filed against the company, search for stories in the financial press that discuss the lawsuit in greater detail than what's included in the notes.

Significant events aren't the only sources of red flags. You may also see signs of trouble in the way the company values assets or in decisions it makes to change accounting policies. The notes involving the long-term obligations the company has to its retirees may also be a good spot to find some potential red flags.

TIP

The financial press often mentions red flags that analysts spot in companies' financial reports. Read the financial press to pick up the potential problem spots, and look for the details in the financial statements and the notes to those statements.

Finding out about valuing assets and liabilities

Valuing assets and liabilities leaves room for accounting creativity. If assets are overvalued, you may be led to believe that the company owns more than it actually does. If liabilities are undervalued, you may think the company owes less than it actually does. Either way, you get a false impression about the company's financial position.

TIP

When you don't understand something, ask questions of the firm's investor relations staff until they present the information in a manner that you understand. If you're confused about the presentation of asset or liability valuation, I guarantee that other financial readers are confused as well. I often find that the more convoluted a company's explanation is, the more likely you are to find out that the company is hiding something.

Considering changes in accounting policies

How a company puts together its numbers is just as critical as the numbers themselves. The accounting policies the company adopts drive these numbers. Whenever a firm indicates in the notes to the financial statements that it's changing accounting policies, your red flag needs to go up. I discuss the key accounting policies and how they can impact income in the section "Accounting Policies Note: Laying out the Rules of the Road," earlier in this chapter. You can find more details about accounting policies in Chapter 4.

Changes in accounting policies aren't always a sign of a problem. In fact, many times, the change is related to requirements the Financial Accounting Standards Board (FASB) or the SEC specifies. Regardless of the reason for the change, be sure you understand how that change impacts your ability to compare year-to-year or quarter-to-quarter results.

REMEMBER

If you see a change in accounting methods, but you don't see an indication that the FASB or SEC required it, dig deeper into the reasons for the change and find out how the change impacts the valuation of assets and liabilities or the company's net income. You can find some explanation in the accounting policies note, but if you don't understand the explanation there, call the investor relations department and ask questions.

Decoding obligations to retirees and future retirees

As noted in the "Pondering Pension and Retirement Benefits" section earlier in this chapter, obligations to retirees and future retirees can be a bigger drain on a company's resources than debt obligations. The note to the financial statements related to pension benefits is probably one of the most difficult to understand. Look specifically at the charts that show the company's long-term payment obligations to retirees and the cash available to pay those obligations. If you find any indication that the company may have difficulty meeting the obligations mentioned in either the text of this note or the charts, it may be a sign of a major cash flow problem in the future. Don't hesitate to call and ask questions if you don't understand the presentation.

» Understanding consolidation

» Seeing how companies buy companies

» Exploring consolidated financial statements

» Turning to the notes for details

Chapter 10

Considering Consolidated Financial Statements

Like couples who marry and work to combine two incomes, two sets of financial obligations, and two ways of managing money, situations get complicated when companies decide to join forces or buy other companies and combine their financial statements. This new arrangement can make it much harder for you to find out how each piece of this new entity performs financially. In this chapter, I discuss how to read the more complex financial reports that arise when companies consolidate.

Getting a Grip on Consolidation

One of the ways businesses grow is buying or merging with other companies. When a company buys another, it gobbles up the new one, which loses its identity. But when firms decide to merge, they usually decide jointly how the new company will operate and how to present the financial statements.

Major corporations that own more than 50 percent of a company create financial reports for each division. These entities include subsidiaries, joint ventures, and associates. Here's how they stack up:

- *Subsidiaries* are entities that a larger entity, usually a corporation, controls. The corporation controlling the subsidiary is called the *parent company*. I discuss the various ways a company can become a subsidiary in the next section, "Looking at Methods of Buying up Companies."
- *Joint ventures* are entities in which *venturers* (usually two or more corporations) share joint control over the economic activity.
- *Associates* are entities over which the parent company has significant influence, but not the level of control it has over a subsidiary.

TIP

If a company's financial report mentions these entities in any detail, you find it in the notes to the financial statements. Most times, you know only that a company has subsidiaries or associates, or participates in joint ventures, if you see "Consolidated" noted at the top of the page on the balance sheet (see Chapter 6) or income statement (see Chapter 7).

If you look at Mattel's or Hasbro's statements online (`http://investor.shareholder.com/mattel/financials.cfm`; `http://investor.hasbro.com/annuals.cfm`), you see that each statement indicates that it represents the financial results of the parent company and its subsidiaries. However, you don't see any listing on the balance sheet or income statement of what those subsidiaries are. In fact, unless a company discusses a merger, acquisition, or sale of a subsidiary, associate, or joint venture in the notes to the financial statements, you probably won't see them mentioned individually in the current year's financial report. If no financial transactions occur in the year being reported, the company may only highlight some of its subsidiaries' successes in the narrative pages in the front of the financial report.

REAL WORLD EXAMPLE

General Electric's consolidated statements are among the easier to navigate because almost every line item of the financial statements indicates which note to look for in the notes to the financial statements for more details about that line item. The Association for Investment Management and Research (AIMR) has cited GE as having one of the best practices for presenting financial information. See Figures 10-1 and 10-2.

TIP

You can see GE's complete annual report online at `www.ge.com/ar2012/`.

Most companies play a game of cat-and-mouse, hiding relevant data in the notes to the financial statements, hoping that you won't take the time to find it in the small print. Look at the statements for Hasbro and Mattel on their websites. Neither statement mentions which notes are relevant to the line items on their balance sheets or income statements. You have to scour the notes to find out which material is relevant to which parts of each of their financial statements.

(a)

Statement of Financial Position

	General Electric Company and consolidated affiliates	
At December 31 (In millions, except share amounts)	2012	2011
ASSETS		
Cash and equivalents	**$ 77,356**	$ 84,501
Investment securities (Note 3)	**48,510**	47,374
Current receivables (Note 4)	**21,500**	20,478
Inventories (Note 5)	**15,374**	13,792
Financing receivables—net (Notes 6 and 23)	**258,028**	279,918
Other GECC receivables	**7,961**	7,561
Property, plant and equipment—net (Note 7)	**69,743**	65,739
Investment in GECC	**–**	–
Goodwill (Note 8)	**73,447**	72,625
Other intangible assets—net (Note 8)	**11,987**	12,068
All other assets (Note 9)	**100,076**	111,701
Assets of businesses held for sale (Note 2)	**211**	711
Assets of discontinued operations (Note 2)	**1,135**	1,721
Total assets[a]	**$685,328**	$718,189
LIABILITIES AND EQUITY		
Short-term borrowings (Note 10)	**$101,392**	$137,611
Accounts payable, principally trade accounts	**15,675**	16,400
Progress collections and price adjustments accrued	**10,877**	11,349
Dividends payable	**1,980**	1,797
Other GE current liabilities	**14,895**	14,796
Non-recourse borrowings of consolidated securitization entities (Note 10)	**30,123**	29,258
Bank deposits (Note 10)	**46,461**	43,115
Long-term borrowings (Note 10)	**236,084**	243,459
Investment contracts, insurance liabilities and insurance annuity benefits (Note 11)	**28,268**	29,774
All other liabilities (Note 13)	**68,676**	70,653
Deferred income taxes (Note 14)	**(75)**	(131)
Liabilities of businesses held for sale (Note 2)	**157**	345
Liabilities of discontinued operations (Note 2)	**2,345**	1,629
Total liabilities[a]	**556,858**	600,055
GECC preferred stock (40,000 and 0 shares outstanding at year-end 2012 and 2011, respectively)	**–**	–
Common stock (10,405,625,000 and 10,573,017,000 shares outstanding at year-end 2012 and 2011, respectively)	**702**	702
Accumulated other comprehensive income attributable to GE[b]		
Investment securities	**677**	(30)
Currency translation adjustments	**412**	133
Cash flow hedges	**(722)**	(1,176)
Benefit plans	**(20,597)**	(22,901)
Other capital	**33,070**	33,693
Retained earnings	**144,055**	137,786
Less common stock held in treasury	**(34,571)**	(31,769)
Total GE shareowners' equity	**123,026**	116,438
Noncontrolling interests[c]	**5,444**	1,696
Total equity (Notes 15 and 16)	**128,470**	118,134
Total liabilities and equity	**$685,328**	$718,189

(a) Our consolidated assets at December 31, 2012 include total assets of $46,064 million of certain variable interest entities (VIEs) that can only be used to settle the liabilities of those VIEs. These assets include net financing receivables of $40,287 million and investment securities of $3,419 million. Our consolidated liabilities at December 31, 2012 include liabilities of certain VIEs for which the VIE creditors do not have recourse to GE. These liabilities include non-recourse borrowings of consolidated securitization entities (CSEs) of $29,123 million. See Note 24.

(b) The sum of accumulated other comprehensive income attributable to GE was $(20,230) million and $(23,974) million at December 31, 2012 and 2011, respectively.

(c) Included accumulated other comprehensive income attributable to noncontrolling interests of $(155) million and $(168) million at December 31, 2012 and 2011, respectively.

See accompanying notes.

FIGURE 10-1: *(continued)*

(b)

GE[(a)]		GECC	
2012	2011	2012	2011
$ 15,509	$ 8,382	$ 61,941	$ 76,702
74	18	48,439	47,359
10,872	11,807	—	—
15,295	13,741	79	51
—	—	268,951	288,847
—	—	13,988	13,390
16,033	14,283	53,673	51,419
77,930	77,110	—	—
46,143	45,395	27,304	27,230
10,700	10,522	1,294	1,546
37,936	36,675	62,217	75,612
—	—	211	711
9	52	1,126	1,669
$230,501	$217,985	$539,223	$584,536
$ 6,041	$ 2,184	$ 95,940	$136,333
14,259	14,209	6,277	7,239
10,877	11,349	—	—
1,980	1,797	—	—
14,896	14,796	—	—
—	—	30,123	29,258
—	—	46,461	43,115
11,428	9,405	224,776	234,391
—	—	28,696	30,198
53,093	53,826	16,050	17,334
(5,946)	(7,183)	5,871	7,052
—	—	157	345
70	158	2,275	1,471
106,698	100,541	456,626	506,736
—	—	—	—
702	702	—	—
677	(30)	673	(33)
412	133	(131)	(399)
(722)	(1,176)	(746)	(1,101)
(20,597)	(22,901)	(736)	(563)
33,070	33,693	31,586	27,628
144,055	137,786	51,244	51,578
(34,571)	(31,769)	—	—
123,026	116,438	81,890	77,110
777	1,006	707	690
123,803	117,444	82,597	77,800
$230,501	$217,985	$539,223	$584,536

(a) Represents the adding together of all affiliated companies except General Electric Capital Corporation (GECC or financial services), which is presented on a one-line basis. See Note 1.

In the consolidating data on this page, "GE" means the basis of consolidation as described in Note 1 to the consolidated financial statements; "GECC" means General Electric Capital Corporation and all of its affiliates and associated companies. Separate information is shown for "GE" and "GECC." Transactions between GE and GECC have been eliminated from the "General Electric Company and consolidated affiliates" columns on the prior page.

FIGURE 10-1: GE balance sheet.

(a)

Statement of Earnings

For the years ended December 31 (In millions; per-share amounts in dollars)	General Electric Company and consolidated affiliates 2012	2011	2010
REVENUES AND OTHER INCOME			
Sales of goods	$ 72,991	$ 66,875	$ 60,811
Sales of services	27,158	27,648	39,625
Other income (Note 17)	2,563	5,064	1,151
GECC earnings from continuing operations	—	—	—
GECC revenues from services (Note 18)	44,647	47,701	47,980
Total revenues and other income	147,359	147,288	149,567
COSTS AND EXPENSES (Note 19)			
Cost of goods sold	56,785	51,455	45,998
Cost of services sold	17,525	16,823	25,715
Interest and other financial charges	12,508	14,528	15,537
Investment contracts, insurance losses and insurance annuity benefits	2,857	2,912	3,012
Provision for losses on financing receivables (Notes 6 and 23)	3,891	3,951	7,085
Other costs and expenses	36,387	37,362	38,033
Total costs and expenses	129,953	127,031	135,380
EARNINGS FROM CONTINUING OPERATIONS BEFORE INCOME TAXES	17,406	20,257	14,187
Benefit (provision) for income taxes (Note 14)	(2,504)	(5,738)	(1,039)
EARNINGS FROM CONTINUING OPERATIONS	14,902	14,519	13,148
Earnings (loss) from discontinued operations, net of taxes (Note 2)	(1,038)	(76)	(969)
NET EARNINGS	13,864	14,443	12,179
Less net earnings attributable to noncontrolling interests	223	292	535
NET EARNINGS ATTRIBUTABLE TO THE COMPANY	13,641	14,151	11,644
Preferred stock dividends declared	—	(1,031)	(300)
NET EARNINGS ATTRIBUTABLE TO GE COMMON SHAREOWNERS	$ 13,641	$ 13,120	$ 11,344
AMOUNTS ATTRIBUTABLE TO THE COMPANY			
Earnings from continuing operations	$ 14,679	$ 14,227	$ 12,613
Earnings (loss) from discontinued operations, net of taxes	(1,038)	(76)	(969)
NET EARNINGS ATTRIBUTABLE TO THE COMPANY	$ 13,641	$ 14,151	$ 11,644
PER-SHARE AMOUNTS (Note 20)			
Earnings from continuing operations			
Diluted earnings per share	$ 1.39	$ 1.24	$ 1.15
Basic earnings per share	1.39	1.24	1.15
Net earnings			
Diluted earnings per share	1.29	1.23	1.06
Basic earnings per share	1.29	1.24	1.06
DIVIDENDS DECLARED PER SHARE	0.70	0.61	0.46

See Note 3 for other-than-temporary impairment amounts.

See accompanying notes.

Consolidated Statement of Changes in Shareowners' Equity

(In millions)	2012	2011	2010
GE SHAREOWNERS' EQUITY BALANCE AT JANUARY 1	$116,438	$118,936	$117,291
Increases from net earnings attributable to the Company	13,641	14,151	11,644
Dividends and other transactions with shareowners	(7,372)	(7,502)	(5,162)
Other comprehensive income (loss) attributable to GE	3,744	(6,119)	(2,325)
Net sales (purchases) of shares for treasury	(2,802)	169	300
Changes in other capital	(623)	(3,197)	(839)
Cumulative effect of changes in accounting principles[a]	—	—	(1,973)
Ending balance at December 31	123,026	116,438	118,936
Noncontrolling interests	5,444	1,696	5,262
Total equity balance at December 31	$128,470	$118,134	$124,198

See Note 15 for further information about changes in shareowners' equity.

(a) On January 1, 2010, we adopted amendments to Financial Accounting Standards Board (FASB) Accounting Standards Codification (ASC) 860, *Transfers and Servicing*, and ASC 810, *Consolidation*, and recorded a cumulative effect adjustment. See Notes 15 and 24.

See accompanying notes.

FIGURE 10-2: *(continued)*

(b)

GE[a]			GECC		
2012	2011	2010	2012	2011	2010
$ 73,304	$ 67,012	$ 60,344	$ 119	$ 148	$ 533
27,571	28,024	39,875	—	—	—
2,657	5,270	1,285	—	—	—
7,401	6,584	3,120	—	—	—
—	—	—	45,920	48,920	49,323
110,933	106,890	104,624	46,039	49,068	49,856
57,118	51,605	45,563	99	135	501
17,938	17,199	25,965	—	—	—
1,353	1,299	1,600	11,697	13,866	14,510
—	—	—	2,984	3,059	3,197
—	—	—	3,891	3,951	7,085
17,672	17,556	16,340	19,413	20,447	22,412
94,081	87,659	89,468	38,084	41,458	47,705
16,852	19,231	15,156	7,955	7,610	2,151
(2,013)	(4,839)	(2,024)	(491)	(899)	985
14,839	14,392	13,132	7,464	6,711	3,136
(1,038)	(76)	(969)	(1,186)	(74)	(965)
13,801	14,316	12,163	6,278	6,637	2,171
160	165	519	63	127	16
13,641	14,151	11,644	6,215	6,510	2,155
—	(1,031)	(300)	(123)	—	—
$ 13,641	$ 13,120	$ 11,344	$ 6,092	$ 6,510	$ 2,155
$ 14,679	$ 14,227	$ 12,613	$ 7,401	$ 6,584	$ 3,120
(1,038)	(76)	(969)	(1,186)	(74)	(965)
$ 13,641	$ 14,151	$ 11,644	$ 6,215	$ 6,510	$ 2,155

(a) Represents the adding together of all affiliated companies except General Electric Capital Corporation (GECC or financial services), which is presented on a one-line basis. See Note 1.

In the consolidating data on this page, "GE" means the basis of consolidation as described in Note 1 to the consolidated financial statements; "GECC" means General Electric Capital Corporation and all of its affiliates and associated companies. Separate information is shown for "GE" and "GECC." Transactions between GE and GECC have been eliminated from the "General Electric Company and consolidated affiliates" columns on the prior page.

FIGURE 10-2: GE income statement.

Looking at Methods of Buying up Companies

One of the most common ways companies grow is to buy up smaller companies. Either these smaller companies get completely gobbled up, with no outward sign that they ever existed, or they become subsidiaries operating under the umbrella of the firm that bought them.

A company can take control over another company by using any of three different methods: statutory merger, statutory consolidation, or stock acquisition. Only when a company buys another using the stock acquisition method does it become a subsidiary. Here's a brief overview of the ways one company can buy another:

- **Statutory merger:** This merger occurs when one company acquires all the assets of another and accepts the responsibilities of all its liabilities. The company that's taken over goes out of business and is no longer a separate legal entity. The financial results of the business that disappeared become part of the consolidated financial results of the company that remains.

- **Statutory consolidation:** In this situation, two companies agree to combine to form one new entity; one company does *not* take over the other. When the transaction is complete, only one legal entity survives, either under one of the original names of the two companies or under a completely new name. Their financial results are combined in a consolidated financial statement.
- **Stock acquisition:** In this case, two companies combine, but both remain separate legal entities after the transaction. The company that buys the stock emerges as the parent firm, and the other company becomes the subsidiary. The parent company takes on all the subsidiary's responsibilities and liabilities, and the financial statements of the two are consolidated into the parent company's financial statements.

  TECHNICAL STUFF

  Two types of stock acquisition exist:

  - **Majority interest:** When a company buys more than 50 percent of another company's stock, this represents a *majority interest.* When a company buys 100 percent of another company's stock, but the two businesses don't merge, the subsidiary is called a *wholly owned subsidiary.*
  - **Minority interest:** When a company or individual owns less than 50 percent of a corporation's voting stock, that's a *minority interest.* A consolidated balance sheet that indicates minority interest shows the interests of minority shareholders as a liability, an equity, or between the liabilities and equities sections.

Subsidiaries are the entities left in place after a company acquires another company using the stock acquisition method. If you were a shareholder in the subsidiary before it was bought out, you won't find tracking the company that you originally owned easy. Instead, you'll find that most of the financial detail is now just part of the consolidated financial statements of the larger firm.

REMEMBER

Stock acquisition is the most common method for taking control of another company because it's cheaper than paying for all the company's assets. To control another company, a parent company needs to buy more than 50 percent of its stock. This type of acquisition doesn't require the difficult and more time-consuming negotiations that are necessary to take control of 100 percent of a company. Sometimes after a parent company takes control of another business, it continues buying stock over the next few years until it owns 100 percent of the stock.

Acquiring a company through stock acquisition is also easier than using the other takeover methods because the company's shares are sold on the open market. One company can take over another simply by buying up those open-market shares.

Reading Consolidated Financial Statements

Most major corporations are made up of numerous companies bought along the way to create their empires. The financial statement for such a corporation reflects the financial results for all these entities it bought, as well as the original assets of the company.

After a stock acquisition by the parent company, the subsidiary continues to maintain separate accounting records. But in reality, the parent company controls the subsidiary, so it no longer operates completely independently. By accounting rules, the parent company must present its subsidiary's and its own financial operations in a consolidated manner (even though the two companies may be separate legal entities). The parent company does so by publishing *consolidated financial statements,* which combine the assets, liabilities, revenue, and expenses of the parent company with those of its affiliates (that is, its subsidiaries, associates, and joint ventures).

WARNING

If you hold a minority interest (see the previous section for more information on minority interest) in the subsidiary of a parent company, the consolidated financial statements don't give you the information you need to make decisions about your holdings. But in addition to having its report included in the consolidated financial statements, a subsidiary with minority shareholders must report its financial results separately from its parent company.

When a company owns all the common stock of its subsidiaries, it doesn't need to publish reports about the subsidiaries' individual results for the general public to peruse. Shareholders don't even need to know the results of these subsidiaries.

In preparing consolidated financial statements, the parent company must eliminate numerous transactions between itself and its affiliates before presenting the statements to the public.

For example, the parent company must eliminate such transactions for accounts receivable and accounts payable, to avoid counting revenue twice and giving the financial report reader the impression that the consolidated entity has more profits or owes more money than it actually does. Other key transactions that a parent company must eliminate when preparing consolidated financial statements include the following:

- **Investments in the subsidiary:** The parent company's books show its investments in a subsidiary as an asset account. The subsidiary's books show the stock that the parent company holds as shareholders' equity. Instead of double-counting this type of transaction, the parent company eliminates it on the consolidated statements by writing off one transaction.

- **Advances to the subsidiary:** If a parent company advances money to a subsidiary or a subsidiary advances money to its parent company, both entities carry the opposite side of this transaction on their books (that is, one entity gains money while the other one loses it, or vice versa). Again, companies avoid the double transaction on the consolidated statements by getting rid of one transaction.
- **Interest revenue and expenses:** Sometimes a parent company loans money to a subsidiary, or a subsidiary loans money to a parent company; in these business transactions, one company may charge the other one interest on the loan. On the consolidated statements, any interest revenue or expenses that these loans generate must be eliminated.
- **Dividend revenue and expenses:** If a subsidiary declares a dividend, the parent company receives some of these dividends as revenue from the subsidiary. Anytime a parent company records revenue from its subsidiaries on its books, the parent company must eliminate any dividend expenses that the subsidiary recorded on its books.
- **Management fees:** Sometimes a subsidiary pays its parent company a *management fee* for the administrative services it provides. These fees are recorded as revenue on the parent company's books and as expenses on the subsidiary's books.
- **Sales and purchases:** Parent companies frequently buy products or materials from their subsidiaries, and their subsidiaries buy products or materials from them. In fact, most companies that buy other companies do so within the same industry as a means of getting control of a product line, a customer base, or some other aspect of that company's operations.

  However, the consolidated income statements can't show these sales as revenue and can't show the purchases as expenses. Otherwise, the company is double-counting the transaction. Accounting rules require that parent companies eliminate these types of transactions.

As you can see, these major transactions are all critical for determining whether a company made a profit or loss from its activities. Eliminating assets, liabilities, revenue, and expenses from public view makes determining a subsidiary's financial results nearly impossible for shareholders or creditors. But if these transactions are included, the value of the parent company's stock is distorted because the transactions are counted twice. The shareholders of the parent company can't know the true value of the company's assets and liabilities in such a case; the income statement doesn't reflect the company's true revenues and expenses.

TECHNICAL STUFF

The Securities and Exchange Commission (SEC) and Financial Accounting Standards Board (FASB) tried to address the problem that shareholders and creditors of a subsidiary face by requiring parent companies to provide *segment reporting* (reporting about subsidiaries, business units, and divisions of the company), which you also find in the notes to the financial statements.

Looking to the Notes

The eliminations to adjust for reporting subsidiary results mentioned in the previous section don't show up in the parent company's financial reports unless some portion of the stock acquisition takes place in the year that's being reported. When the acquisition or some financial impact of that acquisition does take place in the year that's being reported, you need to look to the notes to the financial statements to get details about any financial impacts.

In the first note to the consolidated financial statement, the company indicates that the financial statements represent the results of the parent company, *not* its affiliates. The company also includes some statement about the eliminated transactions. Just to give you an example of how this is worded, here's the information from GE's notes.

REAL WORLD EXAMPLE

Here, verbatim, is how GE explains its presentation of the number in its financial statements:

- Financial data and related measurements are presented in the following categories:
- GE: This represents the adding together of all affiliates other than General Electric Capital Corporation (GECC), whose continuing operations are presented on a one-line basis, giving effect to the elimination of transactions among such affiliates.
- GECC: This represents the adding together of all affiliates of GECC, giving effect to the elimination of transactions among such affiliates.
- Consolidated: This represents the adding together of GE and GECC, giving effect to the elimination of transactions between GE and GECC.
- Operating Segments: These comprise our eight businesses, focused on the broad markets they serve: Power & Water, Oil & Gas, Energy Management, Aviation, Healthcare, Transportation, Home & Business Solutions and GE Capital.
- Prior-period information has been reclassified to be consistent with how we managed our businesses in 2012.

Note that you don't find out what subsidiaries fall under GE in this explanation. You don't find that detail in Mattel's or Hasbro's notes, either, as I discuss in Chapter 9. Few companies provide that detail. Sound like a confusing house of cards? Yep, it sure is, which is what makes reading consolidated financial statements so difficult!

Mergers and acquisitions

If a company completes a merger or acquisition in the year that's reported on the consolidated financial statement, you find a special note in the notes to the financial statements. Otherwise, if you want to find out any details about how the mergers and acquisitions may still be impacting the company financially, you have to start digging.

TECHNICAL STUFF

For example, if a company issues additional shares of stock to buy a subsidiary, the value of the stock held by shareholders before the acquisition is *diluted*, which means that the same earnings or assets must be divided among a greater number of pieces. To see how this works, imagine an example involving 100 shares of stock and a company profit of $100. In this scenario, each share of stock claims $1 of earnings. If, after the acquisition, 150 shares of stock are outstanding, each share of stock can claim only 67 cents of the $100 of earnings. This diluted ownership impacts the amount of dividends or the portion of ownership you have in the company for the rest of the time you own that stock.

You can see how you need to play a game of cat-and-mouse to find all the little pieces of cheese laid out in the financial statements. Companies don't make information easily accessible, and they often hide the financial impact of an acquisition or merger on the value of your shares by writing the notes to the financial statements in such a convoluted way that you have to be a detective to sort out the relevant details.

Goodwill

Another important note you can check out to find the impact of mergers and acquisitions on the consolidated financial statements is the note that explains goodwill. *Goodwill* is the amount of money a company pays in excess of the value of the assets when it buys another company (see Chapters 4 and 6 for more details). For example, suppose a company has $100 million in assets, and another company offers to buy it for $150 million. The extra $50 million doesn't represent tangible assets like inventory or property; it represents extra value because of customer loyalty, store locations, or other factors that add value. Goodwill is a factor only in the case of a merger or acquisition that involves acquiring 100 percent of the subsidiary or other affiliate.

Liquidations or discontinued operations

Whenever a company sells a subsidiary or other affiliate or discontinues its operations, a note to the financial statements regarding this transaction appears in the year in which the transaction first occurred. After the first year, any impact that a sale or a discontinuance of operations has on a company's operating results is usually buried in other notes. Just like with mergers and acquisitions, you have to play detective to find out any ongoing impact that these changes have had on the company.

The company includes information in the notes about any profits or losses related to the liquidation of an asset or discontinued operations. Because these transactions can impact financial statements over a number of years, the fine print includes financial impacts for the years prior to the year being reported, as well as anticipated future impacts.

REMEMBER

When reading the consolidated financial statements and their related notes, be sure you look for any mention of the impact of previous mergers or acquisitions of affiliates and how those transactions may still be impacting the financial statements.

You may find notes related to impacts on the balance sheet, income statement, shareholders' equity, or cash flows. Transactions involving affiliates can impact any of these statements.

3 Analyzing the Numbers

IN THIS PART . . .

Find out how to test the profitability to determine whether a company has made any money.

Find out how to test the liquidity to ensure that a company has the resources to pay its bills.

Find out where the cash comes in and goes out, and ensure that a company is able to generate the cash it needs.

- » Getting a handle on the price/earnings ratio
- » Diving into the dividend payout ratio
- » Examining return on sales
- » Reviewing return on assets
- » Understanding return on equity
- » Working with margins

Chapter 11 Testing the Profits and Market Value

Well, did the company make any money? Everyone, and I mean *everyone* with a financial stake in the company — executives, investors, debtors, employees — wants the answer to that question. Investors especially want to know whether the company's stock is worth the price they have to pay.

You may think the answer is a simple yes or no, but the answer always depends on many factors. How well did the business make use of its resources in order to make a profit? Was that profit high enough based on the resources the firm had on hand and compared with that of similar companies? Did the company pay out a fair share of its earnings to its investors? Did it reinvest the right amount of money in its coffers for future growth?

In this chapter, I show you how to answer these key questions with calculations that help you test a company's profitability and market value: price/earnings ratio (P/E), dividend payout ratio, return on sales (ROS), return on assets (ROA), and return on equity (ROE). I also review how to calculate the profit margins — both the operating margin and the net margin.

To help you understand the validity of these profitability tests, I compare the results of the two leading toy companies, Mattel and Hasbro, and I compare their results with those of the toy industry in general. If you want to follow along, you need the financial statements of Mattel (`http://investor.shareholder.com/mattel/financials.cfm`) and Hasbro (`http://investor.hasbro.com/annuals.cfm`). You can download those at each of the company's websites, or you can order an annual report by calling the company's investor relations office.

The Price/Earnings Ratio

The profit number you hear discussed most often in the financial news is the *price/earnings ratio*, or the *P/E ratio*. Basically, the P/E ratio looks at the price of the stock versus its earnings. For example, a P/E ratio of 10 means that, for every $1 in company earnings per share, people are willing to pay $10 per share to buy the stock. If the P/E is 20, then people are willing to pay $20 per share for each $1 of company earnings.

Why are people willing to pay more per dollar of earnings on some stock? Because the people who buy the more expensive stock believe the stock has greater potential for growth. This ratio is used when valuing stocks and is one of the oldest measurements in the world of stock exchanges.

WARNING

On its own, the P/E ratio means little, but as part of an overall evaluation of a company, the P/E ratio helps you interpret earnings results. Never make a decision on whether to buy or sell a stock based solely on the P/E ratio. Nonetheless, a negative P/E or a P/E of zero is a major trouble sign, indicating that a company isn't profitable.

Figuring out earnings per share

Earnings per share represents the amount of income a company earns per share of stock on the stock market. The firm calculates the *earnings per share* (EPS) by dividing the total earnings by the number of shares outstanding. Companies often use a weighted average of the number of shares outstanding during the reporting period because the number of shares outstanding can change as the company sells new shares to outside investors or company employees. In addition, companies sometimes buy back shares from existing shareholders, reducing the number of shares available to the general public.

A weighted average is calculated by totaling the number of shares available during a certain period of time and dividing that number by the number of periods included. For example, if the weighted average is based on a monthly average, the number of shares outstanding on the stock market at the end of each month is totaled and divided by 12 to find the weighted average. This calculation can also be done with a weekly or daily figure. If weekly stock totals are used, the total of these periods is divided by 52. If daily numbers are used, the total is divided by 365.

Calculating the P/E ratio

To get the P/E ratio, divide the market value per share of stock by earnings per share of stock:

Market value per share of stock ÷ Earnings per share of stock = P/E ratio

TIP

Many websites help you find the market value per share of stock. Yahoo! Finance (`finance.yahoo.com`) is one of my favorites for easily finding historical stock data.

The P/E formula comes in three flavors, which vary according to how earnings per share is calculated: trailing, current, and forward earnings.

- **Trailing P/E:** You calculate a trailing P/E by using earnings per share from the last four quarters, or 12 months of earnings. This number gives you a view of a company's earnings ratios based on accurate historical data.
- **Leading or projected P/Es:** The other two types of P/E ratios are calculated using analysts' expectations, so they're sometimes called leading or projected P/Es.
  - The *current P/E ratio* is calculated using earnings that analysts expect during the current year.
  - A *forward P/E ratio* is based on analysts' projections for the next year.

WARNING

Any P/E ratio that uses future projected results is only as good as the analyst making those projections. So be careful when you see the terms *leading, projected, current,* or *forward P/E.*

REMEMBER

Any type of P/E ratio is just one of many profitability ratios to consider. This ratio gives you a good idea of what the public is willing to pay per share of stock based on the company's historical earnings (trailing P/E) or what the analysts project you can consider paying per share of stock based on future earnings (current P/E or forward P/E). It gives you no guarantee of what the company will earn or what the stock price will be in the future.

Practicing the P/E ratio calculation

Now that you understand the basics behind the P/E ratio, I show you how to calculate it using real-world numbers from Hasbro and Mattel. As I mention earlier in this chapter, the company calculates earnings per share, which represents the total earnings divided by the number of shares outstanding. Remember that the number of shares outstanding can change as the company sells new shares to investors or buys them back from existing shareholders.

When a company reports its earnings per share, it usually shows two numbers: basic and diluted. The firm calculates the *basic EPS* using a weighted average of all shares currently on the market. The *diluted EPS* takes into consideration all future obligations to sell stock. For example, this number takes into account employees who have stock options to buy stock in the future, or bondholders who hold bonds that are convertible to stock.

REAL WORLD EXAMPLE

To practice using the formula to calculate P/E ratios, I use numbers from Mattel's and Hasbro's income statements. Table 11-1 shows Mattel's basic and diluted EPS for 2012, 2011, and 2010. Table 11-2 shows the same information for Hasbro.

TABLE 11-1 Mattel's Earnings per Share (EPS)

Net Income (Loss)	Earnings per Share		
	2012	2011	2010
Basic	2.25	2.20	1.88
Diluted	2.22	2.18	1.86

TABLE 11-2 Hasbro's Earnings per Share (EPS)

Net Income (Loss)	Earnings per Share		
	2012	2011	2010
Basic	2.58	2.88	2.86
Diluted	2.55	2.82	2.74

In the following examples, to calculate how the public valued the results for Mattel and Hasbro at the end of June 2013 using the 2012 annual report, I use the stock price at the time the market closed on June 20, 2013. I also use the diluted earnings per share, which more accurately represents the company's outstanding shareholder obligations.

Mattel closed at $44.02, and Hasbro closed at $43.81. Even though Mattel's diluted earnings per share were 36 cents per share lower than Hasbro, Hasbro's stock sold for slightly less than Mattel, by 21 cents per share.

Here's Mattel's P/E ratio:

$44.02 (Market value) ÷ $2.22 (2012 Diluted EPS) = 19.90 (P/E ratio)

Note that the P/E ratio is shown without a dollar sign. P/E is not a dollar value, but instead shows the number of times the price outweighs the earnings of the company.

So Mattel investors were willing to pay $19.90 for every $1 of earnings by Mattel in 2013. Following is Hasbro's P/E ratio:

$43.81 (Market value) ÷ $ 2.55 (2007 Diluted EPS) = 17.18 (P/E ratio)

Hasbro investors were willing to pay $17.18 for every $1 of earnings by Hasbro in 2013.

These numbers show a dramatic improvement for Mattel over its results five years ago, after the scandal involving toy recalls from China in 2007. At that time, Mattel's P/E ratio was just $13.08, whereas Hasbro's was $18.40. In 2013, the tables turned: Investors were willing to pay more per dollar of earnings for Mattel stock.

Using the P/E ratio to judge company market value (stock price)

In comparing Mattel's and Hasbro's P/E ratios, you can conclude that, on June 20, 2013, investors believed that Mattel had better chances of improving its earnings performance than Hasbro and, therefore, were willing to pay a higher price for each share of Mattel's stock. You must dig deeper into the numbers, the quarterly reports for the first half of 2013, and general financial press coverage to determine why investors were more bullish on Mattel than Hasbro. But this one quick calculation lets you know which stock investors favor.

How do you know what a reasonable P/E ratio is for a company? Historically, the average P/E ratio for stock falls between 15 and 25. This ratio depends on economic conditions and the industry the company's in. Some industries, such as technology, regularly maintain higher P/E ratios in the range of 30 to 40.

In addition to comparing two companies, you need to compare the P/E calculation to the industry of the companies. Doing so allows you to gauge stock price or market value not only for the companies whose annual reports you're analyzing, but also for other companies in the same business.

TIP

One way you can find out the average industry P/E is to look up a company on Yahoo! Finance (`finance.yahoo.com`). On its home page, you see a link for industry information. Toy companies fall into the Toys & Games industry category. In June 2013, Mattel and Hasbro beat out all other industry players by a significant margin. The next-closest toy and games company was Gaming Partners International Corporation, with a P/E of 12.15.

The P/E is a good quick ratio for picking potential investment candidates, but you don't want to use this ratio alone to make a buying or selling decision. After you pick your targets, read and analyze the annual reports and other information about the company before making a decision to invest.

TIP

If you want to start your research on potential investment opportunities based on leaders or laggards in an industry, you can find a summary for all industry statistics at `http://biz.yahoo.com/ic/index.html`. You may wonder why someone would even consider laggards as investment opportunities. Well, you can sometimes find a company that many investors think is a dog but is actually terribly undervalued and doing the right things to recover from its current slump. This style of investing is called *value investing.*

When investors are bullish, they tend to bid up the price of stock and end up paying higher prices for the stock than it may actually be worth. This price-bidding war also drives up the P/E ratio.

REMEMBER

The market sets stock prices based solely on the price at which someone is willing to sell a stock and the price at which someone is willing to buy a stock.

REAL WORLD EXAMPLE

During the Internet and technology stock bubble of the late 1990s and early 2000s, P/E ratios hit highs in the hundreds and tumbled dramatically after the bubble burst. Even big names, such as Microsoft, had P/E ratios over 100 that dropped back to realistic levels when the bubble burst. In July 2004, Microsoft's P/E was 41.37, so you can see that investors can seriously overbid even a top company. By June 2008, Microsoft's P/E had dropped dramatically to 16.14. In 2013, Microsoft still carried a much lower P/E than in 2004. In June 2013, the P/E was 17.11. Its new operating system, Windows 8 didn't do as well as expected, and the losses in the European courts hurt the company's future earnings potential. Investors are no longer willing to overpay for its stock.

WARNING

Be careful when you see P/Es creeping above their historical averages. Usually you're encountering a sign that a correction is looming on the horizon and will bring stock prices down to realistic levels. Do your homework while you wait for the correction, and be ready to jump in after the correction and pick up the stocks you want on sale.

Understanding variation among ratios

You'll probably find varying P/E ratios for the same company because the number used for EPS can vary depending on which method the company chooses for calculating EPS. The diluted EPS is the one you generally want to use. This figure is based on the current number of shares on the market, as well as shares promised to employees for purchase in the future and shares promised to creditors who may decide to convert a debt into a stockholding (if that's part of the debt agreement). So diluted earnings gives you the most accurate picture of the actual earnings per share of stock now available on the market or committed for sale in the future.

But when companies put out a press release, they tend to use whatever EPS looks most favorable for them. Companies can choose among four basic ways to calculate EPS:

- **Reported EPS:** Companies calculate this EPS number by using general accounting principles and report it on the financial statements. They show it in two formats: basic and diluted. Most times, the diluted EPS number is the best one to use, but it's sometimes distorted by one-time events, such as the sale of a division or a one-time charge for discontinued operations. Be sure to read the notes to the financial statements to determine whether you need to adjust the EPS figure for unusual events. Chapter 9 discusses the notes to the financial statements in great detail.
- **Pro forma EPS:** You almost always find this EPS in a company's press release because it makes the company look the best. In most cases, this figure excludes some of the expenses or income the firm uses in the official financial reports. The company adjusts these official numbers to take out income that won't recur, such as a one-time gain on the sale of marketable securities, or expenses that won't recur, such as the closing of a large division.

  REMEMBER

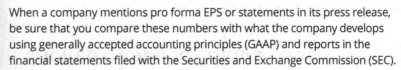

  When a company mentions pro forma EPS or statements in its press release, be sure that you compare these numbers with what the company develops using generally accepted accounting principles (GAAP) and reports in the financial statements filed with the Securities and Exchange Commission (SEC).
- **Headline EPS:** This EPS is the one you hear about on TV and read about in the newspapers. The earnings per share numbers used may be basic EPS, diluted EPS, pro forma EPS, or some other EPS that's calculated based on analysts' projections, so you have absolutely no idea what's behind the numbers or the P/E ratio calculated using it. It's likely the most unreliable EPS, and you don't want to use it for your evaluation.
- **Cash EPS:** Companies calculate this EPS by using *operating cash flow* (cash generated by business operations to produce and sell its products). Operating cash can't be manipulated by accounting rules as easily as net income, so some analysts believe this EPS is the purest. When you see this number, be sure that

it's based on operating cash and isn't just a fancy way of saying EBITDA (earnings before interest, taxes, depreciation, and amortization). You can judge this by calculating the cash EPS using the EBITDA reported on the financial statements and the net cash from operations reported on the statement of cash flows. Only the net cash figure gives you a true picture of cash flow.

REMEMBER

The P/E ratio is an ever-changing number based on the day's market price. It's also a number that's hard to depend on unless you know the calculations behind it. Companies can calculate the earnings per share in many different ways — using basic EPS, diluted EPS, pro forma EPS, cash EPS, headline EPS, and projected or leading EPS. Reading the financial reports and checking the calculation for yourself is the only way you can truly determine a company's P/E and what's included in its calculation.

The Dividend Payout Ratio

The dividend payout ratio looks at the amount of a firm's earnings that it pays out to investors. Using this ratio, you can determine the actual cash return you'll get by buying and holding a share of stock.

Some companies pay a portion of their earnings directly to their shareholders using dividends. Growth companies, which reinvest all their profits, rarely pay out dividends, but older, mature companies usually do. Older companies that no longer need to reinvest large sums in growing their businesses pay out the highest dividends.

To determine how well investors did with their stock holding, you can calculate the *dividend payout ratio.*

Determining dividend payout

To find the dividend payout ratio, divide yearly dividend per share (the total amount per share paid out to investors during the year in dividends) by earnings per share:

Yearly dividend per share ÷ Earnings per share = Dividend payout ratio

REAL WORLD EXAMPLE

You can use numbers from Mattel's 2012 income statement to practice calculating the dividend payout ratio:

\$1.24 (Dividends per share) ÷ \$2.22 (Diluted EPS) = 55.86% (Dividend payout ratio)

Mattel paid out 55.86 percent of its diluted earnings per share to investors in 2012. If you subtract this percentage from 100 percent, you can find how much the company plowed back into its operations toward future growth. In Mattel's case, it reinvested 44.1 percent of its earnings in the growth of the company. You can find the earnings reinvested in the company over the years in the retained earnings line in the shareholders' equity section of the balance sheet. (See Chapter 6 for a more detailed discussion of shareholders' equity.) Each year, any additional retained earnings are added to this line item. Mattel's retained earnings were more than $3,5 billion during its lifespan, according to the 2012 balance sheet.

Following are numbers from Hasbro's 2007 income statement. You can use them to calculate the dividend payout ratio.

$1.44 (Dividends per share) ÷ $2.55 (Diluted EPS) = 56.5% (Dividend payout ratio)

Hasbro paid out 56.5 percent of its diluted earnings per share to investors and plowed 43.5 percent (subtract 56.5 from 100) back into the company to use for future growth. Hasbro's retained earnings on its 2012 balance sheet were more than $3.3 billion.

Digging into companies' profits with dividends

Should the dividend payout ratio make a difference to you? In the past, investors expected dividend payouts. In fact, dividends made up as much as 40 percent of most investors' portfolio returns about 20 years ago. But investors' priorities have changed in the past 20 years. Today investors look toward *capital gains*, which are the profits investors make when selling a share of stock for more than they paid for that stock, for portfolio growth.

The big question is what better serves the investor and the company: immediate cash payouts of dividends or long-term growth resulting from reinvesting profits each year? The answer to this question isn't an easy one. Younger companies rarely pay dividends because they need the money for growth, but as companies mature, the correct answer is more difficult to determine. For example, Microsoft held billions in cash and refused to pay dividends for years, claiming that it may need the cash for growth. Not until investors screamed long and loud did Microsoft finally pay its first dividend in 2003: only 8¢ per share, or a total of about $857 million! In 2012, Microsoft paid 92 cents per share in dividends. Microsoft held $73.79 billion in cash and short-term investments at the end of June 2012.

TIP

Definitely check how the dividend payout ratio compares with that of similar companies. If the dividend payout ratio is considerably smaller than that of other similar companies, be sure you understand what the company does with the money and whether it's making good use of the funds it's reinvesting. If the company pays out a significantly larger portion of earnings to investors than most other companies in the industry, it may not have any good ideas for growth and is therefore just milking the cash cow, which may eventually run dry.

WARNING

High dividend payout ratios may be a sign that a decrease in profits is on the way. If a company continually increases its dividend payout ratio even as profits fall, you've encountered a warning sign that future trouble is brewing.

WHO HAS THE HIGHEST DIVIDEND PAYOUT RATIOS?

Investors who purchase stock primarily for current income look to industries that traditionally have high dividend payout ratios. Utility companies traditionally have some of the highest dividend payout ratios, but you find good dividend payers in many mature, older industries. If you want to look for a good stock to buy based on dividend payout, here are two key factors to consider:

- **Cash stash:** When you read the annual report, pay close attention to how much cash the company reports on its books. Remember that the dividend comes from extra cash flow. Most companies need to hold on to some of their cash so they have money for acquisitions, research and development, and other capital needs to keep them competitive, even if they're not in a high-growth industry. Use your calculation of the dividend payout ratio to determine how much cash the company is using to cover its dividends and how much cash it's saving for future needs. If the firm is paying out most of its cash and saving very little, it may be a sign that the cash could run out at some point because the business is no longer reinvesting anything in maintaining its market or updating its products. Eventually, the company will lose out to competition and earn less, bringing in less cash.
- **Dividend consistency:** As you read the annual report, also look for information about dividends paid out over the past few years. You can find that information for the past three years at the bottom of the income statement. You can get information for more than three years by looking up the company at Yahoo! Finance and other financial websites. You want to find companies that pay dividends at a consistent level or, even better, that are able to increase their dividend payouts regularly.

TIP

If the dividend payout ratio looks extremely high or extremely low, look at the financial statements before you get too concerned. Did some extraordinary event, such as a significant loss from a plant closing or the sale or purchase of a subsidiary, dramatically impact net income? A one-time event that impacts net income can explain an unusually high or low dividend payout ratio and needn't raise a red flag for investors.

Return on Sales

You can test how efficiently a company runs its operations (that is, the making and selling of its products) by calculating its *return on sales* (ROS). This ratio measures how much profit the company is producing per dollar of sales. By analyzing the numbers in the income statement using ROS, you can get a picture of the company's profit per dollar of sales and gauge how much extra cash the company is bringing in per sale.

Remember that the firm needs that cash to cover its expenses, develop new products, and keep itself competitive. Investors also hope that, at some point in the future, they may even be paid some dividends. At the very least, investors want to be sure the company is generating enough cash from sales to keep itself competitive in the market through advertising, new product development, and new market development.

Figuring out ROS

TIP

To calculate ROS, divide the net income before taxes by sales. You can find both numbers on the income statement. Net sales (sometimes called net revenue) is the top number on the income statement. Net income before taxes is in the expense section of the income statement, just before tax expenses are reported.

Net income before taxes ÷ Sales = Return on sales

REAL WORLD EXAMPLE

You can calculate Mattel's ROS based on information in its income statement for 2012:

$776,464,000 (Net income before taxes) ÷ $6,420,881,000 (Sales) = 12.1% (ROS)

Mattel made 12.1 percent on each dollar of sales. Compare that number with Hasbro's ROS using numbers on its income statement for 2012:

$335,999,000 (Net income before taxes) ÷ $4,088,983 (Sales) = 8.2% (ROS)

Hasbro made 8.2 percent on each dollar of sales.

Investors can use the ROS ratio to determine how much profit a company is making on a dollar of sales. In comparing Mattel and Hasbro, you can see why Mattel's P/E is higher: Mattel is getting considerably better return on sales than Hasbro.

Reaching the truth about profits with ROS

In reading analysts' reports on Mattel and Hasbro, I found that Hasbro's historical ROS has been about 7 percent, so the results for Hasbro in the preceding section show minimal improvement. Mattel is stagnating with its efforts to improve operating income. Its ROS in 2001 was 12.5 percent, and it dropped to 11.8 percent in 2007, but that percentage was headed in the right direction in 2012, at 12.1 percent. Mattel wants to get back to its previous historical average of about 15 to 16 percent.

REMEMBER

ROS is just one part of the puzzle. You need to fully analyze the information you see in the annual reports to find all the pieces and make a determination about whether to invest in a company. This chapter focuses on profitability. You also need to analyze a company's liquidity, which I discuss in Chapter 12, and its cash flow, which I discuss in Chapter 13.

Return on Assets

You can judge how well a company uses its assets by calculating the *return on assets* (ROA). If the ROA is a high percentage, the company is likely managing its assets well. As an investor, that consideration is important because your shares of stock represent a claim on those assets. You want to be sure that the company is using your claim wisely. If you haven't invested yet, be sure your investment will go toward stock in a company that invests its assets well. As with all ratios, you need to compare results with those of similar companies in an industry for the numbers to mean anything.

TIP

To calculate ROA, divide net income by total assets. You can find net income at the bottom of the income statement, and you can find total assets at the bottom of the assets section of the balance sheet.

Net income ÷ Total assets = Return on assets

Doing some dividing to get ROA

REAL WORLD EXAMPLE

Using the numbers from Mattel's income statement and balance sheet, you can determine its ROA:

$776,464,000 (Net income) ÷ $6,526,785(Total assets) = 11.9% (ROA)

So Mattel made 11.9 percent on each dollar of assets. Compare this number with Hasbro's ROA:

$335,999,000 (Net income) ÷ $4,325,387 (Total assets) = 7.8% (ROA)

Hasbro made 7.8 percent on each dollar of assets. Mattel earned about 4 percent more than Hasbro on each dollar of assets.

Ranking companies with the help of ROA

The ROA ratio shows you how much a company earns from its assets or capital invested. This ratio gives investors and debtors a clear view of how well a company's management uses its assets to generate a profit. Both *shareholders' equity* (claims on assets by shareholders) and *debt funding* (claims on assets by creditors) factor into this calculation, meaning that the ratio looks at the income generated using money raised by borrowing funds from creditors and selling stock to shareholders.

ROA can vary significantly, depending on the type of industry. Companies that must use their capital to maintain manufacturing operations with factories and expensive machinery have a much lower ROA than companies that don't require heavy manufacturing, like service companies. Businesses with low asset requirements average an ROA of 20 percent or higher, whereas companies that require a large investment in assets can have ROAs below 5 percent.

Return on Equity

Return on equity (ROE) measures how well a company does earning money for its investors. In fact, you'll probably find it easier to determine an ROE for a company than an ROA. Although the ROE is an excellent measure of how profitable the company is in comparison with other companies in the industry, you want to examine the ROA as well because that ratio looks at returns for both investors and creditors.

Calculating ROE

TIP

You calculate ROE by dividing net income the company earned (which you find at the bottom of the income statement) by the total shareholders' equity (which you find at the bottom of the equity section of the balance sheet):

Net income ÷ Shareholders' equity = Return on equity

REAL WORLD EXAMPLE

You can figure out Mattel's ROE based on its 2012 income statements and balance sheets:

$776,464,000 (Net income) ÷ $3,067,044 (Shareholders' equity) = 25.3% (ROE)

Mattel made 26 percent on each dollar of shareholders' equity. Following is Hasbro's ROE, also based on 2012 income statements and balance sheets:

$335,999,000 (Net income) ÷ $1,507,379 (Shareholders' equity) = 22.3% (ROE)

Hasbro made 22.3 percent on each dollar of assets. Comparing Mattel and Hasbro, you can see that Mattel generated more than Hasbro on its shareholders' equity. It's another reason investors pay more for Mattel stock.

Reacting to companies with ROEs assistance

WARNING

Investors most often cite the ROE ratio when they want to see how well a company is doing for them. Looking at that ratio can be a huge mistake because ROE ignores the impact of debt on profitability and thus doesn't give investors the full picture of a company's financial position. ROE doesn't consider the impact of a company's debt position on its future earnings potential.

REAL WORLD EXAMPLE

Comparing ROE to ROA for Mattel and Hasbro, you can see that both companies' ROEs look better than their ROAs:

	ROA	ROE
Mattel	11.9%	25.3%
Hasbro	7.8%	22.3%

TIP

The primary reason ROE often looks better than ROA is that ROE doesn't include debt.

When you see comparisons of company statistics, you frequently find an ROE but see no mention of an ROA. Many companies believe that ROA is primarily a statistic to be used by management and the company's debtors. Take the extra time to determine the company's ROA and compare it with the ROA of other firms in the industry. You get a much better idea of how well the company generates its profit when you take both debt and equity into consideration.

The Big Three: Margins

You need to investigate three types of margins when you evaluate a company based on its financial reports. *Margins* show you how much financial safety the company has after its costs and expenses. Each of the three margins I discuss — gross margin, operating margin, and net profit margin — shows what the company has left to work with at various stages of the profit calculation.

Dissecting gross margin

Gross margin looks at the profit margin based solely on sales and the cost of producing those sales. It gives you a picture of how much revenue is left after subtracting all the direct costs of producing and selling the product. These costs can include discounts offered, returns, allowances, production costs, and purchases. I talk about these costs in greater detail in Chapter 7.

To calculate gross margin, divide gross profit by net sales or revenues:

Gross profit ÷ Net sales or revenues = Gross margin

TIP

You can find gross profit at the bottom of the sales or revenue section of the income statement. Net sales are at the top of the same section.

REAL WORLD EXAMPLE

Using numbers from Mattel's income statement, you can calculate its gross margin:

$3,409,197 (Gross profit) ÷ $6,420,881 (Net sales) = 53.1% (Gross margin)

Mattel made a gross profit of 46.5 percent on each dollar of sales. Compare this number with Hasbro's gross margin (using numbers from its income statement). Hasbro doesn't show gross profit, so you must calculate it first by subtracting cost of goods sold ($1,671,980) from net revenues:

$2,417,003 (Gross profit) ÷ $4,088,983 (Net sales) = 59.1% (Gross margin)

Hasbro has about 6 percent more revenue left after it subtracts its direct costs than Mattel has, which shows that Hasbro has better cost controls on the purchase or production of the toys it's selling.

Investigating operating margin

The *operating margin* takes the financial report reader one step further in the process of finding what's left over for future use and looks at how well a company controls costs, factoring in any expenses not directly related to the production and sales of a particular product. These costs include advertising, selling (sales staff, sales offices, sales materials, and other items directly related to the selling process), distribution, administration, research and development, royalties, and other expenses.

Selling and advertising expenses aren't factored into the cost of goods sold, which were subtracted out before calculating gross margin, because these expenses usually involve the sale of a number of products or even product lines. These expenses can rarely be matched to a specific sale of a specific product in the same way that the cost of actually manufacturing or purchasing that product can be matched.

Divide operating profit by net sales or revenues to calculate the operating margin:

Operating profit ÷ Net sales or revenues = Operating margin

TIP

You can find net sales or revenues at the top of the income statement and find the operating profit at the bottom of the expenses-from-operations section on the income statement.

REAL WORLD EXAMPLE

Using numbers from Mattel's income statement, you can calculate the operating margin:

$1,021,015 (Operating profit) ÷ $6,420,881 (Net sales) = 15.9% (Operating margin)

Mattel made an operating margin of 15.9 percent on each dollar of sales. Compare this number with Hasbro's operating margin (using numbers from its income statement):

$551,785,000 (Operating profit) ÷ $4,088,983 (Net sales) = 13.5% (Operating margin)

Hasbro made an operating profit of 13.5 percent on each dollar of sales.

You can see that the tables have turned. Now that all indirect expenses are factored into the equation, you can see that Hasbro lost its big advantage over Mattel on costs. Hasbro's operating profit is 2.4 percent lower than Mattel's.

One key expense factor that hurts Hasbro is that its royalty expenses (more than $302 million) are much higher than Mattel's. Hasbro buys the rights to toys instead of developing them in-house, so it must pay royalties on its toys.

Mattel traditionally develops more of its toys in-house and has much lower royalty payments. In fact, when you look at Mattel's income statement, you don't even see royalties separated out from other selling and administrative expenses.

REMEMBER

Companies with an operating margin that's higher than the industry average usually can better hold down their cost of goods sold and operating expenses. Maintaining a higher operating margin means the company has more price flexibility during hard times. If a company with a higher operating margin must lower prices to stay competitive, more room is available to continue earning profits even when they must sell products for less.

Catching the leftover money: Net profit margin

The *net profit margin* looks at a company's bottom line. This calculation shows you how much money the company has left after it has deducted all expenses — whether from operations related to the production and selling of the company's products or from nonoperating expenses or revenue not related to the company's sales of products or services.

For example, one nonoperating revenue item is interest earned on a company's bond holdings. That money isn't generated by operations but is still considered earnings for the company. After the operating income line on the income statement, you most likely see a line for interest expense. This line represents the interest the company paid out on corporate debt. You also see income taxes expense, which indicates the amount the company paid in taxes. These items are two of the biggest charges left to subtract from operating income. The only exception to this rule is if a large extraordinary charge from a special event, such as discontinued operations or the purchase or sale of a division, appears on the income statement. Any extraordinary charges also appear on the income statement after the operating income line.

To find net profit margin, divide net profit by net sales or revenues:

Net profit ÷ Net sales or revenues = Net profit margin

TIP

You find the net profit at the bottom line of the income statement; it may also be called net income or net loss. Net sales or revenue is on the top line of the income statement.

REAL WORLD EXAMPLE

You can calculate the net profit margin using numbers from Mattel's income statement:

$776,464,000 (Net profit) ÷ $6,420,881,000 (Net sales) = 12.1% (Net profit margin)

Mattel made a net profit of 10.05 percent on each dollar of sales. Now calculate Hasbro's net profit margin using numbers from its income statement:

$335,999,000 (Net profit) ÷ $4,088,983 (Net sales) = 8.2% (Net profit margin)

Hasbro made a net profit of 8.2 percent on each dollar of sales. Comparing Mattel's and Hasbro's net profit margins, Mattel appears to be more successful than Hasbro at generating a net profit per dollar of sales. The key question investors must then ask is whether Mattel will perform as well in the future.

LOOKING TO THE FUTURE

When you decide to invest in a company, you want to consider one that has a good history of managing its assets and making a profit. Even more important, you need to know the company's growth prospects.

As a new investor, you're most interested in future growth because it's how you make your money. If the company stagnates and the stock price doesn't go up, your investment sees little profit. If the company grows at a rate of 10 to 15 percent per year or more, you'll likely see an ever-increasing value of your stock purchase. If you're looking at a mature company that has a solid market base but isn't expected to grow, you need to be more concerned about what that company pays out to its investors in dividends than about its growth prospects.

» Calculating various debt and income ratios

» Looking at debt in relation to equity and capital

Chapter 12
Looking at Liquidity

Making money is great, but if a business ties up too much of its money in nonliquid assets (such as factories it can't easily sell) or carries too much debt, it isn't going to be around long to make more money. A company absolutely must have the cash it needs to carry out day-to-day operations and pay its debt obligations if its owners want to stay in business.

Lenders who have money wrapped up in a company follow debt levels closely. They definitely want to be sure they're going to get their money back, plus interest. As an investor, you need to take a close look at a company's debt, too, because your investment can get wiped out if the company goes bankrupt. So if you're investing in a company, you want to be certain that the company is liquid and isn't on the road to debt troubles.

So how do you make sure that the firm you invest in isn't about to spiral down the toilet, taking all your money with it? Well, you need to check out the company's ability to pay its bills and pay back its creditors. But looking at one company doesn't give you much information. Instead, compare the company with similar companies, as well as with the industry average. Doing so gives you a better idea of where the company stands.

In this chapter, I show you how to calculate a company's ability to pay the bills by looking at debt ratios, comparing its debt to its equity, and comparing its debt to its total capital. (If you're starting to sweat and/or your brain is shutting down because of the impending mathlete workout, don't worry — these calculations aren't as difficult as they sound!)

Finding the Current Ratio

One of the most commonly used debt-measurement tools is the *current ratio*, which measures the assets a company plans to use over the next 12 months with the debts it must pay during that same period. This ratio lets you know whether the company will be able to pay any bills due over the next 12 months with assets it has on hand. You find the current ratio by using two key numbers:

- **Current assets:** Cash or other assets (such as accounts receivable, inventory, and marketable securities) the company will likely convert to cash during the next 12-month period
- **Current liabilities:** Debts the company must pay in the next 12-month period, including accounts payable, short-term notes, accrued taxes, and other payments

I talk more about current assets and current liabilities in Chapter 6.

Calculating the current ratio

The formula for calculating the current ratio follows:

Current assets ÷ Current liabilities = Current ratio

Using information from the balance sheets for Mattel and Hasbro, here are their current ratios for the year ending December 2007:

Mattel

$3,556,805,000 (Current assets) ÷ $1,716,012,000 (Current liabilities)
= 2.07 (Current ratio)

So Mattel has $2.07 of current assets for every $1 of current liabilities.

Hasbro

$2,508,702,000 (Current assets) ÷ $960,435,000,000 (Current liabilities)
= 2.13 (Current ratio)

So Hasbro has $2.61 of current assets for every $1 of current liabilities.

What do the numbers mean?

REMEMBER

The key question to ask is whether a company's current ratio shows that it's able to cover short-term obligations. Generally, the rule of thumb is that any current ratio between 1.2 and 2.0 is sufficient for a business to operate. Keep in mind that the ratio varies among industries.

WARNING

A current ratio below 1 is a strong danger sign that the company is headed for trouble. A ratio below 1 means the company is operating with *negative working capital;* in other words, its current debt obligations exceed the amount of money it has available to pay those debts.

A company also can have a current ratio that's too high. Any ratio over 2 means the firm isn't investing its assets well. The company can probably put some of those short-term assets to better use by investing them in growth opportunities.

However, many lenders and analysts believe that the current ratio isn't a good enough test of a company's debt-paying ability because it includes some assets that aren't easy to turn into cash, such as inventory. A company must sell the inventory and collect the money before it has cash to work with, and doing so can take a lot more time than using cash that's already on hand, or just collecting money due for accounts receivable, which represent customer accounts for items already purchased.

Determining the Quick Ratio

Stricter than the current ratio is a test called the *quick ratio* or *acid test ratio,* which measures a company's ability to pay its bills without taking inventory into consideration. The calculation includes only cash on hand or cash already due from accounts receivable. Unlike the current ratio, the quick ratio doesn't include money anticipated from the sale of inventory and the collection of money from those sales. To calculate this ratio, you use a two-step process: First, find the assets that a company can quickly turn into cash; then divide those quick assets by the current liabilities.

Calculating the quick ratio

Here's the two-step process you use to find the quick ratio:

1. **Determine the quick assets.**

   Quick assets = Cash + Accounts receivable + Short-term investments

2. **Calculate the quick ratio.**

Quick assets ÷ Current liabilities = Quick ratio or acid test ratio

REAL WORLD EXAMPLE

Using information from Mattel's and Hasbro's balance sheets, I take you through the two-step process. *Note:* I added only two figures to find the quick assets for Mattel and Hasbro because both companies combine cash and short-term investments or marketable securities on their balance sheets.

Mattel

Quick assets = $1,335,711,000 + $1,226,833,000 = $2,562,544,000

$2,562,544,000 (Quick assets) ÷ $1,716,012 (Current liabilities) = 1.49 (Quick ratio)

So Mattel has $1.49 of quick assets for every $1 of current liabilities.

Hasbro

Quick assets = $849,701+ $1,029,959 = $1,879,660,000

$1,879,660,000 (Quick assets) ÷ $960,435,000 (Current liabilities) = 1.96 (Quick ratio)

So Hasbro has $1.96 of quick assets for every $1 of current liabilities.

Hasbro is in a better position than Mattel based on the quick ratio, but both companies have a quick ratio of well over 1, so they should have no problem paying their bills.

What do the numbers mean?

REMEMBER

A company is usually considered to be in a good position as long as its quick ratio is over 1. A quick ratio below 1 is a sign that the company will likely have to sell some short-term investments to pay bills or take on additional debt until it sells more of its inventory.

If you're looking at statements from companies in the retail sector, you're more likely to see a quick ratio under 1. Retail stores often have a lot more money tied up in inventory than other types of businesses. As long as the company you're evaluating is operating at or near the quick ratio of similar companies in the industry, you're probably not looking at a problem situation, even if the quick ratio is under 1.

WARNING

Remember that a quick ratio of less than 1 can be a sign of trouble ahead if the company isn't able to sell its inventory quickly. Other issues that can cause problems include slow-paying customers and accounts receivable that aren't collected when billed. In Chapters 15 and 16, I take a closer look at how you can assess inventory and accounts receivable turnover.

Investigating the Interest Coverage Ratio

Although the current and quick ratios look at a company's ability to pay back creditors by comparing items on the balance sheet, the *interest coverage ratio* looks at income to determine whether the company is generating enough profits to pay its interest obligations. If the company doesn't make its interest payments on time to creditors, its ability to get additional credit will be hurt; eventually, if nonpayment goes on for a long time, the company may end up in bankruptcy.

The interest coverage ratio uses two figures that you can find on the company's income statement: earnings before interest, taxes, depreciation, and amortization (also known as EBITDA; check out Chapter 7 for more information); and interest expense (also in Chapter 7).

Calculating the interest coverage ratio

Here's the formula for finding the interest coverage ratio:

EBITDA ÷ Interest expense = Interest coverage ratio

Calculating this ratio may or may not be a two-step process. Many companies include an EBITDA line item on their income statements. If a company hasn't included this line item, you have to calculate EBITDA yourself.

REAL WORLD EXAMPLE

Mattel and Hasbro don't have an EBITDA line item, so I show you how to figure that out before you try to calculate the ratio.

Mattel

Mattel reports operating income before it lists its interest and tax expenses. Mattel doesn't have a line item for amortization or depreciation, so you need to look at the cash flow statement to find that amortization totaled $16,746,000 and depreciation totaled $157,536,000. Therefore, in Mattel's case, EBITDA was

$945,045 (Income before taxes) + $16,746,000 + $157,536,000 = $1,119,327,000. Then, to get the interest coverage ratio:

> $1,119,327,000 (EBITDA) ÷ $88,835,000 (Interest expense)
> = 12.60 (Interest coverage ratio)

Thus, Mattel generates $12.60 income for every $1 it pays out in interest.

Hasbro

Hasbro reports amortization expenses of $50,569,000 on the income statement (I talk more about amortization in Chapters 4 and 6). It also reports $99,718,000 for depreciation of plant and equipment on the statement of cash flows, so you need to add those expenses back in to find the EBITDA:

> $453,402,000 (Income before taxes) + $50,569,000 (Amortization on income statement) + $99,718,000 (Depreciation of plant and equipment)
> = $603,689,000 (EBITDA)
>
> And then:
>
> $603,689,000 (EBITDA) ÷ $91,141,000 (Interest expense)
> = 6.62 (Interest coverage ratio)

Hasbro generates $6.62 for every $1 it pays out in interest.

What do the numbers mean?

Both companies clearly generate more than enough income to make their interest payments. A ratio of less than 1 means a company is generating less cash from operations than needed to pay all its interest.

REMEMBER

Lenders believe that the higher the interest coverage ratio is, the better. You should be concerned about a company's fiscal health anytime you see an interest coverage ratio of less than 1.5. This means the company generates only about $1.50 for each $1 it pays out in interest. That's operating on a tight budget. Any type of emergency or drop in sales may make it difficult for the company to make its interest payments.

Comparing Debt to Shareholders' Equity

How a company finances its operations involves many crucial decisions. When a firm uses debt to pay for new activities, it has to pay interest on that debt, plus pay back the principal amount at some point in the future. If a company uses shareholders' equity (stock sold to investors) to finance new activities, it doesn't need to make interest payments or pay back investors.

Finding the right mix of debt and equity financing can have a major impact on a company's cost of capital. Too much debt can be both risky and costly. However, if a company has too high a level of equity, investors may believe that it isn't properly leveraging its money. *Leverage* is the degree to which a business uses borrowed money. For example, a company typically buys a new building by using a combination of a mortgage (debt) and cash (from a new stock issue or retained earnings, which is the equity side of the equation). When a company uses leverage, its cash can go a lot further.

Suppose that you have $50,000 to pay for a home. This amount isn't enough to buy the home you want, so you use that money as a deposit on the home and get a mortgage for the rest of the money due. If the house price is $250,000 and you put down $50,000, you can use the mortgage to leverage that cash so you can afford the home. In this scenario, the mortgage covers 80 percent of the purchase price. Any cash you earn beyond your monthly mortgage payment can go toward paying your other bills and buying food and other things you need or want.

TIP

As an investor, you want to know how a company allocates its debt versus its equity. To determine this, use the *debt to shareholders' equity* (see the following section). You also want to check the company's *debt-to-capital ratio* (see the upcoming section "Determining Debt-to-Capital Ratio"), which lenders use to determine how much they'll lend and to monitor a company's debt level.

Calculating debt to shareholders' equity

To calculate debt to shareholders' equity, divide the total liabilities by the shareholders' equity. This ratio shows you what portion of a company's capital assets is paid by debt and what portion is financed by equity.

Here's the formula you use to calculate debt to shareholders' equity:

Total liabilities ÷ Shareholders' equity = Debt to shareholders' equity

REAL WORLD EXAMPLE

I use the numbers from Mattel's and Hasbro's 2007 balance sheets to show you how to calculate the debt to shareholders' equity ratio.

Mattel

$3,459,741,000 (Total liabilities) ÷ $3,067,044 (Shareholders' equity)
= 1.08 (Debt to shareholders' equity)

Mattel used $1.29 from creditors for every $1 it had from investors. Therefore, Mattel depends a bit more on money it raised by borrowing than on money it raised by selling stock to investors.

Hasbro

$2,818,008,000 (Total liabilities) ÷ $1,507,379,000 (Shareholders' equity)
= 1.87 (Debt to shareholders' equity)

Hasbro used $1.87 from creditors for every $1 it had from investors. Therefore, Hasbro used a greater proportion of borrowed money from creditors to operate its company than Mattel did.

What do the numbers mean?

A debt to shareholders' equity ratio that's greater than 1 means that the company finances a majority of its activities with debt. A ratio under 1 means that the company depends more on using equity than debt to finance its activities.

In most industries, a 1:1 ratio is best, but it varies by industry. You can best judge how a company is doing by comparing it with similar companies and the industry averages.

As the ratio creeps higher above 1, a firm's finances get more risky, especially if interest rates are expected to rise. Alarm bells tend to sound when you see a company near or above 2. Lenders consider a business that carries a debt load this large a credit risk — which means the company has to pay much higher interest rates to finance its capital activities.

Determining Debt-to-Capital Ratio

Lenders take another look at debt using the *debt-to-capital ratio*, which measures a company's leverage by looking at what portion of its capital comes from debt financing.

Calculating the debt-to-capital ratio

You use a three-step process to calculate the debt-to-capital ratio:

1. **Find the total debt.**

   Total debt = Short-term borrowing + Long-term debt + Current portion of long-term debt + Notes payable

2. **Find the capital.**

   Capital = Total debt + Equity

3. **Calculate the debt-to-capital ratio.**

   Total debt ÷ Capital = Debt-to-capital ratio

REAL WORLD EXAMPLE

To show you how to calculate the debt-to-capital ratio, I use the information from Mattel's and Hasbro's 2007 balance sheets.

Mattel

First, to find out Mattel's total debt, add up Mattel's short-term and long-term debt obligations:

Short-term borrowings	$9,844,000
Current portion of long-term debt	$400,000
Long-term debt	$1,100,000
Total debt	$1,509,844,000

Next, add the total debt to total equity to figure the number for capital:

$3,067,044,000 (Equity) + $1,509,844,000 (Debt) = $4,576,888,000 (Capital)

Finally, calculate the debt-to-capital ratio:

$1,509,844,000 (Total debt) ÷ $4,576,888,000 (Capital) = 0.33 (Debt-to-capital ratio)

So Mattel's debt-to-capital ratio was 0.33 to 1 in 2007.

Hasbro

First, to find out Hasbro's total debt, add up Hasbro's short-term and long-term debt obligations:

Short-term borrowings	$224,365,000
Current portion of long-term debt	$0
Long-term debt	$1,396,421,000
Total debt	$1,620,786,000

Then add the total debt to total equity to find out the number for capital:

$1,507,379,000 (Equity) + $1,620,786,000 (Debt) = $3,128,165,000 (Capital)

Finally, calculate the debt-to-capital ratio:

$1,620,786,000 (Total debt) ÷ $3,128,165,000 (Capital) = 0.52 (Debt-to-capital ratio)

So Hasbro's debt-to-capital ratio was higher than Mattel's, at 0.52 to 1.

What do the numbers mean?

Lenders often place debt-to-capital ratio requirements in the terms of a credit agreement for a company to maintain its credit status. If a company's debt creeps above what its lenders allow for the debt-to-capital ratio, the lender can *call* the loan, which means the business has to raise cash to pay off the loan. Companies usually take care of a call by finding another lender. The new lender likely charges higher interest rates because the company's higher debt-to-capital ratio makes the company appear as though it's a greater credit risk.

REMEMBER

Generally, companies are considered to be in good financial shape with a debt-to-capital ratio of 0.35 to 1 or less. If a company's debt-to-capital ratio creeps above 0.50 to 1, lenders usually consider the company a much higher credit risk, which means it has to pay higher interest rates to get loans.

Take note of the ratio and how it compares with the ratios of similar companies in its industry. If the company has a higher debt-to-capital ratio than most of its competitors, lenders probably see it as a much higher credit risk.

WARNING

A company with a higher-than-normal debt-to-capital ratio faces an increasing cost of operating as it tries to meet the obligations of paying higher interest rates. These higher interest payments can spiral into more significant problems as the cash crunch intensifies. In a worst-case scenario, the company can seek bankruptcy protection from its creditors to continue operating and to restructure its debt. Many times its stock value plummets — and may have no value at all if the company emerges from bankruptcy.

» Determining a company's solvency

» Gauging financial strength by looking at debt

» Checking cash sufficiency

Chapter **13**

Making Sure the Company Has Cash to Carry On

No business can operate without cash. Unfortunately, the balance sheet (see Chapter 6) and income statement (see Chapter 7) don't tell you how well a company manages its cash flow, which is critical for measuring a company's ability to stay in business. To find this important information, you need to turn to the *statement of cash flows,* also known as the *cash flow statement,* which looks at how cash flows into and out of a business through its operations, investments, and financing activities.

In this chapter, I show you some basic calculations that help you determine the cash flow from sales and help you find out whether the cash flow is sufficient to meet the company's cash needs. Throughout the chapter, I use Mattel and Hasbro (two leading toy companies) as examples to show you how to use these tools to evaluate a company's financial health. You can find Hasbro's financial statements, as well as its complete annual report, at www.hasbro.com and Mattel's at www.mattel.com.

Measuring Income Success

Looking at whether a company is generating enough cash income can help you determine the company's *solvency* — its capability to meet its financial obligations (in other words, its ability to pay all its outstanding bills). If a firm can't pay its bills, its creditors aren't going to be happy, and it could be forced to file bankruptcy or discontinue operations. In this section, I show you two ratios that can help you determine a company's solvency based on its sales success.

Calculating free cash flow

The first step in determining a company's solvency is to find out how much money the company earns from its operations that it can actually put into a savings account for future use — in other words, a company's *discretionary cash*. This money is also called the *free cash flow*.

A business with significant cash flow has a lot of flexibility to decide whether it wants to use its discretionary cash to purchase additional investments, pay down more debt, or add to its liquidity, which means to deposit additional funds in cash and *cash equivalent accounts* (including checking accounts, savings accounts, and other holdings that the company can easily convert to cash). The formula for calculating the free cash flow is a simple one:

Cash provided by operating activities - Capital expenditures - Cash dividends = Free cash flow

TIP

Cash flows from operating activities are located at the bottom of the operating activities section of the statement of cash flows. Capital expenditures appear in the investing activities section of the cash flow statement. Cash dividends paid show up in the financing activities section of the statement of cash flows.

Mattel

Using Mattel's 2007 and 2006 cash flow statements, I show you how to calculate the free cash flow in thousands:

	2007	2006
Cash provided by operating activities	$1,275,650	$664,693
Minus capital expenditures		
Purchases of tools, dies, and molds	($108,070)	($102,193)
Purchases of other property, plant, and equipment	($110,978)	($88,721)

	2007	2006
Minus cash dividends	($423,378)	(4316,503)
Free cash flow	$633,224	$790,282

As you can see, Mattel's free cash flow increased significantly from 2011 to 2012, by a total of about $476 million. Mattel's cash flow provided by operating activities almost doubled in that time period, from $665 million to $1,276 million.

Clearly, Mattel is recovering strongly after its bout with toxic products from China in 2007. Mattel is doing well. But if you find that a company is having trouble maintaining its previous cash levels, that issue may or may not be a sign of trouble. It may mean that the company decided to maintain lower cash levels and invest in new opportunities, or it may mean that it's having difficulty generating new cash. You can't determine that with this calculation — it tells you that the company may have a problem, but it doesn't tell you just what the problem may be. The formula merely tells you that you must seek additional information by continuing the financial analysis of other line items (such as *Accounts receivable* and *Inventory*) and by reading the notes to the financial statements (see Chapter 9) or management's discussion and analysis (see Chapter 5).

Hasbro

Now I show you how to calculate the free cash flow by using Hasbro's 2007 and 2006 cash flow statements, in thousands:

	2007	2006
Cash provided by operating activities	$534,796	$396,069
Minus capital expenditures		
Purchases of property, plant, and equipment	(112,091)	(99,402)
Minus cash dividends	(225,464)	(154,028)
Free cash flow	$197,241	$142,639

Hasbro's free cash flow shows some improvement from 2011 to 2012, but not as significant as Mattel's. The increase from 2011 to 2012 is just $54.6 million so Hasbro has no trouble maintaining its cash flow levels — it's actually improving its cash flow.

What do the numbers mean?

Unquestionably, the more free cash flow a company has, the better it's doing financially. A company with significant free cash flow is in a strong position to weather a financial storm, whether it's a recession, a slowdown in sales, or another type of financial emergency.

REMEMBER

If a company's free cash flow number is negative, it must seek external financing to fund its growth. Negative or very low free cash flow numbers for young growth companies that need to make significant investments in new property, plant, or equipment most likely do not indicate a big problem. But you still want to look deeper into the financial reports, especially the notes to the financial statements (see Chapter 9), to find out why the cash flow is so low and how the managers plan to raise additional capital. This caveat is especially true if you see a negative free cash flow for an older company, which immediately raises a red flag.

Figuring out cash return on sales ratio

You can test how well a company's sales are generating cash using the *cash return on sales ratio.* This ratio looks at profitability from cash rather than from the accrual-based income perspective. Remember, the accrual-based income perspective means that income and expenses are recognized when the transaction is complete, so there's no guarantee that cash has been received. I talk more about this in Chapter 4.

Making sure a business is properly managing its cash flow is critical when assessing the company's ability to stay in business and pay its bills. Sales are the primary way a company generates its cash.

Here's the formula for calculating the cash return on sales ratio, which specifically measures cash generated by sales:

Net cash provided by operating activities ÷ Net sales = Cash return on sales

TIP

You can find the line item *Net cash provided by operating activities* on the cash flow statement in the operating activities section, and you find N*et sales* or *Net revenue* at the top of the income statement.

Mattel

I use Mattel's cash flow and income statements to show you how to calculate the cash return on sales ratio:

$1,275,650,000 (Net cash provided by operating activities) ÷ $6,420,881,000 (Net sales) = 19.87% (Cash return on sales)

From looking at this equation, you can see that 19.87 percent of the dollars that Mattel generates from its sales provide cash for the company. Mattel's *net profit margin* (the bottom line, or how much the company makes after subtracting all costs and expenses), which I show you how to calculate in Chapter 11, is 12.1 percent. When you take a closer look at the inflow of cash, you can see that a significant portion of cash from operating activities was increases in accounts payable, accrued liabilities, and income taxes payable. So $312,634,000 in cash will be paid out early in 2013 to cover the bills due. That figure makes the cash position look better at the end of 2012. Even if you reduce the cash from operations by this number, Mattel still raises 15 percent of its cash from operations.

Hasbro

Using Hasbro's cash flow and income statements, I show you how to calculate the cash return on sales ratio:

> $534,796,000 (Net cash provided by operating activities) ÷ $4,088,983,000 (Net sales) = 13.08% (Cash return on sales)

You can see that 15.7 percent of the dollars that Hasbro generates from its sales provide cash for the company. Hasbro's net profit margin is 8.2 percent (see Chapter 11), which is a strong sign that Hasbro is efficiently converting its sales to cash.

What do the numbers mean?

The cash return on sales looks at the efficiency with which a company turns its sales into cash. Mattel's results show that it's more efficient than Hasbro at turning its sales dollars into cash.

Checking Out Debt

In addition to noting how much cash a company generates from sales, you need to look at the cash flow going out of the company to pay its debts. Whenever a business can't pay its bills or the interest on its debt, it runs the risk of supply cutoffs and possible insolvency. Few vendors will continue sending products to a company that doesn't pay its bills, and most creditors will seek ways to collect a debt if they don't receive the interest and principal due on that debt.

You can check out a company's ability to pay its debt by looking at its debt levels and the cash available to pay that debt. You do this by collecting numbers related to debt levels from the balance sheet and comparing them with cash outflow numbers from the statement of cash flows.

Determining current cash debt coverage ratio

You can determine whether a company has enough cash to meet its short-term needs by calculating the *current cash debt coverage ratio*. You calculate this number by dividing the cash provided by operating activities by the average current liabilities.

Here's the two-step formula for calculating the current cash debt coverage ratio:

1. **Find the average current liabilities.**

   Current liabilities for current year + Current liabilities for previous year ÷ 2 = Average current liabilities

2. **Find the current cash debt coverage ratio.**

   Cash provided by operating activities ÷ Average current liabilities = Current cash debt coverage ratio

TIP

You can find current liabilities for the current year and the previous year on the balance sheet. You can find cash provided by operating activities on the statement of cash flows.

Mattel

Using the cash provided by operating activities from Mattel's 2007 cash flow statement and the average of its current liabilities from its 2007 and 2006 balance sheets, I show you how to calculate the current cash debt coverage ratio. Using the two-step process, I first calculate the average current liabilities; then I use that number to calculate the ratio:

1. **Calculate average current liabilities.**

   $1,716,012,000 (2012 current liabilities) + $960,435,000 (2011 current liabilities) ÷ 2 = $1,377,470,000 (Average current liabilities)

2. **Calculate the ratio for the current reporting year.**

   $1,275,650,000 (Cash provided by operating activities, 2012) ÷ $1,377,470,000 (Average current liabilities) = 0.93 (Current cash debt coverage ratio)

TIP

To determine whether a company's cash provided by activities is improving, you also want to calculate the ratio for the previous reporting year. In this case:

$664,693,000 (Cash provided by operating activities, 2011) ÷ $1,377,470,000 (Average current liabilities) = 0.48.2 (Current cash debt coverage ratio)

This comparison shows you that Mattel's cash position improved from the end of 2011 to the end of 2012.

Hasbro

Now I use the cash provided by operating activities from Hasbro's 2012 cash flow statement and the average of its current liabilities from its 2012 and 2011 balance sheets to show you how to calculate the current cash debt coverage ratio:

1. **Calculate average current liabilities.**

   $960,435,000 (2012 current liabilities) + $942,344,000 (2011 current liabilities) ÷ 2 = $951,390,000 (Average current liabilities)

2. **Calculate the ratio for the current reporting year.**

   $534,796,000 (Cash provided by operating activities, 2012) ÷ $951,390,000 (Average current liabilities) = 0.56 (Current cash debt coverage ratio)

For comparison's sake, calculate the ratio for the previous reporting year as well:

$396.069.000 (Cash provided by operating activities, 2011) ÷ $951.390.000 (Average current liabilities) = 042 (Current cash debt coverage ratio)

What do the numbers mean?

The current cash debt coverage ratio looks at a company's ability to pay its short-term obligations. The higher the ratio, the better.

REMEMBER

A negative "cash provided by operating activities" number is a possible danger sign that the company isn't generating enough cash from operations. You need to investigate why its cash from operations is insufficient. Look for explanations in the notes to the financial statements or in the management's discussion and analysis. If you don't find the answers there, call the company's investor relations department. Also look at analysis written by the financial press or independent analysts.

It's not unusual for growth companies to report negative cash from operations because they're spending money to grow the company. However, companies can't sustain a negative cash flow for long, so be sure you understand the company's long-term plans to improve its cash position.

Computing cash debt coverage ratio

You also want to look at a company's ability to pay debt that's due over the long term. Current liabilities include only debt that a company must pay in the next 12 months. Long-term liabilities are debts that a company must pay beyond that 12-month period. If you see signs that a firm may have difficulties meeting long-term debt, that, too, is a major cause for concern. Although you may find that a company generates enough cash to meet its current liabilities, if long-term debt levels are too high, the company will eventually run into trouble paying off its debt and meeting its interest obligations. You can measure a company's cash position to meet long-term debt needs by using the *cash debt coverage ratio.*

The formula for the cash debt coverage ratio is a two-step process:

1. **Find the average total liabilities.**

   (Current year total liabilities + Previous year total liabilities) ÷ 2
   = Average total liabilities

2. **Find the cash debt coverage ratio.**

   Cash provided by operating activities ÷ Average total liabilities
   = Cash debt coverage ratio

TIP

You can find the current- and previous-year total liabilities on the balance sheet. You can find cash provided by operating activities on the statement of cash flows.

Mattel

Using the cash provided by operating activities from Mattel's 2012 cash flow statement and the average of its total liabilities from its 2012 and 2011 balance sheets, I show you how to calculate the cash debt coverage ratio. Using the two-step process, I first calculate the average total liabilities; then I use that number to calculate the ratio:

1. **Calculate average total liabilities.**

   $3,459,741,000 (2012 total liabilities) + $2,818,008,000 (2011 total liabilities) ÷ 2
   = $3,260,388,000 (Average total liabilities)

2. **Find the cash debt coverage ratio.**

   $1,275,650,000 (2012 cash provided by operating activities) ÷ $3,260,388,000
   (Average total liabilities) = 0.39 (Cash debt coverage ratio)

To judge whether a company's cash provided by activities is improving, you calculate the ratio for both the current reporting year and the previous reporting year:

$664,693,000 (2012 cash provided by operating activities) ÷ $3,260,388,000 (Average total liabilities) = 0.20 (Cash debt coverage ratio)

This ratio serves as evidence that Mattel's cash position improved from the end of 2011 to the end of 2012. Its cash position worsened because less cash came into the company from inventories and more went out in accounts payable. Mattel's total debt increased between 2011 and 2012 by about $398.7 million, according to its balance sheet.

Hasbro

To show you how to calculate the cash debt coverage ratio, I use the cash provided by operating activities from Hasbro's 2012 cash flow statement and the average of its total liabilities from its 2012 and 2011 balance sheets:

1. **Calculate average total liabilities.**

   $2,818,008,000 (2012 total liabilities) + $2,713,259,000 (2011 total liabilities) ÷ 2 = $2,765,634,000 (Average total liabilities)

2. **Calculate the cash debt coverage ratio for the current reporting year.**

   $534,796,000 (2012 cash provided by operating activities) ÷ $2,765,634,000 (Average total liabilities) = 0.19 (Cash debt coverage ratio)

Calculate the ratio for the previous year as well:

$396,069,000 (2011 cash provided by operating activities) ÷ $2,765,634,000 (Average total liabilities) = 0.14 (Cash debt coverage ratio)

Taking total liabilities into consideration, Hasbro ended 2012 in a stronger cash position than in 2011, but Mattel's cash improvement was much greater. Much of that improvement, though, came from the delay in payments, as discussed earlier.

What do the numbers mean?

The cash debt coverage ratio looks at a company's ability to pay its long-term debt obligations. As you can see, when long-term debt is taken into consideration, Mattel's cash position was still better than Hasbro's, but not as strong as when looking only at current liabilities. Both Mattel and Hasbro carry a larger part of their debt as long-term debt. So calculating only one ratio — current cash debt coverage ratio or cash debt coverage ratio — doesn't give you the full picture of a company's financial health. You need to look at both ratios to be certain that the company is generating enough cash to cover both its short-term and long-term debt. In Chapter 9, I talk more about this debt structure difference when looking at the explanations given in the notes to the financial statements.

REMEMBER

As with the current cash debt coverage ratio, if you find a negative cash from operations number, be sure to look for an explanation in the notes to the financial statements or in the management's discussion and analysis to find out why the cash flow from operations is negative. If you don't find it there, call the company's investor relations office to get the answers to your questions.

Calculating Cash Flow Coverage

Debt and the interest paid on that debt are not a company's only cash requirements. Businesses also need cash for capital expansion to grow the company (including new plants, tools, and equipment) and pay dividends to investors.

As a shareholder, you make money only when the company's stock goes up in price. The stock market rewards a company with good growth potential by bidding up the price of its stock. Firms that show low growth prospects usually have few buyers and end up with lower stock prices. So you want to invest in companies that not only generate enough cash to pay their bills, interest, and the principals on their long-term debts, but also have money left over to pay dividends to their shareholders and grow their company. Remember that many growth companies don't pay dividends at all, but instead reinvest all profits toward future growth.

REMEMBER

You can test whether a company is generating enough cash to cover its capital expenditures, pay its dividends, and pay its debt obligations by calculating the cash flow coverage ratio.

Finding out the cash flow coverage ratio

You use a two-step process to calculate the cash flow coverage ratio:

1. **Calculate the company's cash requirements.**

   Add the following:

   Capital expenditures (listed in the investing activities section of the cash flow statement)

   Cash dividends paid (listed in the financing activities section of the cash flow statement)

Interest expenses (listed on the income statement)

Current portion of long-term debt (listed in the financing activities section of the cash flow statement)

2. **Calculate the cash flow coverage ratio.**

   Cash provided by operating activities ÷ Cash requirements = Cash flow coverage ratio

TIP

You can find cash provided by operating activities on the statement of cash flows.

Mattel

REAL WORLD EXAMPLE

I use Mattel's financial statements to show you how to calculate its cash flow coverage ratio:

1. **Find Mattel's cash requirements.**

Capital expenditures	$730,950,000
Plus cash dividends paid	$423,378,000
Plus interest paid	$88,524,000
Plus current portion of long-term debt	$400,000,000
Cash requirements	$1,130,950,000

   For capital expenditures, I used two line items on the cash flow statement: *Purchases of tools, dies, and molds* and *Purchases of other property, plant, and equipment*. For current portion of long-term debt, I used the *Payments of long-term debt* line item on the cash flow statement.

2. **Calculate the cash flow coverage ratio.**

   $1,275,650,000 (2012 cash provided by operating activities) ÷ $1,130,950,000 (Cash requirements) = 1.13 (Cash flow coverage ratio)

Mattel generated more than enough cash from its operations to pay all its cash requirements for 2012. The 1.13 cash flow coverage ratio means that Mattel generated enough cash to cover 112 percent of its cash requirements. If a company doesn't raise enough cash from operations, it must cover the rest of the cash it needs by either borrowing money or drawing down cash on hand from activities in previous years. Any firm that must draw down savings to maintain its operating activities is likely showing signs of trouble. Anytime a company can't meet its cash requirements, you want to seriously reconsider investing in it.

Hasbro

Now I use Hasbro's financial statements to show you how to calculate its cash flow coverage ratio:

1. **Find Hasbro's cash requirements.**

Capital expenditures	$112,091,000
Plus cash dividends paid	$316,503,000
Plus interest paid	$93,957,000
Cash requirements	$522,551,000

   For capital expenditures, I used the *Additions to property, plant, and equipment* line item on the cash flow statement. Hasbro had no current long-term debt payments in 2012.

2. **Calculate the cash flow coverage ratio.**

   $534,796,000 (2012 cash provided by operating activities) ÷ $522,551,000 (Cash requirements) = 1.02 (Cash flow coverage ratio)

Hasbro generated more than enough cash from its operations to pay all its cash requirements in 2012.

What do the numbers mean?

Both Mattel and Hasbro generated enough cash from operations to pay all their bills. If a company did not generate enough cash, it would have to find sources other than operations to meet the shortfall in its cash requirements.

REMEMBER

Companies that generate more than enough cash have a cash flow coverage ratio of more than 100 percent. The higher the ratio, the better. If you see a company that isn't able to cover its cash requirements and that has little left in cash and short-term investments, raise that red flag.

4 Understanding How Companies Optimize Operations

IN THIS PART . . .

Look at the budget process and understand how it relates to financial reporting.

Explore the efficiency with which the company uses its assets and how quickly it sells its inventory.

Discover some tests you can do to see if a company can collect from its customers.

Dig into how the company keeps its cash flowing.

- » **Examining the budgeting process**
- » **Figuring out how budgets are created**
- » **Understanding the importance of monthly budget reports**
- » **Putting internal budget reports to work**

Chapter 14
How Reports Help with Basic Budgeting

No matter how good the numbers look, you don't know how well a company is really doing until you compare the actual numbers with the company's expectations. *Expectations* (the budget targets a company hopes to meet) are spelled out during the *budgeting process*, in which the company projects its financial needs for the next year. At different times throughout the year, managers use these budgets, along with periodic financial reports, to determine how close the company is to meeting its budget targets.

As an outsider, you don't have access to the company's budgets or the reports related to them. But if you're seeking to find out more about internal financial reports and how to use them effectively, understanding the budgeting process is critical.

This chapter discusses the budgeting process and how it complements financial reporting. A well-planned budgeting process not only helps a company plan for the next year, but also provides managers with key information throughout the year to be sure the company is meeting its goals — and raising red flags when it doesn't reach its goals. The sooner managers recognize a problem, the greater their ability to fix it before the end of the year.

Peering into the Budgeting Process

The budget a company sets for itself relies on a lot of careful calculations and some guesswork about the amount of revenue it expects from the sale of products and services, as well as the expenses it will incur to manufacture or purchase the products it sells and to cover the other operating expenses during the next year. Creating a budget is a lot more complicated than just making a list of expected revenues and expenses. I talk more about the basics of revenue and expenses in Chapters 4 and 7.

Companies use one of two approaches to budgeting:

- **Top-down approach:** Key executives set budgets and give them to department heads to meet. Most employees aren't involved in the budgeting process; instead, the bigwigs impose the numbers on the employees, who are expected to meet them. The big problem with this type of budget process is that the employees don't feel any ownership of the budget and frequently complain that the budget handed down to them is unrealistic, which is why they can't meet expectations.

  Few large corporations use the top-down approach today. You're more likely to find this approach in small businesses run by one person or a small group of partners.

- **Bottom-up approach:** Budgets are created at the department level based on overall companywide goals and guidelines that the board of directors and top executives set. This approach encourages employee participation in the budgeting process, so the employees have more of a sense of budget ownership. Because they help develop the budget, they can't later claim that the budget is unrealistic if it turns out that they don't meet expectations.

REMEMBER

Most management studies show that the bottom-up approach works better because managers and staff members are more likely to take a budget seriously and follow it if they have some involvement in developing it. In this chapter, I focus on the process for bottom-up budget development, which is the most commonly used budgeting process in large corporations today.

Understanding who does what

Everyone has a role to play in bottom-up budgeting. Top executives who are part of a budget committee set companywide goals and objectives. Then starting at the lowest staff levels, each department determines its budget needs. These budgets work their way through the management tree to the top, where the bigwigs pull together numbers from each department to develop a companywide budget.

The budget committee manages the entire process and is responsible for determining budget policies and coordinating budget preparation among departments. Most often this committee includes the president, chief financial officer (CFO), controller, and vice presidents of various functions, such as marketing, sales, production, and purchasing.

Even before the departments start to develop their budgets, the budget committee develops rules that all departments must follow. These rules likely include a request to hold all budgets to a certain percentage increase in costs, and possibly even a reduction in costs. These guidelines help departments develop budgets that meet company needs while proposing something the departments can live with throughout the year.

The budget committee doesn't mandate what the department's actual budget should be or how the department should find a way to keep its costs down; it leaves those decisions to each individual department. One department may decide it can cut costs by reducing staff, another may determine that it can cut costs by better controlling the use of supplies, and yet another may decide that cutting back on the use of rental equipment or temporary help can meet its cost-cutting goals. By leaving these choices to the departments instead of mandating the numbers from the top, companies give employees a stake in meeting their budget goals.

After the budgets are developed at the section and department levels, the budget committee gives final approval for all budgets. The committee also resolves any disputes that may arise in the budget process. Budget disputes can occur when different departments have conflicting goals to meet. For example, say the manufacturing department is mandated to cut costs, while the sales department must increase sales to meet its goals. The manufacturing manager may decide to cut costs in a way that lowers product-quality standards. However, the sales manager may believe that this cost-cutting method will create problems in maintaining customer satisfaction and will ultimately hurt sales. The budget committee acts as the mediator for this kind of decision-making process.

Setting goals

To develop companywide budget guidelines, the budget committee must first determine the goals for the company. Before the committee can set those goals, it gathers information about where the company stands financially, how the company fits into the bigger economic picture, and how it stacks up against its competitors. This information forms the basis for what the committee determines it needs to accomplish during the next year, such as increasing market share, increasing profit, or entering a new market area. Sections and departments can then estimate the resources they need to meet those goals.

The first critical step for goal setting is to develop a *sales forecast* (a projection of the number of sales the company will make during the year), usually involving the staff of several departments, including marketing, sales, and finance. Much of the data this staff collects is from industry research reports, as well as from actual company numbers from the accounting, finance, and marketing departments.

TECHNICAL STUFF

These factors must be considered to develop an accurate sales forecast:

- **Past sales success:** By looking at a breakdown of sales by product or service for the past three to five years, a company can look for trends and make a best guess about future sales growth potential.
- **Potential pricing policy:** By looking at past sales, a company can determine whether the current pricing policy is viable or whether changes are needed. Products that are moving quickly off the shelves may be able to sustain a price increase, and products that aren't moving may need a price cut to stimulate sales. Pricing isn't set solely based on sales success or failure, of course; costs for producing the product or providing the service are a key factor as well.
- **Data on unfilled orders and backlogs:** This data helps a company determine which product lines or services it may need to modify to meet demand.
- **Market research:** This research includes potential sales and competitive data for the entire industry, as well as forecasts for the individual company. This information lets the committee know where the company fits in the industry and what potential the industry may have in the next year.
- **Information about general economic conditions:** This research gives the budget committee an overview of expected economic conditions for the next year so it knows whether there's potential for growth or a possible reduction in sales. For example, if the economy has seen a slowdown during the past three years but economists are now predicting a market recovery, the company may need to increase manufacturing goals to meet anticipated increasing demand.
- **Industry economic conditions:** A company monitors these conditions to determine whether the industry in which it operates is set for a growth spurt or a downturn, or is expected to perform at the same level in the next year.
- **Industry competition data:** Reviews of competitors' marketing strategies, advertising, and other competitive factors must also be considered when developing future goals to stay competitive within the industry. The company must review this information to determine where it sits in relation to its competitors and whether new competitors on the horizon may challenge the company's products or services.
- **Market share data:** A company collects this data, which is the percentage of the market held by the company's products, to help set goals — whether

to increase market share or maintain current levels. Growth potential depends on increasing market share, but if the company already holds nearly 100 percent of the market, as Microsoft does in the operating systems market for personal computers, room for growth may not exist. In that case, marketing strategists focus on tactics for maintaining that market share.

In addition to the hard numbers, a company collects information from staff members at all levels to get a firsthand view of what's actually happening in the field. This information includes reports about exchanges with customers, vendors, and contractors. Real-world data that a company collects from sales staff, customer service staff, purchasers, and other employees gives the company additional information and allows it to test the numbers.

Building Budgets

After the budget committee finishes data collection (see the preceding section), it can determine sales goals for the company. After the committee establishes goals, it uses them to develop *strategies* — the actual methods used to reach the goals — and build budgets that reflect the resources needed to carry out the strategies. Although the budget committee sets companywide goals and global strategies, each section and department translates those broad goals and strategies into specific goals and strategies for its own staff.

REMEMBER

Armed with its goals and strategies, each department develops its specific budget. Not all departments develop their budgets at exactly the same time because some departments depend on others to make budget decisions. For example, sales revenue must be projected before the company can make decisions about production levels and just about every other aspect of its operations.

Common budget categories include the following, which I organize according to the order in which they're produced:

- **Sales budget:** Sales managers start their budget planning by forecasting sales levels and the gross revenue they anticipate those levels will generate. Most other budgets depend on the goals set by sales, so this budget is usually the first to be developed. Without a sales budget, production managers don't know how many products to produce, and purchasing managers don't know how many items to buy.
- **Production budget:** If the company manufactures its own product, this budget is the next one to be developed. The production department looks at the beginning inventory left from the previous planning period and plans what additional inventory is needed, based in part on the forecasts in the

sales budget. Production planning can be a difficult development task. Making sure they have a just-right level of inventory means that production managers must be sure they plan for the right amount of raw materials, the efficient use of production facilities, and an appropriate number of staff members to produce the products to meet customer needs on time.

- **Inventory purchases budget:** For companies that don't manufacture their own products, the budgeting process focuses on purchasing needed inventory and being sure it's delivered on time to meet customer needs. Similar issues drive purchasing concerns because a company wants to be sure it has enough product on hand to meet customer demand. At the same time, it doesn't want too many products left over, because that means resources were wasted on inventory and could have been better used to meet other company needs.
- **Direct materials budget:** This budget controls the raw materials needed to meet the production schedule. The last problem any company wants to face is not having enough materials on hand to keep the product line moving, thus risking a factory shutdown. But the company also wants to avoid keeping too many materials on hand because doing so increases warehousing expenses. Also, holding raw materials too long can result in material spoilage.
- **Direct labor budget:** This budget is unique to manufacturing companies and depends on the production budget. Companies work hard to determine how much staff they need to meet production needs. If they hire too few people, they have to deal with overtime charges or, in the worst cases, production shortfalls. If companies hire too many people, they may end up spending more than necessary on salaries or may have to lay off employees — which is a huge blow to morale.
- **Selling and administrative expense budgets:** Many smaller departments are involved in getting a product to market and supporting those sales. These departments include accounting, finance, marketing, human resources, mailroom, and materials management. After sales revenue is known and the cost of selling those goods has been determined, the remaining resources are divided up between the company's selling and administrative needs.
- **Master budget:** After everyone signs off on each of the department and section budgets, the accounting department prepares a master budget, which the company uses as a road map to test how well each department is doing in meeting its budget expectations.
- **Cash budget:** After all the budgets are completed and combined into a master budget, the accounting department develops a cash budget that estimates the monthly cash needs for each department. Based on this budget, the finance department determines whether operations will generate enough cash to meet needs or whether the company needs other financing to maintain its cash flow.

When all the budget planning is complete, the accounting department develops a budgeted income statement (see Chapter 7 for more information on income statements) to test whether the budgeting process has created a budget that truly meets profit planning goals. If the answer is no, the budget committee has to decide where budget changes are needed to meet company goals. A lot of negotiating is often necessary between the budget committee and the company's top managers to determine budget changes.

REMEMBER

If the budget committee imposes unrealistic changes on the budget for a department, little budget compliance from that department is likely to happen, and financial difficulties may develop throughout the year. Budgets that department and section managers can live with have a better chance of producing expected results and meeting goals.

Providing Monthly Budget Reports

No matter how thoroughly prepared it may be, a budget is useless if it's not matched to actual revenue and expenses. So throughout the budget period, the accounting department prepares monthly *internal financial reports* (reports that summarize financial results) for the managers, who use these reports to identify where the budget is going right or wrong. Many of these internal financial reports have a system of red flags that identify areas where the actual results aren't meeting budget expectations.

Each company has its own style for internal reports, but most reports include similar types of information. The report is usually broken into five columns:

- **Red flag:** A symbol, such as an asterisk, is usually used in the first or last column to identify problem line items in a budget. Some companies skip the symbol and instead add a column with an explanation of the variances between actual and budgeted numbers.
- **Line item:** This column lists the budget categories as they appear on the section or department budget.
- **Budget amount:** This column states the dollar amount allocated for the period of the internal financial report.
- **Actual amount:** This column states how much the company spent during the period of the internal financial report.
- **Difference:** This column shows how close (or far apart) the actual and budgeted numbers are.

Many companies also include a year-to-date section on the internal financial reports that shows the same information on a year-to-date basis in addition to the information specific to the month or quarter. See Table 14-1 for a sample income statement.

TABLE 14-1 **Income Statement, ABC Company, March 2013 (Confidential, for Internal Use)**

Flag	Line Item	Budget	Actual	Difference
*	Sales	$1,400,000	$1,200,000	($200,000)
	Cost of goods sold	(700,000)	(650,000)	50,000
*	Gross margin	700,000	550,000	($150,000)
	Expenses			
	Advertising	(150,000)	(150,000)	
	Administrative	(300,000)	(275,000)	25,000
	Interest	(25,000)	(35,000)	(10,000)
*	Net income	$225,000	$90,000	($135,000)

Table 14-1 shows an internal report for March 2013 for a fictitious company called ABC Company. In this example, a flag appears automatically on the report if the difference is greater than $100,000, but each company determines its own designated levels for red flags. A small company may flag items for a difference of just $5,000, and a large corporation may flag items for differences at much higher levels.

Although Table 14-1 uses an income statement format, internal reports have no required format; each company develops its own report format, depending on what works best for the company.

In Table 14-1, you can see that flags have been marked next to the line items *Sales*, *Gross margin*, and *Net income*. Flags were thrown because those line items show differences of more than $100,000; therefore, management needs to investigate them.

A glance at Table 14-1 shows that the key problem is lower than expected sales revenue. Sales were budgeted for $1.4 million, and the actual sales were $200,000 less, at $1.2 million. That difference is shown on the report's first line. Management first needs to determine why sales are lower than forecast and then must develop strategies for correcting the problem. The fact that cost of goods sold and administrative expenses are lower than budgeted could be a sign that management recognized the problem after a previous month's report and already initiated cost-cutting programs.

After looking at the report in Table 14-1, executives have to determine what the problem is and what other changes may be needed to get the budget back in line. If external factors such as economic conditions are to blame, the best the company can do is revise the budget to meet current economic conditions so that it can avoid further slippage in net income.

REMEMBER

Internal financial reports aren't important just to find out about the bad news; good news can also require critical actions. For example, if sales are much higher than expected, a company may need to put plans in place to be sure it can meet the unexpected demand without losing sales. After all, customers don't want to wait weeks or months to get their products, and they may seek out a competitor to fulfill their needs if products aren't available when they're ready to buy.

If conditions change from expectations, a company can more easily make a midyear correction if budgets have been accurately prepared. The company knows what was expected, and it can tweak its revenues or expenses to correct a problem long before the shortfall becomes disastrous.

In Chapter 17, I talk about strategies companies use to keep cash flowing when internal financial reports don't meet expectations.

Using Internal Reports

Inside your company, you probably see much more detailed reports than the sample in Table 14-1. Department heads see only the budget line items related to their own departments, and only the budget committee and departments responsible for developing budget reports have access to companywide internal reports.

The internal financial report managers receive are usually based on the budget they develop. The line items listed are directly related to their department functions. Any line item whose difference exceeds the difference allowed by the company is flagged, and you need to find out why. Sometimes the answer is clear. For example, if you know sales were higher or lower than expected, you simply need to report why and tell what you're doing to correct any problems. Other times, the answer requires some digging on your part.

After a report arrives at your office door, you don't have much time to figure out what the differences are and what they mean for your department. If the differences are big, you can probably expect a call from your manager as soon as he sees his copy. When I was managing the finances for five departments, I knew I could expect a call from my manager even before I got my copy of the report. An entire day's activities could be changed if a major difference showed up on an internal financial report, and I had to find out why.

TIP

Your best bet is to keep a good working relationship with someone in the accounting department who can help you sort through the details. Hopefully, you'll find that the difference was based solely on a coding error, and the revenue or expense was just put in the wrong place. Otherwise, you'll likely have to come up with some solution to correct the problem rather quickly.

» Comparing inventory valuation systems

» Counting inventory turnover

» Measuring fixed assets turnover

» Assessing total asset turnover

Chapter 15
Turning Up Clues in Turnover and Assets

Testing how well a company manages its assets is a critical step in measuring how effectively it uses its resources. Inventory is the most important asset for generating cash for any company that sells a product.

Many factors directly impact the cost of selling a product, including producing the product, purchasing the products or materials not produced in-house, storing the product until it's sold, and shipping the product to the customer or store where it's sold. And if a company doesn't sell its product fast enough, the product may become obsolete or damaged before it's sold.

In this chapter, I review the measures you can use to gauge how well a company manages its assets, especially its inventory, and how quickly the company sells the inventory.

Exploring Inventory Valuation Methods

A company must know the value of its inventory to complete its balance sheet. In addition, the company must set a value for the items it sells in order to include a *cost of goods sold* number on its income statement (see Chapter 7). How that value is calculated depends on the accounting method the company uses. Five different methods are acceptable for determining the value of inventory, and each one can result in a different *net income.* These methods include the following:

- **Last in, first out (LIFO) inventory system:** This system assumes that the last item put onto the shelf is the first item sold. Each time a product is purchased or manufactured to be put on the shelves, it costs a different amount. Most times, the cost goes up, so the last item put on the shelf likely costs more than the first item. Therefore, the goods sold first in the LIFO system are the highest-priced goods, which raises the cost of goods sold number and lowers the net income. Stocking a shelf by leaving the older items in place and just adding the newly received products in front of them is a lot quicker. For example, hardware stores often use this method when restocking products that rarely change, like hammers and wrenches. Be aware that a company must use the same method for all its inventory.
- **First in, first out (FIFO) inventory system:** This system assumes that the first item put on the shelf is the first item sold. Just as for LIFO, the cost of goods purchased or manufactured differs each time they're bought or made. Usually, prices increase, so in the case of FIFO, the first item put on the shelf likely has a lower cost than the last item. Because the first item is the one sold first, the cost of goods sold will likely be lower than for a company that uses the LIFO method. Therefore, the cost of goods sold number will be lower and the net income will be higher. For example, grocery stores must worry about spoilage, so they put the newly received products behind the older ones to be sure that the older products sell first, before they spoil.
- **Average costing inventory system:** This system doesn't try to specify which items sell first or last, but instead calculates the average cost of each unit sold. This method gives a company the best picture of its inventory cost trends because the ups and downs of prices don't impact the company's inventory. Instead, the inventory value levels out through the year. The net income actually falls somewhere between the net income figures based on LIFO and FIFO.
- **Specific identification inventory system:** This system tracks the value of each individual product in a company's inventory. For example, car dealers track the value of each car in their stock by using this method. The net income is calculated by subtracting the cost of goods sold that have been specifically identified from the price at which the items are sold.
- **Lower of cost or market inventory system:** This system sets an inventory value based on whichever cost is lower: the actual cost of inventory or its current market value. Companies whose inventory values can change numerous times, even throughout a day, most often use this valuation method. For example, dealers in precious metals, commodities, and publicly traded securities commonly use this system.

In most cases, companies use the LIFO, FIFO, or average costing inventory system. Specific identification inventory comes into play only with companies that sell major items that each have a unique set of add-ons, such as cars or high-end computers. Therefore, each product has a different cost of goods sold value. The lower of cost or market inventory system primarily applies to companies that sell marketable securities and precious metals.

REMEMBER

The way a company values its inventory has a major impact on its bottom line. The reason is that the figure a company uses on its income statement for cost of goods sold depends on the costs it assigns to the inventory it sold during the period that income statement covers. The inventory's value shown on the balance sheet is what's left over and still held by the company, so the *ending inventory's value* is the value of the goods the company still holds. This is listed as a current asset on the balance sheet.

TRACKING INVENTORY

Inventory-tracking methods for large corporations can be a highly honed science that involves extensive computer programming and management, or they can be as simple as taking a count of what's in stock. Companies use one of the following two systems to keep track of their goods on hand:

- **Periodic inventory tracking:** A company periodically counts inventory on hand to verify how many of the products are left on the shelves (if the company has retail outlets) and how many are left to be sold in the warehouse (or in cartons in the back of a store, if the company has retail outlets). Most companies that use periodic inventory tracking do a physical count at least monthly, and possibly as often as daily, depending on the company's sales volume.
- **Perpetual inventory system:** Using this system, a company gets an updated inventory count after each sale. If you get a receipt that lists a long string of numbers next to each product's name, the company most likely uses a perpetual inventory system. The long string of numbers is the tracking number assigned to the inventory in the computer system.

You've probably been the victim of a company's perpetual inventory system if you've tried to buy something at a store when the cash register is down. I've actually been in stores that couldn't make a sale because the cash register was down, and the store had no way to manually handle the sale.

If you're a company outsider, you won't be able to get the details you need to calculate the value of the products left in inventory. In fact, many times, only the company insiders directly involved in inventory decision making have access to cost details. Many companies consider actual inventory costs to be a trade secret, and they don't want their competitors to know the details. Nonetheless, understanding what's behind those numbers and how different inventory methods can impact the bottom line is important for understanding financial reports.

TIP

If you're comparing two companies that use two different methods, you need to take that factor into consideration when doing the comparisons. You can find out in the notes to the financial statements which method a company uses.

To calculate a company's cost of goods sold, you must know the value assigned to the *beginning inventory* (which is the same as the ending inventory for the previous period and is also the same as the inventory number you find on the balance sheet). The beginning inventory is the number that's used at the beginning of the next accounting period, so any purchases made during this period are added onto the beginning inventory. Finally, you need to number how much inventory is left at the end of the accounting period, which is called the *ending inventory*. Using those figures, here's the formula for calculating the cost of goods sold:

1. **Find the value of the goods available for sale.**

   Beginning inventory + Purchases = Goods available for sale

2. **Calculate the value of items sold.**

   Goods available for sale – Ending inventory = Value of items sold

Applying Three Inventory Valuation Methods

To give you an idea of how inventory can impact the bottom line, the following sections use an inventory scenario to take you through the calculations for cost-of-goods value by using the three key methods: average costing, FIFO, and LIFO.

In all three cases, I use the same beginning inventory, purchases, and ending inventory for a one-month accounting period in March.

1. **100 (Beginning inventory) + 500 (Purchases) = 600 (Goods available for sale)**
2. **600 (Goods available for sale) – 100 (Ending inventory) = 500 (Items sold)**

Three inventory purchases were made during the month:

March 1	100 at $10
March 15	200 at $11
March 25	200 at $12

The beginning inventory value was 100 items at $9 each.

Average costing

Before you can use the average costing inventory system, you need to calculate the average cost per unit.

100 at $9	= $900 (Beginning inventory)

Plus purchases:

100 at $10	= $1,000 (March 1 purchase)
200 at $11	= $2,200 (March 15 purchase)
200 at $12	= $2,400 (March 25 purchase)

Cost of goods available for sale = $6,500

Average cost per unit:

$6,500 (Cost of goods available for sale) ÷ 600 (Number of units) = $10.83 (Average cost per unit)

When you know the average cost per unit, you can calculate the cost of goods sold and the ending inventory value pretty easily by using the average costing inventory system:

Cost of goods sold	500 at $10.83 each	=	$5,415
Ending inventory	100 at $10.83 each	=	$1,083

So the value of cost of goods sold using the average costing method is $5,415. This figure is the one you see as the *Cost of goods sold* line item on the income statement. The value of the inventory left on hand, or the ending inventory, is $1,083. This number is the one you see as the inventory item on the balance sheet.

FIFO

To calculate FIFO, you don't average costs. Instead, you look at the costs of the first units the company sold. With FIFO, the first units sold are the first units put on the shelves. Therefore, beginning inventory is sold first, then the first set of purchases, then the next set of purchases, and so on.

To find the cost of goods sold, add the beginning inventory to the purchases made during the reporting period. The remaining 100 units at $12 are the value of ending inventory. Here's the calculation:

Beginning inventory: 100 at $9	=	$900
March 1 purchase: 100 at $10	=	$1,000
March 15 purchase: 200 at $11	=	$2,200
March 25 purchase: 100 at $12	=	$1,200
Cost of goods sold	=	$5,300
Ending inventory:		
From March 25: 100 at $12	=	$1,200

In this example, the cost of goods sold includes the value of the beginning inventory plus the purchases on March 1 and 15 and part of the purchase on March 25. The units that remain on the shelf are from the last purchase on March 25. The cost of goods sold is $5,300, and the value of the inventory on hand, or the ending inventory, is $1,200.

LIFO

To calculate LIFO, start with the last units purchased and work backward to compute the cost of goods sold. The first 100 units at $9 in the beginning inventory end up being the same 100 at $9 for the ending inventory. Here's the calculation:

March 25 purchase: 200 at $12	=	$2,400
March 15 purchase: 200 at $11	=	$2,200
March 1 purchase: 100 at $10	=	$1,000
Cost of goods sold	=	$5,600
Ending inventory:		
From beginning inventory: 100 at $9	=	$900

So the *Cost of goods sold* line item that you find on the income statement is $5,600, and the *Value of the inventory* line item on the balance sheet is $900.

How to compare inventory methods and financial statements

Looking at the results of each method side by side shows you the impact that the inventory valuation system has on the net income statement:

Income Statement Line Item	Averaging	FIFO	LIFO
Sales	$10,000	$10,000	$10,000
Cost of goods sold	$5,415	$5,300	$5,600
Income	$4,585	$4,700	$4,400

LIFO gives the lowest net income figure and the highest cost of goods sold. Companies that use the LIFO system have higher costs to write off on their taxes, so they pay less in income taxes. FIFO gives companies the lowest cost of goods sold and the highest net income, so companies that use this method know that their bottom line looks better to investors.

Results for the inventory number on the balance sheet also differ using these methods:

	Averaging	FIFO	LIFO
Ending inventory	$1,083	$1,200	$900

REMEMBER

LIFO users are likely to show the lowest inventory balance because their numbers are based on the oldest purchases, which, in many industries, cost the least. This situation is exactly opposite if you look at an industry in which the cost of goods is dropping in price — then the oldest goods can be the most expensive. For example, computer companies carrying older, outdated equipment can have more expensive units sitting on the shelves if they try to use the LIFO method, even though the units may not be worth anywhere near what the company paid for them.

Determining Inventory Turnover

The big question you have for any company is how quickly it sells its inventory and turns a profit. As long as a company turns over its inventory quickly, you probably won't find outdated products sitting on the shelves. But if the company's inventory moves slowly, you're more likely to find a problem in the valuation of its inventory.

You use a three-step process to find out how quickly product is moving out the door.

Calculating inventory turnover

Here's the three-step formula for calculating a company's inventory turnover:

1. **Calculate the average inventory (the average number of units held in inventory).**

   Beginning inventory + Ending inventory ÷ 2 = Average inventory

2. **Calculate the inventory turnover (the number of times inventory is completely sold out during the accounting period).**

   Cost of goods sold ÷ Average inventory = Inventory turnover

3. **Calculate the number of days it takes for products to go through the inventory system, according to the accounting policies in the notes to the financial statements.**

   365 ÷ Inventory turnover = Number of days to sell all inventory

In this calculation, you find out the number of days it takes the company to sell its entire inventory.

REAL WORLD EXAMPLE

I use Mattel's and Hasbro's 2012 income statements and balance sheets to show you how to calculate inventory turnover and the number of days it takes to sell that inventory. Both companies use the FIFO inventory system to value their inventory, according to the accounting policy in their notes to the financial statements.

Mattel

1. **Find the average inventory.**

   Use the inventory on hand December 31, 2011, as the beginning inventory, and use the inventory remaining on December 21, 2012, as the ending inventory.

   $487,000,000 (Beginning inventory) + $465,057,000 (Ending inventory) ÷ 2 = $476,028,500 (Average inventory)

2. **Calculate the inventory turnover.**

   You need the cost of goods sold figure on the 2012 income statement to calculate the inventory turnover.

   $3,011,684,000 (Cost of goods sold) ÷ $476,028,500 (Average inventory) = 6.33 (Inventory turnover)

   This figure means that Mattel completely sold out its inventory 6.33 times during 2007.

3. **Find the number of days it took for Mattel to sell out all its inventory.**

   365 (Days) ÷ 6.33 (Inventory turnover) = 57.7

As an investor reading this report, you can assume that, on average, Mattel sells all inventory on hand every 57.7 days. Remember, though, that isn't true for every toy that Mattel makes. Popular toys may sell out, and new stock may be needed every month, whereas less popular toys may sit on the shelf for several months or more. This calculation gives you an *average* for all types of toys sold.

Hasbro

1. **Calculate the average inventory.**

   Use the inventory on hand December 31, 2011, as the beginning inventory, and use the inventory remaining on December 21, 2012, as the ending inventory.

   $333,993,000 (Beginning inventory) + $316,049,000 (Ending inventory) ÷ 2 = $325,021,000 (Average inventory)

2. **Calculate the inventory turnover.**

   To do so, use the cost of goods sold number on the 2012 income statement.

   $1,671,980,000 (Cost of goods sold) ÷ $325,021,000 (Average inventory) = 5.14 (Inventory turnover)

3. **Find the number of days it took for Hasbro to sell off its inventory.**

   365 (Days) ÷ 5.14 (Inventory turnover) = 70.95

So Hasbro sells its entire inventory every 71 days. Mattel is selling its toys faster.

What do the numbers mean?

Hasbro takes more than 71 days to sell all its inventory, and Mattel sells out every 57.7 days. Mattel turns over its inventory about six times a year, whereas Hasbro turns it over about five times per year. To judge how well both companies are doing, check the averages for the industry — you can do so online at Bizstats (`http://bizstats.com/`). Start by clicking on the selection for industry financial benchmark reports. Input the annual sales number. Using the stats for Miscellaneous Manufacturing, I find that 6.84 is the average inventory turnover ratio in the industry. So Mattel is slightly below average, at 6.33, and Hasbro, at only 5.14, has more room for improvement.

TIP

If the company you're evaluating has a slower than average inventory turnover, look for explanations in the management's discussion and analysis and the notes to the financial statements to find out why the company is performing worse than its competitors. If the rate is higher, look for explanations for that as well; don't get too excited until you know the reason. The better numbers may be because of a one-time inventory change.

Investigating Fixed Assets Turnover

Next, you want to test how efficiently a company uses its fixed assets to generate sales, a ratio known as the *fixed assets turnover. Fixed assets* are assets that a company holds for business use for more than one year and that aren't likely to be converted to cash anytime soon. Fixed assets include items such as buildings, land, manufacturing plants, equipment, and furnishings. Using the fixed assets turnover ratio, you can determine how much per dollar of sales is tied up in buying and maintaining these long-term assets versus how much is tied up in assets that are more quickly used up.

REMEMBER

If the economy goes sour and sales drop, reducing variable costs is much easier than reducing costs for maintaining fixed assets. The higher the fixed assets turnover ratio, the more nimble a company can be when responding to economic slowdowns.

Calculating fixed assets turnover

Here's the fixed assets turnover ratio formula:

Net sales ÷ Net fixed assets = Fixed assets turnover ratio

REAL WORLD EXAMPLE

I show you how to calculate this ratio by using the net sales figures from Mattel's and Hasbro's income statements and the fixed assets figures from their balance sheets. For both companies, use the line item *Property, plant, and equipment, net.* (If a company doesn't calculate its fixed assets for you, you have to add several line items together, such as *Buildings, tools,* and *equipment.*)

Mattel

$6,420,881,000 (Net sales) ÷ $4,088,983,000 (Net fixed assets) = 10.82 (Fixed assets turnover ratio)

Hasbro

$4,088,983,000 (Net sales) ÷ $230,414,000 (Net fixed assets) = 17.75 (Fixed assets turnover ratio)

What do the numbers mean?

A higher fixed assets turnover ratio usually means that a company has less money tied up in fixed assets for each dollar of sales revenue that it generates. If the ratio is declining, it can mean that the company is overinvested in fixed assets, such as plants and equipment. To improve the ratio, the company may need to close some of its plants and/or sell equipment it no longer needs.

TIP

You can tell whether a company's fixed assets turnover ratio is increasing or decreasing by calculating the ratio for several years and comparing the results. The balance sheet includes two years' worth of data, so in this example, you may be able to find the financial statements for 2010 online (if not, you can request them). Then you'd have the data for 2012 and 2011 on the 2012 balance sheet, and you'd have the data for 2010 and 2009 on the 2010 balance sheet.

Tracking Total Asset Turnover

Finally, you can look at how well a company manages its assets overall by calculating its total asset turnover. Instead of just looking at inventories or fixed assets, the *total asset turnover* measures how efficiently a company uses all its assets.

Calculating total asset turnover

Here's the formula for calculating total asset turnover:

Net sales ÷ Total assets = Total asset turnover

REAL WORLD EXAMPLE

I use information from Mattel's and Hasbro's income statements and balance sheets to show you how to calculate total asset turnover. You can find the net sales at the top of the income statement and the total assets at the bottom of the assets section on the balance sheet. Here are the calculations:

Mattel

$6,420,881,000 (Net sales) ÷ $6,526,785,000 (Total assets) = 0.98 (Total asset turnover)

Hasbro

$4,088,983,000 (Net sales) ÷ $3,237,063,000 (Total assets) = 0.95 (Total asset turnover)

What do the numbers mean?

Mattel and Hasbro have similar asset ratios, so their efficiency in using their total assets to generate revenue is about equal. Both companies hold more than half their assets in current assets, which means that they're relatively liquid and can respond quickly to industry changes.

REMEMBER

A higher asset turnover ratio means that a company is likely to have a higher return on its assets, which some investors believe can compensate if the company has a low profit ratio. By *compensate,* I mean that the higher return on assets could mean increased valuation for the company and, therefore, a higher stock price.

In addition to looking at this ratio, when determining stock value, you need to calculate the profit ratios and return on assets. (I show you how to calculate these in Chapter 11.) Aside from inventory turnover, another key asset to consider is accounts receivable turnover, which I discuss in Chapter 16.

- Discovering the ins and outs of accounts receivable
- Considering the nuts and bolts of accounts payable
- Digging into discount offers

Chapter 16 Examining Cash Inflow and Outflow

Is the money flowing? That's the million-dollar, and sometimes multimillion-dollar, question. Measuring how well a company manages its inflow and outflow of cash is crucial to being able to stay in business. Cash is king in business — without it, you can't pay the bills.

In this chapter, I review the key ratios for gauging cash flow and show you how to calculate them. In addition, I explore how companies use their internal financial reporting to monitor slow-paying customers, and I discuss whether paying bills early or on time is better — and how you can test that issue.

Assessing Accounts Receivable Turnover

Sales are great, but if customers don't pay on time, the sales aren't worth much to a business. In fact, someone who doesn't pay for the products he takes is no better for business than a thief. When you're assessing a company's future prospects, one of the best ways to judge how well it's managing its cash flow is to calculate the accounts receivable turnover ratio.

A balance sheet lists customer credit accounts under the line item *Accounts receivable*. Any company that sells its goods on credit to customers must keep track of whom it extends credit to and whether those customers pay their bills.

REMEMBER

Financial transactions involving credit card sales aren't figured into accounts receivable, but are handled like cash. The type of credit I'm referring to here is *in-store credit*. In this case, the bill the customer receives comes directly from the store or company where the customer purchased the item.

When a store makes a sale on credit, it enters the purchase on the customer's credit account. At the end of each billing period, the store or company sends the customer a bill for the purchases she made on credit. The customer usually has between 10 and 30 days from the billing date to pay the bill. When you calculate the *accounts receivable turnover ratio*, you're seeing how fast the customers are actually paying those bills.

Calculating accounts receivable turnover

Here's the three-step formula for testing accounts receivable turnover:

1. **Calculate the average accounts receivable:**
2. **Find the accounts receivable turnover ratio:**

   Net sales ÷ Average accounts receivable = Accounts receivable turnover ratio

3. **Find the average sales credit period (the time it takes customers to pay their bills):**

   52 weeks ÷ Accounts receivable turnover ratio = Average sales credit period

TIP

If you work inside the company, an even better test is to use annual credit sales instead of net sales because net sales include both cash and credit sales. But if you're an outsider reading the financial statements, you can't find out the credit sales number.

I show you how to test accounts receivable turnover by using Mattel's and Hasbro's 2012 income statements and balance sheets.

Mattel

1. **Calculate the average accounts receivable:**

   ($1,226,833,000 + $1,029,959,000) ÷ 2 = $1,236,760,000

2. **Find Mattel's accounts receivable turnover ratio for 2012:**

   $6,420,881,000 (Net sales) ÷ $1,236,760,000 (Average accounts receivable) = 5.19 times

3. **Find the average credit collection period:**

   52 weeks ÷ 5.19 (Accounts receivable turnover ratio) = 10.02 weeks

Mattel's customers averaged about 10.2 weeks to pay their bills.

Comparing this data with the previous year's is a good way to see whether the situation is getting better or worse. If you use the same process to calculate Mattel's 2011 average credit collection period, you find that the answer is 5.07 weeks, meaning that the company took slightly longer in 2011 to collect than it did in 2012. To understand the significance of this, look at what's happening with similar companies, as well as what's happening within the industry as a whole. It may be an internal company problem, or it may be an industry-wide problem related to changes in the economic situation.

Hasbro

1. **Calculate Hasbro's average accounts receivable:**

   ($1,029,959,000 + $1,034,580,000)/2 = $1,032,270,000

2. **Calculate Hasbro's accounts receivable turnover ratio for 2012:**

   $4,088,983,000 (Net sales) ÷ $1,032,270,000 (Average accounts receivable) = 3.96 times

3. **Calculate the average sales credit period:**

   52 weeks ÷ 3.96 (Accounts receivable turnover ratio) = 13.13 weeks

Hasbro's accounts receivable turned over at a rate slower than Mattel's.

Is that an improvement or a step backward for Hasbro? Using the 2011 numbers, you find that Hasbro took 12.52 weeks to collect from its customers. So the company experienced deterioration in its accounts receivable collection.

What do the numbers mean?

The higher an accounts receivable turnover ratio is, the faster a company's customers are paying their bills. Most times, the accounts receivable collection is directly related to the credit policies that the company sets. For example, a high turnover ratio may look very good, but that ratio may also mean that the company's credit policies are too strict and that it's losing sales because few customers qualify for credit. A low accounts receivable turnover ratio usually means that a company's credit policies are too loose, and the company may not be doing a good job of collecting on its accounts. In the case of Mattel and Hasbro, the slow pay rates may be indicative of the economic environment in the toy industry since the 2008 bubble burst, not a major problem with their credit approval processes.

FINDING THE RIGHT CREDIT POLICY

Setting the right accounts receivable policy can have a major impact on sales. For example, a company may require customers to pay within ten days of billing or close the accounts. That may be too strict, and customers may end up having to walk out of the store because they can't charge to the account. Another common credit policy that may be too strict is one that requires too high of a salary level to qualify, forcing too many customers to go elsewhere to buy the products they need.

Looking at the other side of the coin, a credit policy that's too loose may give customers 60 days to pay their accounts. By the time the company realizes that it has a nonpaying customer, the customer may have already charged a large sum to the account. If the customer never pays the amount due, the company has to write it off as a bad debt.

Hasbro's customers took an average of 13.13 weeks to pay their bills in 2012. Mattel's customers paid quicker, at 10.02 weeks. Both companies waited more than two months to get paid. The amount sitting in accounts receivable for Mattel decreased by about $20 million between 2011and 2012. Hasbro also experienced a decrease in accounts receivable of almost $5 million.

Both companies seem to be improving their collections after what was one of the most severe downturns in the economy since the Great Depression.

Taking a Close Look at Customer Accounts

If you work inside a company and have responsibility for customer accounts, you get an internal financial report called the *accounts receivable aging schedule.* This schedule summarizes the customers with outstanding accounts, the amounts they have outstanding, and the number of days that their bills are outstanding. Each company designs its own report, so they don't all look the same. Check out Table 16-1 to see an example of an accounts receivable aging schedule.

Looking at the aging schedule, you can quickly see which companies are significantly past due in their payments. Many firms begin cutting off customers whose accounts are more than 60 or 90 days past due. Other firms cut off customers when they're more than 120 days past due. No set accounting rule dictates when to cut off customers who haven't paid their bills; this decision depends on the accounting policies the company sets.

TABLE 16-1 Accounts Receivable Aging Schedule for ABC Company, as of July 31, 2012

Customer	30–45 Days	46–60 Days	61–90 Days	Over 90 Days	Total
DE Company	$100	$50	$0	$0	$150
FG Company	$200	$0	$0	$0	$200
HI Company	$200	$100	$100	$50	$450
JK Company	$300	$150	$50	$50	$550
Total	$800	$300	$150	$100	$1,350

In the aging schedule example for ABC Company, the JK Company looks like its account needs some investigating. Although a company can carry past-due payments because of a dispute about a bill, after that dispute goes beyond 90 days, the company awaiting payment may put restrictions on the other company's future purchases until its account gets cleaned up. HI Company seems to be another slow-paying company that may need a call from the accounts receivable manager or collections department.

Many times, a company salesperson makes the first contact with the customer. If the salesperson is unsuccessful, the business initiates more severe collection methods, with the highest level being an outside collection agency. Companies with strong collection practices place a gentle reminder call when an account is more than 30 days late and push harder as the account goes more past due.

When a business decides that it probably will never collect on an account, it writes off the account as a bad debt in the Allowance for Bad Debt Account. Each company sets its own policies about how quickly it writes off a bad debt. A company usually reviews its accounts for possible write-offs at the end of each accounting period. I talk more about accounts receivable and their impact on cash flow in Chapter 17.

Finding the Accounts Payable Ratio

A company's reputation for paying its bills is just as important as its ability to collect from its own customers. If a company develops the reputation of being a slow payer, it can have a hard time buying on credit. The situation can get even more serious if a company is late paying on its loans. In that case, the business can end up with increased interest rates while its credit rating drops lower and lower. I discuss the importance of a good credit rating in Chapter 21.

You can test a company's bill-paying record with the accounts payable turnover ratio. In addition, you can check how many days a company takes to pay its bills by using the days in accounts payable ratio. Keep reading to find out how to calculate these ratios.

Calculating the ratio

The *accounts payable turnover ratio* measures how quickly a company pays its bills. You calculate this ratio by dividing the cost of goods sold (you find this figure on the income statement) by the average accounts payable (you find the accounts payable figures on the balance sheet).

Here's the formula for the accounts payable turnover ratio:

Cost of goods sold ÷ Average accounts payable = Accounts payable turnover ratio

REAL WORLD EXAMPLE

I use Mattel's and Hasbro's income statements and balance sheets for 2012 to compare their accounts payable turnover ratios.

Mattel

1. **Find the average accounts payable:**

   $334,999,000 (2011 accounts payable) + $385,375,000 (2012 accounts payable) ÷ 2 = $360,187,000 (Average accounts payable)

2. **Use that number to calculate Mattel's accounts payable turnover ratio:**

   $3,011,684 (Cost of goods sold) ÷ $360,187,000 (Average accounts payable) = 8.4 times

Mattel turns over its accounts payable 8.4 times per year.

Hasbro

1. **Find the average accounts payable:**

   $134,864,000 (2011 accounts payable) + $139,906,000 (2012 accounts payable) ÷ 2 = $137,385,000 (Average accounts payable)

2. **Calculate Hasbro's accounts payable turnover ratio:**

   $1,671,980 (Cost of goods sold) ÷ $137,385,000 (Average accounts payable) = 12.7 times

Hasbro turns over its accounts payable 12.7 times per year, which is faster than Mattel.

What do the numbers mean?

The higher the accounts payable turnover ratio, the shorter the time between purchase and payment. A low turnover ratio may indicate that a company has a cash-flow problem. Hasbro is paying its bills more rapidly than Mattel.

REMEMBER

Each industry has its own set of ratios. The only way to accurately judge how a company is doing paying its bills is to compare it with similar companies and the industry.

Determining the Number of Days in Accounts Payable

The *number of days in accounts payable ratio* lets you see the average length of time a company takes to pay its bills.

If a company is taking longer to pay its bills each year, or if it pays its bills over a longer time period than other companies in its industry, it may be having a cash-flow problem. Similarly, if a company pays its bills slower than other companies in the same industry, that could be a problem, too.

Calculating the ratio

Use the following formula to calculate the number of days in accounts payable:

> Average accounts payable ÷ Cost of goods sold × 360 days = Days in accounts payable

Note: The industry uses 360 days rather than a full year's 365 to make this calculation based on an average 30-day month (30 × 12 = 360).

REAL WORLD EXAMPLE

I use Mattel's and Hasbro's balance sheets and income statements to find the number of days in accounts payable ratio. I don't have to calculate average accounts payable because I already did so when I calculated the accounts payable turnover ratio (see the section "Finding the Accounts Payable Ratio," earlier in this chapter).

Mattel

$360,187,000 (Average accounts payable) ÷ $3,011,684,000 (Cost of goods sold) × 360 = 43.1 days

Mattel takes about 43.1 days to pay its bills, or about 6.2 weeks, which is about 4 weeks less than it takes Mattel to collect from its customers — 10.02 weeks, as the accounts receivable turnover ratio shows. Therefore, Mattel is receiving cash from its customers at a slower rate than it's paying out in cash to its vendors and suppliers. This issue may be a factor in the need for short-term borrowings of $9,844 million, as the balance sheet shows.

Hasbro

$137,385,000 (Average accounts payable) ÷ $1,671,980,000 (Cost of goods sold) × 360 = 29.6 days

Hasbro takes about 29.6 days, or 4.2 weeks, to pay its bills. Hasbro's accounts receivable turnover ratio shows that its customers take slightly more than 13.12 weeks to pay their bills. Therefore, Hasbro must pay its bills more quickly than its customers pay theirs, which could cause a cash-flow problem.

What do the numbers mean?

WARNING

If the number of days a company takes to pay its bills increases from year to year, it may be a red flag indicating a possible cash-flow problem. To know for certain what's happening, compare the company with similar companies and the industry averages.

Just as accounts receivable prepares an aging schedule for customer accounts, companies prepare internal financial reports for accounts payable that show which companies they owe money to, the amount they owe, and the number of days for which they've owed that amount.

Deciding Whether Discount Offers Make Good Financial Sense

One common way companies encourage their customers to pay early is to offer them a discount. When a discount is offered, a customer (in this case, the company that must pay the bill) may see a term such as "2/10 net 30" or "3/10 net 60" at the top of its bill. "2/10 net 30" means that the customer can take a 2 percent discount if it pays the bill within 10 days; otherwise, it must pay the bill in full within 30 days. "3/10 net 60" means that if the customer pays the bill within 10 days, it can take a 3 percent discount; otherwise, it must pay the bill in full within 60 days.

REMEMBER

Taking advantage of this discount saves customers money, but if a customer doesn't have enough cash to take advantage of the discount, it needs to decide whether to use its credit line to do so. Comparing the interest saved by taking the discount with the interest a company must pay to borrow money to pay the bills early can help the company decide whether using credit to get the discount is a wise decision.

Calculating the annual interest rate

The formula for calculating the annual interest rate is:

([% discount] ÷ [100 – % discount]) × (360 ÷ Number of days paid early)
= Annual interest rate

I calculate the interest rate based on the early payment terms I stated earlier.

For terms of 2/10 net 30

You first must calculate the number of days that the company would be paying the bill early. In this case, it's paying the bill in 10 days instead of 30, which means it's paying the bill 20 days earlier than the terms require. Now calculate the interest rate, using the annual interest rate formula:

(2 [% discount] ÷ 98 [100 – 2]) × (360 ÷ 20 [Number of days paid early]) = 36.73%

That percentage is much higher than the interest rate the company may have to pay if it needs to use a credit line to meet cash-flow requirements, so taking advantage of the discount makes sense. For example, if a company has a bill for $100,000 and takes advantage of a 2 percent discount, it has to pay only $98,000, and it saves $2,000. Even if it must borrow the $98,000 at an annual rate of 10 percent, which would cost about $544 for 20 days, it still saves money.

For terms of 3/10 net 60

First, find the number of days the company would be paying the bill early. In this case, it's paying the bill within 10 days, which means it's paying 50 days earlier than the terms require. Next, calculate the interest rate, using this formula:

(3 [% discount] ÷ 97 [100 – 3]) × (360 ÷ 50 [Number of days paid early]) = 22.27%

Paying 50 days earlier gives the company an annual interest rate of 22.27 percent, which is likely higher than the interest rate it would have to pay if it needed to use a credit line to meet cash-flow requirements. But the interest rate isn't nearly as good as the terms of 2/10 net 30. A company with 3/10 net 60 terms will probably still choose to take the discount, as long as the cost of its credit lines carries an interest rate that's lower than the rate that's available with these terms.

What do the numbers mean?

For most companies, taking advantage of these discounts makes sense as long as the annual interest rate calculated using this formula is higher than the one they must pay if they borrow money to pay the bill early. This becomes a big issue for companies because, unless their inventory turns over very rapidly, 10 days probably isn't enough time to sell all the inventory purchased before they must pay the bill early. Their cash would come not from sales but, more likely, from borrowing.

If cash flow is tight, a company has to borrow funds using its credit line to take advantage of the discount. For example, if the company buys $100,000 in goods to be sold at terms of 2/10 net 30, it can save $2,000 by paying within 10 days. If the company hasn't sold all the goods, it has to borrow the $100,000 for 20 days, which wouldn't be necessary if it didn't try to take advantage of the discount. I assume that the annual interest on the company's credit line is 9 percent. Does it make sense to borrow the money?

The company would need to pay the additional interest on the amount borrowed only for 20 additional days (because that's the number of days the company must pay the bill early). Calculating the annual interest of 9 percent of $100,000 equals $9,000, or $25 per day. Borrowing that money would cost an additional $500 ($25 times 20 days). So even though the company must borrow the money to pay the bill early, the $2,000 discount would still save it $1,500 more than the $500 interest cost involved in borrowing the money.

» Delaying bill payments to increase cash flow

» Collecting accounts receivable more quickly

» Using a receivables securitization program

» Ordering less inventory

» Finding quick cash

Chapter 17
How Companies Keep the Cash Flowing

Managers sometimes face a shortage of cash to pay the bills, and they need to find ways to fix the problem. They can use different strategies to get their hands on cash quickly when running a business.

In this chapter, I review the pros and cons of the possible fixes available when a manager finds a red flag about a company's cash flow.

Slowing Bill Payments

Short on cash? Well, maybe you can just let your bills slide. It may not be the most responsible policy, but sometimes doing so can get a company through a fiscal rough patch — as long as its suppliers are relatively patient. When businesses buy on credit and don't have to pay cash upon receipt of the goods, this is called *trade financing.* Often businesses must pay for those goods within 30, 60, or 90 days. When cash gets tight, one of the first strategies many small business owners (and even some large corporations) use is to pay their bills more slowly, and sometimes even pay them late, to make it through a cash crunch.

This practice is known as *stretching accounts payable* or *riding the trade*. Some companies use this strategy as long as their suppliers and vendors tolerate the late payments — in other words, until they threaten nondelivery of goods. The primary advantage of this plan is that the manager or business owner doesn't need to look for a way to borrow additional money to pay operating expenses. The big disadvantage is that companies can build bad reputations among their suppliers and vendors and are less likely to get trade financing in the future.

Paying bills early can be an even bigger advantage for companies than delaying payments for as long as possible. In Chapter 16, I talk about how much money companies can save by taking advantage of trade discounts instead of paying bills on time.

WARNING

Although slowing bill payment may be the easiest way to deal with a cash-flow problem, it's the option with the least advantages and the greatest potential for hurting business operations in the long term, especially when vendors and suppliers finally decide to stop providing the necessary goods.

TIP

When reading a financial report, you can test to see whether a company may be choosing a bill-paying delay strategy by calculating its accounts payable turnover ratio (see Chapter 16). If the turnover of accounts payable is slowing from one year to the next, it may be a sign that the company has a cash-flow problem.

Speeding Up Collecting Accounts Receivables

If a company owes more money than it has, clearly, it needs to bring in more money. A business whose cash is tight often brings in more money by speeding up the collection of its *accounts receivables* — money that customers who bought on credit or people who borrowed from the company owe. To collect the money, the company must make changes to its credit policies, focusing on one or more of these five basic variables:

- **Credit period:** Companies can change the length of time they give their customers to pay for their purchases. A liberal credit period can give customers 60 or 90 days to pay, whereas a conservative credit period can allow as few as 10 days.
- **Credit standards:** In times of trouble, the company can loosen the policies it uses to determine a customer's credit eligibility. For example, a company that requires customers to have an income level of at least $50,000 to get a $1,000

credit line may decide to offer that same credit line to customers with an income of only $30,000. This policy change increases the credit-customer base and allows more people to buy on credit; however, the change can also increase the number of customers who have difficulty paying their bills.

- **Collection period:** Companies with strict collection policies can begin contacting slow payers or prohibiting them from making further purchases, even if their account is just a few days late. Other companies wait 60 days or longer before they follow up on late accounts. Shortening the credit period can get more cash in the door quickly, but this policy can also cause customers to buy fewer products or to move their business to another store.
- **Discounts:** Companies can encourage their customers to pay their bills earlier by using a discount program. I discuss using discount programs in greater detail in Chapter 16. For example, a company can offer customers a 2 percent discount for paying their bills within 10 days of receiving the bill, but if the customers wait 30 days to pay their bills, the company expects the payment in full. Deciding to add or change a discount program may speed up cash collections, but it lowers the profit margin on sales because these discounts bring in less revenues.
- **Fees and late payments:** Companies must decide whether they want to charge late fees or interest to customers who don't pay on time. Companies with a strict collection process charge a late fee one day after a bill's due date and start adding interest for each day that the payment is late. Companies with a liberal collection policy don't charge late fees or add interest charges to late payers. To encourage on-time payment, a company could charge a $25 late fee when a bill is paid ten days after it's due. This strategy encourages slow payers to pay more quickly, but it can also chase customers away if one of the company's competitors doesn't impose late fees or interest charges.

Before a company that's trying to speed up its incoming cash flow makes any changes to its credit policy, it must look at a number of financial variables to determine the long-term impact the change may have on its sales and profit margin. Stricter accounts receivable policies are likely to honk off customers and increase staff workload, whereas looser policies may encourage more sales but result in more bad debt that a company has to write off.

To fully assess the possible ramifications of the change, top executives must discuss with managers in the sales, marketing, accounting, and finance departments the potential impact of the changes in credit policy.

For instance, any change in credit policy increases the staff's workload. When a company eases its credit standards and increases the number of customers who can buy on credit, it needs more staff to manage its accounts receivable and keep track of all the new customer accounts. If the company decides to make its credit standards stricter and require a more time-consuming credit check before establishing new customer accounts, it has to hire more staff or an outside vendor to do those credit checks. Either way, a stricter policy costs more money and may drive customers away.

REMEMBER

So before they change their credit policies, companies must carefully assess the potential cash inflow change and potential staff costs, as well as the impact a policy change may have on customers. Though at first glance the change may look like a good idea for improving cash flow, its long-term impact may actually reduce sales or profits.

TIP

You can test whether a company is having problems collecting from its customers by calculating its accounts receivable turnover ratio. To find out how to calculate this ratio, turn to Chapter 16.

Borrowing on Receivables

Instead of delving into the complicated realm of credit policy changes, many companies use a *receivables securitization program.* In this case, I'm talking about accounts receivable, which include all accounts of customers who buy on credit. In this type of program, a company sells its receivables to an outside party — usually a bank or other financial institution — to get immediate cash, and as the receivables come in from customers, the company repays the financial institution. Most companies retain the *servicing rights* of the receivables, which means that they continue to collect from customers and receive servicing fees for administering that collection.

Two standard options for selling receivables follow:

- **Selling the receivable for less than it's worth:** For example, a program's terms may dictate that the company gets 92 cents for each dollar of receivables, which, in essence, is equivalent to an 8 percent interest rate.
- **Paying interest as if the company had taken out a loan secured by a physical asset, such as a building:** For example, the company's credit terms for the securitization program may set up an annual interest rate of 8 percent. But for customers who pay their bills within 30 days, the amount of interest the company actually pays on the accounts receivable loan is only 1/12 of 8 percent for the one month it borrowed the money while waiting for a customer to pay.

In addition, companies usually have to pay upfront charges of 2 to 5 percent to set up the program.

REMEMBER

The biggest advantage of using a receivables securitization program is that the company has immediate access to cash. The biggest disadvantage is that the company ends up with less than the full value of the receivables when it collects from its customers because of discounts or any interest paid on those receivables.

TIP

You can find out whether a company uses a securitization program by reading the notes to the financial statements. If a company does use this type of financing, it includes in the notes information about money it has borrowed on a short-term basis, called *short-term financing.*

Reducing Inventory

Companies in a cash-flow crunch sometimes decide to reduce their on-hand inventory. Doing so certainly reduces the amount of cash the company must lay out to pay for that inventory, but it also can result in lost sales if customers come in to buy a product and don't find it on the shelves. Customers may then be more likely to go to a competitor than wait for the product to arrive.

Many companies use a *just-in-time inventory system,* which means the product shows up at a company's door just before it's needed. To set up this type of system, a company must know how many sales it normally makes over a period of time and how long it takes to get new products.

Then the company calculates when it must order new products so that it receives them just before the shelves become empty. This system reduces the inventory a company has to store in its warehouses and the cash payments it must make to suppliers and vendors for the products it purchases. When done correctly for a product that moves quickly off the shelves, the system works well — the company may even sell the product and collect cash before it needs to pay the bills. This strategy certainly helps a company manage its cash flow and reduce the amount of cash it must borrow to pay for inventory.

The big disadvantage of using a just-in-time inventory system is that estimates are sometimes wrong. For example, a company decides when and how much it needs to reorder based on historical sales data. If a product's popularity increases dramatically before the company can adjust its inventory purchasing process, store shelves may be empty for days before new products arrive — just when the public is rushing to get the product. As a result, the company loses sales to a competitor who still has the product on its shelves. Any cash that customers would have paid for those goods that weren't available is cash that's permanently lost to the company.

Other times, a just-in-time inventory system breaks down because a problem occurs in the supply chain. For example, if a customer orders a product from a company in Singapore and a major storm shuts down the manufacturing plant for a week or more, product deliveries are delayed. The company selling the product may be left with empty shelves because the inventory on hand ran out and the new inventory won't show up for a few weeks, until the manufacturing plant can restore its operations and begin shipping products again. This could result in a lot of lost cash to the company because customers would be forced to buy the goods elsewhere.

TIP

Using financial reports, you can test how quickly a company's inventory turns over by calculating the inventory turnover ratio, which I discuss in Chapter 15. However, you won't be able to tell whether the company regularly runs out of products on its shelves by reading the financial reports. You can determine that issue only by periodically stopping by stores to find out.

REMEMBER

Although reducing inventory does save the company cash up front that it would normally pay to buy that inventory, inventory reduction can actually result in a loss of sales and less cash in the long run if customers have to go elsewhere to find the products they want. Inventory reduction makes sense only when the company believes the product is sitting too long on the shelves and customer interest in buying the product is low.

Getting Cash More Quickly

The most flexible way for a company to keep its cash moving is to have numerous options in place so it can borrow cash when needed or speed up cash receipts. Companies can choose from among the following options to keep their cash flowing:

- **Credit cards:** Credit cards can be a great way for a company to conserve cash and pay bills. Banks offer a range of credit cards, debit cards, and other short-term cash options to help companies maintain cash flow. Banks can put controls on these cards to ensure that a company's employees don't abuse them.
- **Lines of credit:** Lines of credit allow companies to access cash as needed. The bank or financial institution sets a maximum amount of credit that the company can borrow and gives the company checks or allows it to transfer cash into a checking account.

- **An unsecured line of credit:** This type of credit isn't backed by the company's assets, which means that if the company can't pay back the loan, the financial institution can't seize the company's assets.
- **A secured line of credit:** This type of credit is backed by the company's assets, so the bank can foreclose and take possession of the asset that backs the line of credit if the company fails to pay back the loan.

- **Lockbox services:** Companies can set up these services with a bank so that they pay their bills directly to the bank, using a lockbox; then the bank deposits the money directly into the company's account. This method can speed up cash flow because the bank deposits the funds upon receipt, eliminating the day or longer it normally takes for checks accepted by the company to be processed in-house and then deposited in the bank. However, electronic banking and bill paying has eliminated the need for many lockbox services.
- **Electronic bill payment:** Many businesses allow customers to pay their bills online and send in bills by e-mail to speed up the cash collection process. When they get money from customers more quickly, companies speed up their incoming cash flow.
- **Merchant services:** A firm can get access to money much more quickly by using electronic payment systems when accepting credit and debit cards. Most stores now use electronic payment systems rather than paper copies when accepting credit cards. Instead of waiting for paper transactions to yield cash — which sometimes occurs days later — companies can use electronic payment systems to access cash within minutes.
- **Small Business Administration loans:** Small businesses can get low-interest loans guaranteed by the U.S. Small Business Administration (SBA) to assist with cash-flow problems, which helps a small business owner get approval for the needed funds.

5 The Many Ways Companies Answer to Others

IN THIS PART . . .

Checking out the numbers. Discover the role of auditors.

Answering to the government. Explore the various government agencies that regulate financial reporting

Developing international standards. What will they mean for public companies worldwide

Exploring the role of analysts. Can you trust them?.

Communicating with the companies in which you invest. What are the options?

Digging into the games companies play with the numbers on financial reports.

» Getting acquainted with audits and auditors

» Checking out the auditing process

» Exploring accounting standards and principles

Chapter 18

Finding Out How Companies Find Errors: The Auditing Process

Most readers of financial reports don't work for the company whose reports they're reading and, therefore, must depend on the truthfulness of the company's management in reporting its financial statements. Can you depend on the numbers you see?

The question is valid, especially considering the corporate scandals that have rocked Wall Street since the collapse of Enron in December 2001. (To find out more about why the world's largest electricity and natural gas trader filed for bankruptcy, see Chapter 24.) The Enron scandal — followed by financial reporting scandals at other major corporations such as MCI WorldCom, Adelphia, AIG, and many others — led investors to be wary about the numbers companies put in their financial reports.

In this chapter, I explore how third parties get involved to keep company records on the up and up.

Inspecting Audits and Auditors

Company outsiders can't be sure the information they see is an accurate reflection of the company's financial situation unless a disinterested third party reviews the company's operations and financial statements and determines that the reports are free of fraud and misrepresentation. Called an *audit*, this process is crucial for verifying the accuracy of a firm's financial reports.

Every public company that sells stock on one of the public markets must hire an independent certified public accountant (CPA) to audit its financial statements. Investors, financial institutions, vendors, suppliers, and anyone else who depends on knowledge about a company's financial well-being expect these audited statements to be truthful. I talk about the process of auditing a company's books in the following sections, and I discuss the process of taking a company public in Chapter 3.

Looking for mistakes

Even when a company has no desire to mislead investors and others, honest mistakes can happen. Sometimes errors occur because a company's accounting system is flawed or isn't capable of handling changing company conditions, especially when a business is growing rapidly. Other times, a company's accountants present wrong numbers because they don't have a good understanding of the latest accounting principles related to the presentation of some of the numbers.

WARNING

Fraudulent financial reporting results when management decides to deliberately distort the numbers to make the company's financial results look better than they actually are. Sometimes companies withhold negative information to avoid an investor backlash and a drop in stock value. Companies often deceive without the knowledge of the auditors, but sometimes the auditors permit deception by bending the rules. Turn to Chapter 23 to get the dirt on fraudulent financial reporting.

Meeting Mr. or Ms. Auditor

To become a licensed CPA, candidates must complete extensive training that includes having at least a bachelor's degree with a major emphasis in accounting, passing a national CPA exam, and showing that they know how to work with the information in the real world by satisfying work experience requirements that vary by state.

To keep a current license, CPAs must take continuing education courses each year. The amount of time devoted to continuing education varies by state.

TECHNICAL STUFF

Each state has a board of accountancy that monitors the activities of its CPAs. The state boards have the right to revoke or suspend a CPA's license if he violates the laws, regulations, or ethics governing CPAs. If a CPA's license is revoked or suspended, she can no longer serve her clients as an independent CPA unless she gets her license reinstated.

CPAs don't just audit financial reports. They also provide tax planning services and consulting to help a company set up its accounting system, develop the needed information systems to manage its accounting functions, evaluate its business, and even assist with personal financial planning. Some CPAs develop other specialties, such as production control and efficiency, to provide additional services to clients.

REMEMBER

To audit a company's financial statements, a CPA must be in public practice and must not be an employee of any organization other than a CPA firm. A CPA's independence from the companies he serves is critical to ensure an independent report.

Examining Records: The Role of the Auditor

The Securities and Exchange Commission (SEC) requires most major corporations to have their financial reports checked by a third party, called an *auditor*, to be sure the reports truthfully portray the company's financial health.

Some partnerships that aren't corporations choose to pay for an audit, but they aren't required to do so. They do it primarily because the banks or financial institutions that loan them money request it. They may also choose to pay for an audit if several partners are involved in the company but only one of the partners runs its day-to-day operations. The partners who aren't involved in the day-to-day activities may want to have the books audited by a CPA to be sure the active partner is accurately reporting the company's financial activities to them.

If you've worked in a business, you know how nervous some managers become when auditors show up at their door. An audit isn't a complete surprise to a business, however. Auditors sit down with top management and an internal audit committee to discuss the audit process and to schedule the audit for a time that's least disruptive to the business. For example, a retail company certainly doesn't want auditors checking out its stores during the end-of-year holiday rush.

Auditors do more than just review financial statements, as you can see in the next three sections, which describe other elements of the auditing process.

Preliminary review

Before auditors show up at a business's door, they meet with key executives and board members from the audit committee to discuss the audit's scope and objectives. For example, an audit may include a complete review of the company's operations, or it may focus on just one aspect of the operation, such as collections from customers. The objectives of a full audit usually are to validate the company's financial statements. The objectives of an audit for one particular part of an operation usually involve reviewing the operation's efficiency or finding possible internal control problems that can lead to theft or fraud.

After the scope of the audit is determined, the auditors meet with key managers to gather information about internal accounting processes, to evaluate existing controls, and to plan how the audit will be conducted inside the company.

The internal accounting manager responsible for the audit then sends a letter to the staff members involved, announcing the audit and who's been assigned to do the audit. In the first meeting with accounting staff, the auditors review the available resources — including personnel, facilities, and funds — that are allocated to the audit. During these initial meetings, the auditors identify areas of special concern.

Auditors then meet with the departments being audited, which may include all departments in a company or just a few that are directly involved in the issues being investigated. The auditors survey key personnel and review financial reports, files, and other information deemed important to the audit. The auditors also review each department's internal control structure. This review helps the auditors determine where holes are in internal control processes and helps them identify the key areas that need to be tested in the field when auditing specific stores or other locations that the company owns.

After all the facts are determined in the preliminary review, the auditors design the audit process that's used in the field to collect needed information and to meet the objectives set out in the initial meetings with top executives and the board of directors.

Fieldwork

Auditors perform *fieldwork* when they visit a company's individual offices and locations to determine whether the internal controls discussed at the company's top levels are actually being implemented properly. For example, if a business requires a certain type of coding when an order is charged to a customer's account and that coding is not being used consistently, some customers may be getting merchandise without getting billed.

In the field, auditors watch a company's employees carry out certain tasks to be sure that they're performing them correctly. Additionally, auditors review files to be sure all the paperwork is in order to back up reports sent to the central corporate offices. For example, if the company requires a manager's signature before a customer is given a refund, the auditor randomly reviews company refund records to be sure that the signature process is being followed.

Although the top manager at a location likely knows when the auditors will arrive, the rest of the staff is usually surprised by their arrival. Any findings during the fieldwork become part of the draft audit report.

After the auditors complete a preliminary review of the specific location with the top managers, they randomly review various records to be sure that employees are following internal control procedures. For example, if an auditor is auditing a bank's operations, she wants to know whether employees are following the bank's procedures for approving a loan. She likely checks random files for loans to be sure all needed approvals are in place.

TECHNICAL STUFF

The type of fieldwork that may be required depends on the business type and the audit's scope. Auditors for a bank visit offices in the corporate headquarters, as well as bank branches, to complete their fieldwork. Auditors for a corporation with retail stores do their fieldwork in the corporate headquarters, regional headquarters, and individual stores. If the scope of the audit is just to review the customer order and bill-paying process, the fieldwork may take place only in the corporate accounts receivable section.

As the auditors work in the field, they discuss any significant discrepancies with top management at the field locations. Auditors often work with management to determine how best to resolve any problems before they complete the final audit report. If a problem can be easily resolved, they can do so orally. If the problems are more serious or complex, auditors compile written reports and circulate them to managers in the field, corporate executives, and board members. These reports summarize the auditors' field findings, identifying problems and making recommendations, before the auditors turn in their final report.

REMEMBER

Most companies work to fix problems internally to avoid being reported to their outside stakeholders: investors, creditors, employees, vendors, and suppliers. If you're a member of top management or the audit committee of the board of directors, you usually find out about problems long before they're detailed in the business press or on the front page of the newspaper, as some company scandals are.

Audit reports from fieldwork aren't released publicly, so when scandals do make it to the front pages, it's usually after a whistle-blower comes forward or the SEC announces an investigation.

Audit report

After auditors complete their fieldwork, they start working on their *audit report*, which presents the audit findings and discusses recommendations for improvement. Auditors review their findings with top management and discuss any disagreement that managers in the field may have with the findings. Managers can then comment on the findings before auditors submit a final report to the operating managers, top executives, and the board of directors. Managers are usually given an opportunity to submit their own comments in areas of discrepancy.

If the auditor concludes that changes need to be made within the corporation, managers submit their plans to improve processes based on the auditor's recommendations. If managers disagree with the auditor for some reason, they have to explain in the final report why they disagree and what they plan to do to fix the problem.

Filling the GAAP

Although a CPA's primary role as an auditor is to make sure that a company's financial statements are presented fairly and accurately, he must also ensure that the *generally accepted accounting principles* (GAAP) are followed.

GAAP guidelines help a company determine the amount of financial information it must disclose and help it measure its assets, liabilities, revenues, expenses, and equity. That information makes up the financial statements, including the balance sheet (see Chapter 6), the income statement (see Chapter 7), and the statement of cash flows (see Chapter 8). The GAAP guidelines, which fill bookshelves in an accountant's office, are highly technical explanations of how a company must report the financial information on each line item of these financial statements, such as how to calculate the value of each asset, liability, or equity on the balance sheet, or how to report revenue and expenses on the income statement.

Accounting standards: Four important qualities

The primary accounting standard-setting body in the U.S. is the Financial Accounting Standards Board, or FASB (check out the sidebar "Exploring the FASB"). It's responsible for developing GAAP, as well as updating the already developed GAAP to reflect changes in the ways companies operate. These changes occur as new ways of doing business become common in the business world.

REMEMBER

The FASB specifies four characteristics of useful accounting information that companies need to strive for in their financial reports. These four characteristics form the basis for designing the technical GAAP requirements:

- **Relevance:** Relevant information includes information needed to forecast a company's future earnings or confirm or correct prior expectations. The information must also be timely, which means it must be available to business decision makers before it loses the power to influence decisions. For example, if companies had to report their earnings only every five years, the information wouldn't be relevant to most company outsiders, who need to make decisions about the company more frequently than that.
- **Reliability:** For accounting information to be considered reliable, it must be verifiable, factual, and accurate. The information must also be neutral. In other words, a company can't cherry-pick the information it wants outsiders to see and hide any bad news that it doesn't want to report.
- **Comparability:** Not all companies must collect and present the information in exactly the same way. Some variation is allowed in accounting methods, but a company must disclose what accounting methods it uses. For example, as I discuss in Chapter 15, numerous methods are available for tracking inventory, so companies must state which method they use. This requirement makes comparing results from company to company easier.
- **Consistency:** The company must use the same accounting principles and methods from year to year so that financial report readers can compare results with the results of previous years. If a company changes the accounting principles or methods its financial reports are based on, it must tell the financial report readers about the change and provide information regarding how that change impacts previously reported financial results.

Changing principles: More work for the FASB

GAAP principles aren't set in stone. As business needs and the way companies do business change, so must the principles. The auditing industry is the most sensitive to emerging trends in day-to-day reporting practices, so it tends to be the profession that most frequently alerts the FASB to the need for new principles or changes in old ones. In addition to changes noticed in the field, new legislation or regulatory decisions can be the sources of needed changes in the GAAP.

EXPLORING THE FASB

TECHNICAL STUFF

The FASB was first designated as the organization responsible for establishing standards of financial accounting and reporting in 1973. Both the SEC and the American Institute of Certified Public Accounts (AICPA) recognize the FASB as the authority for setting the standards for financial reports.

The FASB board is made up of seven members who serve full time for five-year terms and are eligible for one additional five-year term. To serve on the FASB, board members must sever all connections with firms or institutions they've been involved with before the appointment.

The FASB's mission is to establish and improve standards of financial accounting and reporting. The board is responsible for the guidance and education of the public, which includes issuers, auditors, and users of financial information. The FASB carries out its mission by

- Seeking to improve the usefulness of financial reporting by focusing on four characteristics: relevance, reliability, comparability, and consistency.
- Maintaining current standards that reflect changes in the methods of doing business and in the economic environment.
- Reviewing promptly any significant areas where financial reporting may be deficient and improving the reporting situation through its standards-setting process.
- Promoting the international convergence of accounting standards to improve financial reporting.
- Improving the common understanding of the nature and purpose of financial report information.

You can access information about FASB working projects and accounting standards online at `www.fasb.org`.

After hearing from all sources about emerging issues, the FASB decides what technical issues it will add to its agenda to change the GAAP. The board looks at a number of factors when deciding whether an issue is worth changing:

» **Pervasiveness of issue:** The board determines how troublesome the issue is to users, preparers, auditors, and others. It also considers whether the practice being questioned impacts many different kinds of companies and whether the issue is likely to be transitory or to persist for a long time. Only issues that are likely to persist over time are considered for further action.

- **Alternative solutions:** The board considers which of the one or more alternative solutions will improve financial reporting in terms of the key characteristics of relevance, reliability, consistency, and comparability.
- **Technical feasibility:** The board determines whether it can develop a technically sound solution or whether the project under consideration must wait for another issue to be decided as part of a different project also underway. If another issue must be decided first, the board holds off working on the issue.
- **Practical consequences:** The board weighs whether the improved accounting solution is likely to be generally accepted and to what extent addressing a particular issue may cause others, such as the SEC or Congress, to act.
- **Convergence possibilities:** The board determines whether its action on the issue will lead to the elimination of significant differences in standards or practices between the U.S. and other countries, with resulting improvement in the quality of U.S. standards.
- **Cooperative opportunities:** The board considers whether there's international support by one or more other standard setters for undertaking the project jointly or through other cooperative means with the FASB.
- **Resources:** The board must determine whether adequate resources and expertise are available within the FASB or whether the FASB can leverage the work of other standard setters.

If the FASB decides it wants to work on an issue, it begins a long process that can take years before the issue is added to the GAAP. This process includes board meetings that are open to the public, exposure drafts circulated for public comment, and additional board meetings and comment periods, if necessary.

» Looking at the 10-Q
» Getting acquainted with the 10-K
» Evaluating internal controls
» Checking out company compliance
» Becoming familiar with the way the board works
» Disclosing insider ownership

Chapter 19
Digging into Government Regulations

You've probably heard all kinds of complaints about the government bureaucracy involved in, and the paperwork required for, corporate reporting. Most corporate executives and managers responsible for answering to the government don't find pleasure in reading through government reporting requirements. This stuff doesn't make great bedtime reading, although some people do find these requirements good to read when they're having a hard time falling asleep — boring!

No matter how boring and frustrating corporate staff may find these government requirements, corporations have no way to bypass the rules. Actually, as a company outsider who needs to know what's happening behind closed doors, you should be glad such stringent regulations exist. Without them, you'd have no idea whether you're getting accurate reports about what the company does and what its growth prospects are.

TIP

If you're researching a company because you're considering investing in it or have already invested, you needn't depend solely on the information the company gives you in its annual and quarterly reports. Visit the Securities and Exchange Commission's (SEC) Edgar website (`www.sec.gov/edgar.shtml`) and read the details in the company's public reports it files with the government.

TIP

I find that one of the best ways to track news about particular companies and new SEC filings is by listing a mock portfolio on one of the financial news websites, such as Yahoo! Finance (finance.yahoo.com). Any news or SEC filing is linked to the opening page of each stock. An asterisk designates when something new is reported about a stock in your mock portfolio, so you know when new information about the company has been posted.

Checking Out the 10-Q

Every quarter, corporations must report their financial results to the SEC (which has primary responsibility for the U.S. government's oversight of public corporations) on Form 10-Q. The 10-Q isn't a blank form that needs to be filled in. Instead, the SEC provides general instructions for the information that must be included and the format in which it must be presented. The 10-Q includes two parts.

Financial information

The financial information required for Part 1 of Form 10-Q isn't much different from the info required for the annual reports. Four items are required:

- **Item 1 — Financial statements:** Included in this section are the balance sheet (see Chapter 6), income statement (turn to Chapter 7), and statement of cash flows (discussed in detail in Chapter 8).
- **Item 2 — Management's discussion and analysis of financial condition and results of operations:** This section includes a discussion and analysis by management of the company's liquidity, resources, and operations, its financial condition, and any changes that occurred during the quarter. I discuss the requirements for this section in greater detail in Chapter 5.
- **Item 3 — Quantitative and qualitative disclosures about market risk:** This section includes discussion about external conditions that impact the company's market, including the impact of inflation, economic conditions that could impact revenue, and competitive forces that may impact the company's future results.
- **Item 4 — Controls and procedures:** This section requires management to disclose the controls and procedures the company has in place to protect its assets and the accuracy of its financial reports. I discuss this requirement in greater detail in the section "Investigating Internal Controls."

Other critical matters

Companies report other important corporation matters that don't fall under the topic of financial results in Part 2 of the 10-Q. This section contains several possible items, but companies need to include only the items relevant to the particular quarter being reported. Following are the items in Part 2:

- **Item 1 — Legal proceedings:** Events involving legal proceedings must be reported only during the quarter in which they first became material and in any future quarters when information related to material developments is available. *Material developments* are proceedings that may have a significant impact on a company's finances.
- **Item 1A -Risk factors:** This section reviews the risks disclosed related to a company's business, financial condition, and cash flows, as well as results of operations that may be materially adversely affected by any of these risks. The trading price of the company's common stock may decline due to these risks.
- **Item 2 — Unregistered sales of equity securities and use of proceeds:** The company must report all equity securities sold by the registrant during the period covered by the report that were not registered under the Securities Act. Information about repurchases of securities also must be included.
- **Item 3 — Defaults upon senior securities:** If a company defaults on its payment of principal or interest on company debt and the default isn't cured within 30 days, the company must report it. The only type of default that doesn't need to be reported is one between a parent company and one of its subsidiaries.
- **Item 4 — Mine safety disclosures:** If applicable, information about mine safety violations or other regulatory matters is reported here.
- **Item 5 — Other information:** This item is a catchall for any issue that hasn't been previously reported on Form 8-K but needs to be reported. I discuss the requirements of Form 8-K in a later section called "Uncovering the Ways Companies Keep in Compliance." A company doesn't have to file an 8-K for an issue reported on a Form 10-Q.
- **Item 6 — Exhibits and reports on Form 8-K:** Any compliance reports filed during the quarter must be attached as an *exhibit* (additional pages that provide this information) on the 10-Q.

Introducing the 10-K

Form 10-K is the official annual report form the SEC requires, and it's the report you're most likely to see as part of the glossy annual report that companies send out to investors. The 10-K includes four parts, which I discuss in this section.

Business operations

In Part 1 of the 10-K, you find the following details about business operations:

- **Item 1 — Business:** This section describes the company's operations with discussions about product lines, major classes of customers, industries in which the company operates, and details about domestic and foreign operations. "Risk factors" (Item 1A) and "Unresolved staff comments" (Item 1B) are also discussed in this section.
- **Item 2 — Properties:** This section describes the property the company owns.
- **Item 3 — Legal proceedings:** This section discusses any legal proceedings the company is involved in and the material impact the lawsuits may have on the company.
- **Item 4 — Mine safety disclosures:** If applicable, information must be provided regarding mine safety violations or other regulatory matters.

Financial data

Part 2 of the 10-K includes information related to any matters that impact the company's financial health. In this part, you find the following items:

- **Item 5 — Market for registrant's common equity, related shareholder matters, and issuer purchases of equity securities:** In this section, you find information about the market for the company's stock, which stock exchange the company is traded on, the quarterly low and high stock prices for the past two years, the approximate number of shareholders, the amount paid in cash dividends for the past two years, and discussion of any restrictions on the company's ability to pay future dividends.
- **Item 6 — Selected financial data:** In this section, you find a five-year summary of selected financial data, including net sales, income or loss from *continuing operations* (company activities that go on each year to make and sell products or services) on a per-share basis, total assets, long-term debt, cash dividends per share of common stock, and information about any redeemable *preferred stock* (stock that can be converted to debt).

» **Item 7 — Management's discussion and analysis of financial condition and results of operations:** In this section, management discusses the company's financial condition and any changes to its condition that have occurred in the past year. Management also discusses the results of operations and analyzes the company's liquidity, resources, and operations. If any major changes in the financial statements took place during the year being reported, the company also discusses those changes in this section.

» **Item 7A — Quantitative and qualitative disclosures about market risk:** This section is where you find management's discussion of external economic factors that impacted the company's operations, such as the effects of inflation. You also find discussion about the company's competition and any major risks to the industry as a whole.

» **Item 8 — Financial statements and supplementary data:** Here's where you find the balance sheet, income statement, and statement of cash flows, as well as all supplementary information for these documents, such as the notes to the financial statements (see Chapter 9) and the auditors' report (see Chapter 5).

» **Item 9 — Changes in and disagreements with accountants on accounting and financial disclosure:** If the company has any disagreements with the auditors about what information must be presented on the financial statements and how to present it, this section is where you find discussion of the differences.

» **Item 9A — Controls and procedures:** Here you find information about the company's internal controls and procedures to avoid fraud and ensure accuracy in the financial statements. I discuss these requirements in greater detail in the section "Investigating Internal Controls."

» **Item 9B - Other information:** This section includes any items that aren't reported on an 8-K during the year, as well as items that are reported on an 8-K but aren't reported elsewhere in the 10-K.

Information about directors and executives

Part 3 of the 10-K takes you behind the scenes of company operations and gives you information about the directors and top executives, including any special compensation packages they receive. Following are the items you can expect to find:

» **Item 10 — Directors and executive officers of the registrant:** Here's where you find out who sits on the company's board of directors, as well as who serves as the company's top executive officers.

» **Item 11 — Executive compensation:** The company must report the compensation packages for all its top executives in this section.

- **Item 12 — Security ownership of certain beneficial owners and management and related stockholder matters:** Here you find details about the stock owned by top executives, board members, senior managers, and any other major shareholders of the company.
- **Item 13 — Certain relationships and related transactions and director independence:** This section is where you find out about large related-party transactions, such as any transactions between the company and its top management team. Companies must also include information about significant transactions with subsidiaries or major shareholders.
- **Item 14 — Principal accounting fees and services:** Here's where you find details about the relationship between the company and its accountants. The company must report the fees billed for each of the past two fiscal years for professional services by the principal accountant for the audit of the company's financial statements, as well as for any services related to the audit. The company must also disclose fees for tax services by professional accountants for tax compliance, tax advice, and tax planning, as well as fees for any additional services that the principal accountant provides. In addition, the company must disclose the audit committee's preapproved policies and procedures related to the work of the principal accountant.

The extras

Part 4 of the 10-K is the catchall for additional exhibits, including any financial statement schedules and any reports the company filed throughout the year and reported on Form 8-K.

Investigating Internal Controls

REMEMBER

When filing Form 10-K with the SEC, companies must also include the management's report on internal controls (which includes rules for how company staff should do their work to avoid theft and fraud). This requirement was added as part of the sweeping changes mandated by the Sarbanes-Oxley Act of 2002, which I discuss in greater detail in Chapter 3.

The management's report on internal controls requires that companies provide the following:

- Statement of management's responsibility for designing, establishing, and maintaining an adequate internal control structure over financial reporting for the company

- Statement identifying the framework management used to evaluate the effectiveness of its internal controls
- Management's assessment, as of the end of the fiscal year being reported, of the effectiveness of the company's internal control structure and procedures for financial reporting
- Attestation report from the company's auditor regarding management's assessment of the internal controls' effectiveness, which assures the 10-K reader that the auditor reviewed the assessment and found it effective

Management must report any weaknesses it finds in its internal controls over financial reporting. If management finds one or more material weaknesses within the company's internal control system, the company can't conclude that its internal controls are effective. The following are some of the key points management must guarantee for its internal control process:

- Maintenance of records that accurately detail and fairly reflect the transactions and dispositions of the company's assets
- Assurance that transactions are recorded as necessary to permit the company to prepare financial statements in accordance with generally accepted accounting principles
- Assurance that receipts and expenditures are made only in accordance with authorizations from management and company directors
- Assurance that management has controls in place to detect and prevent unauthorized acquisition, use, or disposition of company assets that may have a material effect on the financial statements

You may be thinking, "Shouldn't a company have all these controls in place and not need the government to tell it to put them there?" Well, investors who lost billions because of the financial shenanigans at companies like Enron, MCI, and others during the early 2000s sure wish the SEC had more strongly enforced these internal controls before they took their losses.

Uncovering the Ways Companies Keep in Compliance

Sometimes significant changes in a company's financial position occur between the times the company files its financial reports. When that happens, the company must file a special report called an 8-K, which reports any *material changes*

(changes that may have a significant financial impact on the company's earnings) that happen between the times of the quarterly or annual reports.

REMEMBER

The Sarbanes-Oxley Act of 2002 (see Chapter 3) mandates that the SEC review all its compliance requirements regarding financial reporting. In response to the legislation, the SEC issued new rules for Form 8-K, requiring companies to report any material changes within four days of the event. Critical events to be reported on Form 8-K include

- **Business combination:** Any agreement related to a *business combination* (such as a merger combining two companies or consolidating two major divisions into one) or other extraordinary corporate transaction that may be material to the company's financial position. This report must include this information:
  - Date of execution
  - Parties involved
  - Material relationship between the company or its affiliates and any other party involved in the agreement
  - Brief description of the terms and conditions of this agreement

  Companies don't need to disclose any nonbinding agreements or letters of intent, provided that they aren't material to the company.
- **Agreement termination:** Any termination of an agreement that was previously reported, such as the cancellation of a signed contract to provide a significant amount of the company's product to another company if this cancellation means a loss of significant future earnings.
- **Bankruptcy or receivership:** Any plans to declare bankruptcy or enter into *receivership,* a type of bankruptcy in which the company can avoid liquidating itself and instead work with a court-appointed trustee to restructure its debt with the intention of emerging from bankruptcy.
- **Acquisition or disposition:** Any acquisition or sale of major assets outside the course of ordinary business operations. For example, the acquisition of a new company fits the reporting requirement, but the acquisition of new equipment for continuing operations doesn't need a special report on Form 8-K.
- **Financial results:** Any earnings results related to earnings, company operations, or financial conditions that occurred between the quarterly or annual reports and were distributed by press releases or other public means.
- **Financial obligations:** Any direct financial obligations that are material to the company, such as the signing of a long-term debt or lease obligation. The company must include a brief description of the transaction and agreement.

- **Disposal of assets:** Any costs related to the disposal of long-held assets when the company enters into an agreement (usually called an *exit agreement*) to get rid of those assets. The company must also disclose termination of employees under an exit plan.
- **Impairment of asset value:** Any conclusion by the board or an authorized company officer that the value of an asset is significantly impaired — for example, when the value of goodwill is determined to be significantly less than what the company reports on the balance sheet.
- **Changes in stock exchange listing:** Any time the company gets notification that it may be *delisted* (removed) from a stock exchange, or if the company fails to meet the rules or standards set by the stock exchange it's listed on. It must also report any plans to change to a new stock exchange.
- **Accountant change:** Any change in the company's certifying accountant.
- **Unreliable financial reports:** Any conclusion by the company's board of directors, a committee of the board, or an authorized officer that a previously issued financial report can't be relied on for information. You've probably heard press reports indicating that a company plans to restate its financial reports because of an error. Many times those press reports are based on a press release and the Form 8-K.
- **Changes in control of company:** Any departures of directors or principal officers, election of new directors, or appointment of new principal officers.
- **Changes in charter or bylaws:** Any proposed change in the charter or bylaws and its impact on the company's operations.
- **Changes in fiscal year:** Any plans to change a company's fiscal year if the decision is made outside the vote of the shareholders or by amendment to its bylaws. The company must include the date of determination, the date of the new fiscal year, and the form on which the report covering the transition period will be filed.
- **Temporary suspension of trading in the company's employee benefit plans:** Any suspensions of employee benefit plans for a period of time. Most often such suspensions happen when the company changes from one benefit provider to another. However, this change can be a sign of a major decision impacting the company's stock, such as a pending announcement about company earnings, a stock split, a buyback of stock, or an issuance of new stock.
- **Amendments to the company's code of ethics:** Any significant changes to the company's code of ethics.

As you can see from this list, you'd never hear about most of these events if companies weren't required to report them. But this information may be critical to any decision you make about the stock you currently hold or may want to buy.

Digging into Board Operations

Since the passage of the Sarbanes-Oxley Act of 2002 (see Chapter 3), the SEC more closely scrutinizes a company's board operations and the interaction between its board and shareholders. The SEC staff continues to study the act's requirements and to issue new disclosure requirements as they identify problems. Two major changes adopted since initial passage involve these issues:

- Disclosure to investors about the board's nominating committee and the nominating process for new board members
- Disclosure about the means by which the holders of a company's securities can communicate with the board of directors

In most cases, this information appears on the company's website or with its annual reports.

REMEMBER

Note that I refer to "security holders" in some cases and "shareholders" in other cases. Not all security holders are shareholders. Only shareholders have voting rights within the company. Bonds are a type of security, so although bondholders don't have voting rights like shareholders, they do have an interest in who serves on the board.

Understanding the nominating process

The newly adopted rules imposed by Sarbanes-Oxley regarding a public company's nomination process demand that the board specify the following in writing to its shareholders:

- **Whether the nominating committee has a written charter and, if it does, whether it's available on the company's website.** If the charter isn't available on the website, the company must print it as part of its proxy information once every three years.
- **Whether the members of the nominating committee are independent (not directly involved in company operations).**
- **Whether the nominating committee accepts nominations from security holders.** If the company allows nominations, it must include information about how security holders can nominate someone to be on the board. If the company doesn't have a policy to accept nominations from security holders, it must explain why the board has decided not to accept these nominations.

- **Minimum qualifications that the nominating committee believes must be met by a person who's recommended for a position on the company's board of directors.** In addition, the company must list any specific qualities or skills that the nominating committee believes are needed for one or more of the open director's positions.
- **How the company evaluates director nominees, including ones recommended by security holders.** If evaluation is different for committee nominees than it is for security holder nominees, the documentation must specify the differences as well.

After the nominations are set, the company needs to disclose to its shareholders whether the nominee was recommended by a security holder, a nonmanagement director, the chief executive officer, a third-party search firm, or some other source. The board doesn't have to disclose this information about nominees who are executive officers or directors standing for reelection.

The SEC reviews all *proxies* (paper ballots sent to shareholders) to see how the company presents the information concerning its nominating process. If the SEC determines that the company doesn't provide sufficient details, it can ask that the company expand its information.

Contacting board members

A company must put a process in place that permits security holders to send communications to the board of directors or supply a statement from the board explaining why it believes that not doing so is appropriate.

The board must make a public disclosure about its communications process with security holders that includes a description of how security holders can communicate with the board and, if applicable, a list of specific board members who deal with specific topics. If the board decides that not all security holder communications are to be sent directly to board members, it must specify how it selects which communications it sends to board members. It can make this disclosure on the company's website or in annual reports.

Finding Out about Insider Ownership

REMEMBER

As an investor, tracking the ownership of stock by insiders can give you a good idea of how they feel about owning the company's stock. If most of the insiders buy the stock, it's usually a good sign — the insiders believe in the long-term performance of the company. But if you find that insiders primarily sell their holdings, trouble may be brewing.

Forms 3, 4, and 5 are used to file information about holdings by individuals or entities who are directors, officers, or major shareholders (holders of more than 10 percent of the stock). Keep your eye on these three important forms to find out what insiders think of the stock:

- **Form 3:** Filed when an individual or entity first takes ownership of stock
- **Form 4:** Filed when an individual or entity changes ownership of stock
- **Form 5:** Filed as an annual statement summarizing changes in stock ownership of directors, officers, or major shareholders

TIP

You can find forms filed with the SEC at `www.sec.gov/edgar.shtml`, but it's easier to use certain financial websites to track stock transactions made by company insiders. On Yahoo! Finance (`http://finance.yahoo.com/`), after you get to the main page for a particular company, you find a link in the left column for insider transactions. You can also get a list of major stockholders by using the link in the right column for major holdings.

- Developing uniform global financial reporting standards
- Seeing who benefits from standardization
- Examining the differences between reporting systems

Chapter 20
Creating a Global Financial Reporting Standard

As more companies operate globally, the need grows for common financial reporting rules. Today many global companies must prepare financial statements in every country in which they operate, to meet each country's reporting requirements. They also must keep the books according to U.S. generally accepted accounting principles (GAAP) rules (see Chapter 18), if the company is a U.S. company, and must meet the standards of the International Financial Reporting Standards (IFRS), or possibly other standards set by government officials in the country in which they're based.

Financial regulatory institutions plan to meld the standards at some point in the future. Today more than 100 countries use the IFRS as the public reporting standard. The IFRS may be used in almost every country, including the U.S, if the company is based in another country. In this chapter, I explore why a move to develop a global public reporting standard is underway, and I introduce you to the key players who are creating this standard. I also discuss the primary benefits of a worldwide standard and talk about some key differences between the U.S. GAAP and the IFRS.

Why Develop a Worldwide Financial Standard?

Have you ever tried to compare a U.S. company to a company in another country and been frustrated with how difficult it is to be looking at apples to oranges? Financial reporting rules differ from country to country, so you can never be certain you're comparing the same information about assets, liabilities, equity, revenue, or expenses. These differences in reporting can make trying to decide which company's stock to buy very difficult.

Companies that operate in more than one country have bigger problems than ones that operate in only one country because they must report results to each country in which they operate, as well as to the country in which they're based. This can result in numerous different accounting systems that must constantly be translated to match the rules for each set of financial reports.

For example, a global U.S. company operating in Canada can report results using the U.S. GAAP, but Canada is moving toward full adoption of IFRS. If the firm is listed on the London exchange, it must also prepare statements to meet the IFRS, and it needs to prepare another set of statements under the rules of the U.S. GAAP. Imagine doing that for every country in which the business operates. Fortunately for U.S. companies, most countries are now accepting the IFRS standards. At some point in the future, the U.S. may also accept IFRS standards, but that point seems to be getting farther away as the work continues. Anything that can simplify this process benefits both the companies that must prepare the statements and the investors trying to interpret the differences.

Key Moves to Reshape Global Financial Reporting

So how did the process get started to reshape the global financial road map, and who are the key players?

In 2002, the U.S. Financial Accounting Standards Board (or FASB, which issues GAAP rules) and the London-based International Accounting Standards Board (or IASB, which issues the IFRS) entered into the Norwalk Agreement, which lays out a plan to undertake efforts to converge the U.S. GAAP and the IFRS. The primary difference between the two is that the IFRS is more focused on objectives and principles and less reliant on detailed rules than the GAAP.

After much discussion and negotiation, the European Commission began its project on the equivalence of national GAAP and the IFRS and issued a draft report in 2005. The U.S. Securities and Exchange Commission (SEC) followed with its development of the IFRS Road Map in 2005.

In 2006, the FASB and IASB reaffirmed their commitment to converge the two reporting systems and updated the Norwalk Agreement based on findings in the 2005 reports. In 2007, the SEC eliminated the requirement for foreign companies that use the IFRS to reconcile to the GAAP. The first major step in accepting the IFRS in financial reports circulated to U.S. investors.

In 2007, in another major step to accept IFRS reporting requirements by U.S. companies, the SEC issued a "concept release" on the topic of giving U.S. companies a choice between filing their reports based on IFRS or GAAP requirements. A concept release opens up the question and seeks comments. The SEC has not yet permitted U.S. companies to use IFRS reporting requirements for SEC reports, but it did move a step closer in May 2008 when it released a "proposing release" on the matter. The proposing release proposes the change and asks for comments.

In July 2012, the SEC issued a report entitled "Work Plan for Consideration of Incorporating International Reporting Standards into the Financial Reporting System for U.S. Issuers," but it did not make any recommendations for a time frame in which to adopt IFRS. The staff concluded that more analysis and consideration was needed before IFRS could be incorporated into U.S. financial reporting.

The U.S. will be one of the last countries to jump on this bandwagon. Israel adopted the IFRS in 2008, Chile and Korea adopted it in 2009, Brazil adopted it in 2010, and Canada did so in 2011.

So global corporations will be able to adopt IFRS for almost all their reporting, unless they are a U.S.-based corporation.

Who Benefits from a Global Standard and How?

Companies that must prepare the reports, and investors, government agencies, and vendors that must use the reports, all benefit from a global standard. Making an informed decision is hard when companies use varying regulations for reporting their finances.

Investors

Every day, investors seek ways to get high-quality financial information that accurately reflects a company's true financial results. Any investor burned by the mortgage mess in 2007, when key financial institutions kept major holdings off the books, knows how critical accurate financial reporting can be to decision making.

REMEMBER

Although the IFRS wouldn't fix all the problems that cropped up in 2007 and 2008 as financial institutions fessed up to their reporting shenanigans, a global standard would make it harder to hide problems across country borders. As U.S. investors become aware that they no longer have to massage the numbers to compare the results of U.S. companies to companies based outside the U.S., they'll push for IFRS alignment so they can compare apples to apples.

Companies that use IFRS standards tend to have longer annual reports than companies that use GAAP guidelines, and the reports are more transparent. A U.S. report based on GAAP principles may be 60 to 70 pages; a report using the IFRS guidelines may be closer to 110 pages. That difference may seem even more overwhelming to you, but you'll have more information with which to make your decisions.

Capital Markets

Capital markets would benefit from the IFRS because if all companies operate under one set of accounting standards, investors can more easily access multiple foreign markets as they build their investment portfolios. This move would stimulate investment and enable capital flows across borders.

Companies

Companies stand to gain the most from this rule change because it would simplify the financial reporting requirements for companies that operate in more than one country. Allowing U.S. companies who operate globally to use IFRS would have these benefits:

- **Standardized and improved accounting and financial policies:** Companies would no longer have to maintain two or more sets of books to prepare financial statements based on varying rules.
- **More efficient use of resources:** Companies would be able to more easily centralize their accounting processes and simplify the training required for employees if only one set of standards for reporting were required to meet governmental regulations.

- **Improved controls:** The IFRS gives companies more control over statutory reporting, which would reduce the risks related to penalties and compliance problems to meet the regulations of each country in which the company operates.
- **Better cash management:** By having more consistent rules across borders, companies could manage their cash more efficiently.

Key Differences between GAAP and the IFRS

Major reports have been written about the key differences between the GAAP and IFRS standards. I don't have the space to do a comprehensive breakdown of the differences, but I do give you a quick peek at some of the key differences in this section.

TIP

If you want a full comparison, you can download excellent reports from PricewaterhouseCoopers (a major global accounting firm) at `www.pwc.com/us/en/issues/ifrs-reporting/index.jhtml`.

Accounting framework

A significant difference between IFRS and GAAP standards is that the IFRS guidelines permit the revaluation of intangible assets; property, plant and equipment; and investment property. GAAP prohibits revaluations except for certain categories of financial instruments that are carried at fair value.

Many analysts believe that assets are undervalued on the balance sheets of major U.S. corporations that compile their reports based on GAAP, especially when it comes to the value of property and plants. Corporate headquarters and factories that were built 20 to 30 years ago are valued on the balance sheets at cost. These assets likely have appreciated greatly even though the buildings have been depreciated to near zero on the balance sheets.

REMEMBER

If U.S. corporations do decide to switch to IFRS standards, you may see a dramatic increase in the value of assets held by some companies as they revalue their property and plants.

Financial statements

The key financial statements required by both the IFRS and GAAP are similar, but the ways in which the numbers are calculated sometimes differ. Also, IFRS standards require only two years of data for the income statements, changes in equity, and cash flow statements, whereas GAAP requires three years of data for SEC registrants.

I discuss some key differences in the following sections, but if your company is considering a switch to the IFRS, or if you're an investor who really wants to understand how the differences may impact the compilation of numbers for the financial statements, I highly recommend that you download the report from PricewaterhouseCoopers mentioned earlier in the chapter.

Balance sheet

GAAP standards require assets, liabilities, and equity to be presented in decreasing order of liquidity. The balance sheet is generally presented with total assets equaling total liabilities and shareholders' equity. For more details on how the balance sheet is presented, review Chapter 6.

IFRS guidelines don't require any specific format, but entities are expected to present current and noncurrent assets and current and noncurrent liabilities as separate classifications on their balance sheets, except when liquidity presentation provides more relevant and reliable information.

I did review several balance sheets of European companies and didn't find any significant differences in the way the balance sheet was presented. The basic format of the GAAP balance sheet seems to be pretty well accepted globally. In Chapter 6, I include a financial position format, which is sometimes used by companies not based in the U.S.

Income statement

The IFRS guidelines don't prescribe a standard format, but GAAP does require the use of a single-step or multistep format, as shown in Chapter 7. The IFRS prohibits the use of the category "extraordinary items," but GAAP allows an extraordinary line item on the income statement.

Extraordinary items are defined as being both infrequent and unusual. For example, when goodwill is shown as a negative item, it's listed as an extraordinary item on the income statement. In 2007 and 2008, as financial institutions put goodwill in this category from acquisitions gone bad because of the mortgage mess, they usually put it down as an extraordinary item. By separating these items from operating income results, a company can make its net income look better.

REMEMBER

Writing down goodwill doesn't involve the use of cash. Cash is used when a company buys another company for more than the value of its assets. If this happened many years ago, it doesn't impact the current year's operating results.

Statement of recognised income and expense (SoRIE)

The SoRIE is unique to IFRS, but the information is commonly shown at the bottom of the income statement in companies filing reports under the rules of GAAP, or it's presented on a separate document called the *statement of changes in shareholders' equity*. In either case, the information presents the total income and accumulated income over time.

Note: Note that *recognised* is spelled with an *s* instead of a *z*. I use the common British spelling because U.S. corporations don't use this statement; it's primarily for companies in Europe that use a British spelling.

Statement of changes in shareholders' equity

This statement is similar in both the IFRS and GAAP standards, unless a non-U.S. company files a SoRIE. This statement isn't required as a separate document under GAAP rules. A company can choose to present the information about changes in shareholders' equity as part of the notes to the financial statements.

Cash flow statement

In both IFRS and GAAP rules, this statement is presented with similar headings. The IFRS gives limited guidance on what information the statement must include.

GAAP gives more specific guidance for which categories must be included in each section of the statement. Statements can be prepared using the direct or indirect method under either the IFRS or GAAP. I discuss the differences between the direct and indirect methods in Chapter 8.

Revenue recognition

Both the IFRS and GAAP require the recognition of revenue when an item's ownership is transferred to the buyer of the goods, but GAAP gives much more detailed guidance for specific types of transactions. In Chapter 23, I detail the games some companies play with revenue recognition, even under the more detailed GAAP rules. I certainly hope that as the international financial regulators converge the requirements of the two systems, they improve the rules related to the recognition of revenue.

Assets

REMEMBER

One key difference between the IFRS and GAAP rules is that assets can be revalued under the IFRS, as discussed earlier in the "Accounting framework" section. Another key difference is that only research is expensed as a cost of doing business under the IFRS, but both research and development are expensed under the GAAP rules. Under the IFRS, development costs are capitalized and amortized (or written off) over several years.

This policy can have a major impact on a company's bottom line. For example, suppose a company determines that, of the $5 million it spent on bringing a new product to market, $1 million was for research and $4 million was for development of the product after research was concluded. Under the GAAP rules, the $5 million would be expensed in each year of the development, based on when the expenses are recognized (I talk about expense recognition in Chapters 7 and 16). Those expenses would decrease net income significantly.

A company operating under the requirements of the IFRS would report this same scenario differently. It would need to expense the $1 million spent on research only as it was spent, but it could capitalize the $4 million and write it off more slowly as an amortization. Depending on the life span given the value of the development, it could be written off over 10 to 15 years or more, to reduce the impact of development on the bottom line.

TIP

If you're trying to determine which company makes the better investment, you must look carefully at this key difference in research and development. When all global firms use IFRS to file their financial statements, this difference will no longer be a factor when comparing U.S. companies to companies based outside the U.S.

Inventory

Another key difference between IFRS and GAAP standards is the way inventory is valued. All companies that file reports under the IFRS must use FIFO or weighted-average inventory valuation methods (I discuss inventory valuation methods in Chapter 15). Companies filing under GAAP rules can also use LIFO.

FIFO stands for "first in, first out." This type of inventory valuation assumes that the first item in the door is the first item sold. Because prices of goods are usually increasing, the item with the lowest cost likely sells first. LIFO stands for "last in, first out." When this inventory valuation method is used, the last item bought is the first item sold. In this case, the most expensive item is likely sold, and the older, cheaper items remain on the shelf.

REMEMBER

LIFO can increase the cost of goods sold and decrease net income, making it look like a company made less money and, therefore, reducing the company's taxes. FIFO results in a lower cost of goods sold and higher net income.

When comparing companies using two different inventory valuation methods, determining the actual costs of doing business can be difficult. If all companies were required to use either FIFO or the weighted-average inventory valuation methods, comparing apples to apples would be easier. When the two systems are merged in the future, the IFRS requirements on inventory valuation will hopefully be adopted. In fact, the LIFO option may be discontinued under GAAP rules.

Related-party transactions disclosures

In related-party transactions — transactions between, say, a corporation and one of its affiliates — companies filing under IFRS regulations must disclose the compensation of key management personnel in the financial statements. GAAP doesn't require such disclosure.

Hopefully, the IFRS rules will be adopted when the systems converge. Shareholders need to know the compensation of management personnel, and this information should be made visible in the financial statements. U.S. investors will definitely benefit from fuller disclosure in this area.

Discontinued operations

Under the IFRS, if operations are discontinued, the operations and cash flows must be clearly distinguished for financial reporting and must represent a separate line of business or geographical area of operations, including whether a subsidiary is acquired exclusively for the purpose of being sold. That scenario happens often when a company buys another company for a specific purpose and isn't interested in continuing every area of the bought company's operations.

Under GAAP, the lines are more blurred for discontinued operations. A segment, operating segment, reporting unit, subsidiary, or asset group can be shown as separate losses for discontinued operations.

WARNING

Some analysts believe that companies filing under GAAP use this loophole to hide significant problems. I talk more about how discontinued operations are used to clear out deadwood on a balance sheet in Chapter 23. U.S. investors will benefit if clear IFRS lines are drawn for U.S. companies, and fewer problems will be swept under the rug.

Impairment charges

Sometimes an asset loses value. For example, a computer manufacturer may have inventory of older models that can no longer be sold at full price because newer, more advanced models are now available. Their values become *impaired* and must be written down.

Under GAAP, when an impairment charge is recorded in inventory, the company can't reverse the impairment charge if assets subsequently increase in value. Under the IFRS, however, the company is allowed to reverse the impairment charge if assets subsequently go back up in value.

REMEMBER

Both the income statement and the balance sheet can be impacted, as assets whose values have been impaired are adjusted in later years. Investors need to watch the ups and downs of assets, which can impact the profit or loss of a company without a change in operations.

- **Looking at the various kinds of analysts**
- **Exploring the bond-rating agencies**
- **Understanding stock ratings**
- **Getting key information from analysts**

Chapter 21
Checking Out the Analyst–Corporation Connection

Financial analysts regularly get into the act not by talking companies through their mother issues, but by developing rankings that reflect a company's value.

The way analysts view a company can make or break the value of its stock. If a well-respected analyst writes a negative report after seeing a firm's financial reports, its stock price is guaranteed to drop at least temporarily. Red flags analysts raise help you find crucial details to look for when reading a company's financial reports.

This chapter reviews the types of analysts and the ways a company feeds financial information to them.

Typecasting the Analysts

Analysts, many of whom have completed a grueling testing process that takes at least three years to get the designation *Chartered Financial Analyst*, serve different roles for different people:

- **For large investment groups (such as mutual or pension funds):** They determine whether a company's stock price accurately reflects the firm's worth and whether the stock fills a particular niche that the group wants to fill in its overall portfolio-management objectives.
- **For financial institutions:** They analyze a company's debt structure and determine whether the company is bringing in enough money to pay its bills, which helps the institution decide whether to loan the firm money and at what interest rate.
- **For brokerage houses:** They provide individual investors analysis about the companies they're considering for their portfolio. Their reports are available to anyone who uses the brokerage house for stock transactions. Unless you have a very large portfolio and can pay an analyst, the analyst doesn't work specifically for you, so you need to read and analyze financial reports yourself.
- **For bond-rating firms:** They review a company's debt structure, financial health, and bill-paying ability to rate the bonds the company issues.

  TIP

  Reports from bond-rating companies are especially helpful because they focus on any debt problems the company may be facing. You can then check out the financial reports yourself and find the red flags more easily.

You may not realize that several types of analysts master various domains of financial analysis. Regardless of what type of analyst you're dealing with, the one fact you can be sure of as an individual investor is that analysts don't work for you unless you're the one paying them for developing the information. They primarily gear their reports to the needs of the people who do pay them.

This section looks at the various types of analysts and who they primarily serve.

Buy-side analysts

Buy-side analysts work primarily for large institutions and investment firms that manage mutual funds, pension funds, or other types of multimillion-dollar private accounts. Buy-side analysts are responsible for analyzing stocks that portfolio managers are considering for possible purchase and placement in various portfolios their firms manage. In other words, buy-side analysts' bosses are major institutional buyers of stock. Some buy-side analysts work directly for mutual funds or pension funds; others work for independent analyst firms hired by the mutual funds or pension funds.

Buy-side analysts write reports that help portfolio managers determine whether a stock fits the firm's portfolio-management strategy. But the stock may not fit your portfolio's strategy, so you can't necessarily follow their recommendations. Managers of mutual funds that focus on growth stocks look for stocks that fill that niche. Managers of mutual funds that focus on foreign stocks look for stocks that fit that objective. Sometimes a stock that most analysts pan gets a positive report inside a buy-side analytical shop. For example, if portfolio managers are looking for candidates for a value portfolio made up of stocks currently beaten down by the market but with good potential to rebound, buy-side analysts may recommend buying a stock that has just lost half its value.

TIP

You rarely see this type of analyst's research available on the public market, but much of the information does trickle out in the financial press through statements made by mutual fund managers. Morningstar, which is one of the leading groups that rate mutual funds for individual investors, is a good place to get ideas for possible additions to your stock portfolio. On its website (`www.morningstar.com`), you can frequently find stories about which stocks mutual fund managers are buying and why they're buying them. Of course, you can't just buy stock based on these stories. You need to read the financial reports and do your own analysis of these reports.

Sell-side analysts

As an individual investor, you most likely see reports from *sell-side analysts*. These analysts work for brokerage houses or other financial institutions that sell stocks to individual investors. You get reports written by these analysts when you ask your broker for research on a particular stock.

You can't take everything you get from sell-side analysts as gospel. Their primary purpose is to help a company's salespeople make sales. As long as your interests match the interests of the broker and brokerage house, the sell-side analytical reports can be helpful. But as scandals after the Internet and technology stock crash of 2000 showed (see the sidebar "Analyzing the analysts"), conflicts of interest can exist between a brokerage house's need to make money by selling stock and an individual investor's need to make money by owning stock that goes up in value.

Many investors lost 50 percent or more of the money they invested in stock during the 1990s and early 2000s before the stock market crashed. Many brokerage houses were more concerned with making money by selling stocks than they were with helping investors put together stock portfolios that met their goals and took into consideration their tolerance for risk. And investors weren't well served by the analysts, who should have been accurately reporting the risks of investing in many of the companies whose financial reports they analyzed for investors.

WARNING

You must take the responsibility yourself to read and analyze reports. You can't depend on an analyst unless you pay that analyst out of your own pocket to do the analysis.

REAL WORLD EXAMPLE

ANALYZING THE ANALYSTS

During the scandal-ridden technology crash of 2000, sell-side analysts working for brokerage houses were caught between the needs of their firms' investment banking division to help sell new offerings and the needs of their firms' individual investors, who were clients of the salespeople. The investment banking side won, and individual investors got hosed.

By writing glowing reports about the stocks or bonds involved in investment banking deals, sell-side analysts helped pull in new investment banking clients and kept existing clients happy. While the brokerage houses made millions on investment banking deals, individual investors lost big chunks of their portfolios buying analyst-recommended stocks, many of which dropped dramatically in value after the market crash of 2000, leaving investors with ruined portfolios filled with worthless stocks. Overall, investors lost billions.

Then–New York State Attorney General Eliot Spitzer helped expose this entire mess by unearthing e-mails from superstar analysts like Henry Blodget of Merrill Lynch, who wrote positive reports about stocks being sold by his investment banking divisions while privately calling these stocks "dogs," "junk," and "toast." Spitzer charged that Blodget's recommendations helped bring in $115 million in investment banking fees for Merrill Lynch. Blodget got rich, too — he took home about $12 million in compensation, according to Spitzer's findings.

Merrill Lynch wasn't the only company that Spitzer's investigation exposed. Other firms caught in Spitzer's net included Morgan Stanley Dean Witter & Co. and Credit Suisse First Boston. In fact, most brokerage houses that have an investment banking division got caught up in the scandal.

Brokerage companies used to avoid scandals and conflicts of interest by protecting themselves with what's called a *Chinese Wall*. Analysts kept their work separate from the investment banking division (which sells new public offerings of stocks or bonds and arranges mergers and acquisitions), and their compensation wasn't dependent on what business they helped to bring in. At some point in the past 20 years, this wall broke down, and sell-side analysts became partners with the investment banking side to help the firm make money. If a company won new investment banking business, it rewarded analysts with fees or commissions.

TECHNICAL STUFF

Sell-side analysts' Chinese Wall was reconstructed to a certain extent after the tech stock scandals (see the sidebar "Analyzing the analysts"). The Securities and Exchange Commission (SEC) finally got involved in April 2002 and ended up endorsing rulemaking changes developed by the New York Stock Exchange and the National Association of Securities Dealers. These new rules do the following:

- Prohibit investment banking divisions from supervising analysts or approving their research reports.
- Ban the practice of tying analysts' compensation to specific investment banking transactions.
- Prohibit analysts from offering favorable research to bring in investment banking business for a firm.
- Disclose conflicts of interest in research reports and public appearances. Brokerage houses must include information about business relationships with, or ownership interests in, any company that's the subject of an analyst's report.
- Restrict personal trading by analysts in securities of companies they analyze or report on.
- Dictate that a firm disclose data about its historical ratings and a price chart that compares its ratings with closing prices.

As an investor, you can quickly determine whether a conflict exists between your interests and the financial interests of a brokerage house or analyst when you see the new disclosures required. You can also look at the brokerage house's historical ratings for a company's stock and see how successful it has been in accurately reporting the stock's value in the past.

WARNING

When you read a sell-side analyst's report and see that the brokerage firm gets fees for investment banking services from the company that's the subject of the report, realize that the brokerage firm makes more money from its investment banking business than it does from you. Take what you find useful from the report, but be sure to do your own additional research.

Independent analysts

You may wonder whether you can depend on any analysts out there. Well, the answer is yes and no. Certainly, some independent analyst groups — ones that *aren't* paid by a brokerage house or other financial institution but that provide reports for a fee paid by people who want them — report on companies as well. The problem is that independent analyst groups work for people who can afford to pay them, meaning that you must have a portfolio of at least $1 million or be able to pay about $25,000 per year. Few individual investors meet these criteria.

REMEMBER

Many independent analysts do sell the reports through financial websites for a per-report fee to individuals who are researching a specific company. Your rule of thumb about independent analysts' reports must be to take what information you find useful but be sure to do additional research on your own. The report you buy from the independent analyst on a particular company was developed for one of the analyst's clients, not specifically for you.

TIP

After reading about analysts, you may think you don't have a chance to get good information from them. Your best place to find research that isn't tainted by the investment banking business of your brokerage firm is the websites of major investment research firms like Morningstar (`www.morningstar.com`) and Standard & Poor's (`www.standardandpoors.com`). You have to pay fees to access their confidential services, but they're much more reasonable than the cost of using an independent analyst — they can be as low as $100 per year, depending on what information you need.

Bond analysts

Bond analysts are most concerned with a company's liquidity and the company's ability to make its interest payments, repay its debt principal, and pay its bills. They used to have a reputation of doing things with a more cautious eye, but their close relationship to the investment banking side of the house was exposed during the mortgage crisis beginning in 2007. Many of the mortgage debt instruments they rated proved to be rated incorrectly, leading to huge losses for banks, mutual funds, and pension funds.

Before this fiasco, bond analysts were thought to evaluate financial reports, management quality, the competitive environment, and overall economic conditions more carefully. They tended to err on the side of caution, but now this reputation has been shattered. When it comes to rating corporate bonds, it's worth looking at their view, but always do your own research.

TIP

When you're looking to buy stock, pay attention to the warnings of bond analysts. You certainly don't want to invest in a company that can't meet its financial obligations and may go bankrupt. Use bond analysts' red flags to help you find the critical information when you read and analyze financial reports yourself.

Regarding Bond-Rating Agencies

Bond ratings have a great impact on a company's operations and the cost of funding its operations. The quality rating of a company's bonds determines how much interest the firm has to offer to pay in order to sell the bonds on the public bond market. Bonds that are rated with a higher-quality rating are considered less risky, so the interest rates that must be paid to attract individuals or companies to buy those bonds can be lower. Companies that issue bonds with the lowest ratings, which are also known as *junk bonds*, pay much higher interest rates to attract individuals or companies to buy those bonds.

REMEMBER

Bonds are a type of debt for a company. The individual or company that buys a bond is loaning money to the company that it expects to get back. The firm must pay interest on the money that it's borrowing from these bondholders.

You should be familiar with the three key rating agencies, where you can find out what bond analysts think:

- **Standard & Poor's:** Although S&P is well-known for the S&P 500, which is a collection of 500 stocks that form the basis for a *stock market index* (a portfolio of stocks for which a change in price is carefully watched), the company is also one of the primary bond raters. You can find more information at `www.standardandpoors.com`.
- **Moody's Investor Service:** Moody's specializes in credit ratings, research, and risk analysis, tracking trillions of dollars in debt issued in the U.S. and international markets. In addition to its credit-rating services, Moody's publishes investor-oriented credit research, which you can access at `www.moodys.com`.
- **Fitch Ratings:** The youngest of the three major bond-rating services is Fitch Ratings (`www.fitchratings.com`). John Knowles Fitch founded Fitch Publishing Company in 1913, and the business started as a publisher of financial statistics. In 1924, Fitch introduced the credit-rating scales that are very familiar today: AAA to D. Fitch is best known for its research in the area of complex credit deals and is thought to provide more rigorous surveillance than other rating agencies on such deals.

BUILDING BOND RATING'S BIG GUNS

Standard and Poor's is one of the premier bond-rating firms. The company's founder, Henry Varnum Poor, built his financial information company on the "investor's right to know." His first attempt at providing this type of financial information can be found in his 1860 book, *History of Railroads and Canals of the United States,* where he included financial information about the railroad industry. Today Standard & Poor's is a leader in independent credit ratings, risk evaluation, and investment research.

John Moody started his rating service in 1909 and was the first to rate public market securities. He adopted a letter-rating system from the mercantile exchange and credit-rating system that had been used since the late 1800s. By 1924, Moody's ratings covered nearly 100 percent of the U.S. bond market. To this day, Moody's prides itself on ratings based on public information and is written by independent analysts who don't answer to the requests of bond issuers.

Each bond-rating company has its own alphabetical coding for rating bonds and other types of credit issues, such as commercial paper (which are shorter-term debt issues than bonds).

Table 21-1 shows how the companies' bond ratings compare.

TABLE 21-1 **Bond Ratings**

Bond Quality	Moody's	Standard & Poor's	Fitch
Best quality	Aaa	AAA	AAA
High quality	Aa	AA	AA
Upper medium grade	A	A	A
Medium grade	Baa	BBB	BBB
Speculative	Ba	BB	BB
Highly speculative	B	B	B
High default risk	Caa or Ca	CCC or CC	CCC, CC, or C
In default	C	D	DDD, DD, or D

Any company bonds rated in the "speculative" category or lower are considered to be junk bonds. Companies in the "best quality" category have the lowest interest rates, and interest rates go up as companies' ratings drop. A key job of any firm's executive team is to feed bond analysts critical financial data to keep the firm's ratings high. Financial reports are one major component of that information.

TIP

Standard & Poor's (S&P) makes its bond ratings publicly available with links on its website home page. You can search for information about any company's debt ratings.

TIP

Whenever a change occurs in the ratings, the rating services issue a press release with an extensive explanation about why the rating has changed. These press releases can be an excellent source of information if you're looking for opinions on the numbers you see in the financial reports. You can find these press releases on the bond-rating companies' websites, as well as in news links on financial websites.

Regulations for bond-rating agencies changed after passage of the Dodd Frank Wall Street Reform and Consumer Protection Act of 2010. The change became necessary after the failure of bond-rating agencies to properly rate mortgage securities.

Many people see the AAA ratings on bonds that later proved to be junk as a major contributing factor to the crash of 2008 and the collapse of Lehman Brothers. The 2010 legislation imposes new liability exposure on the credit rating agencies. They must improve their internal control requirements. They must also put barriers in place to address conflicts of interest issues. The SEC also now has more oversight responsibility regarding bond-rating companies.

Delving into Stock Rating

Stock ratings for general public consumption are primarily done by sell-side analysts, who seem to err on the side of optimism. You rarely find a stock with a *sell rating* (a recommendation to sell the stock). In fact, when analysts testified in Congress after the analyst scandals in the early 2000s (see the sidebar "Analyzing the analysts," earlier in the chapter), one analyst was heard saying that everybody on Wall Street knows that a *hold rating* (which is intended to mean you should hold the stock but probably not buy more) really means to sell. Some firms use an *accumulate rating*, which you may think means to hold on to the stock or maybe even add more shares, but really means to sell in behind-the-scenes circles on Wall Street.

WARNING

Just like with bond ratings, each firm has its own vocabulary when rating stocks. A *strong buy* from one firm may be called a *buy* in another firm and may be on the *recommended* list in a third firm. You can never know which company is right, but after following a firm's stock ratings for a while, you can understand how its systems work and how accurate it is compared with what actually happens to the price on the stock market.

Because various companies' rankings may differ dramatically, you need to check out ratings from several different firms and research what each firm means by its ratings. A stock that's rated as a "market outperformer" may sound pretty good, but in reality, it's probably not a good investment, which may become clear when you compare rankings of other firms and find that they consider the stock a "neutral" or "hold" stock.

REMEMBER

I don't put much faith in the stock analyst rating system, and you shouldn't, either. As you start doing independent research on a company after reading its financial reports, take everything you read with a grain of salt. Collect all the information you can and then do your own analysis. In Part 3 of this book, I show you how to analyze the numbers in financial reports.

Taking a Look at How Companies Talk to Analysts

Companies not only send out financial reports to analysts, but also talk with analysts regularly about the reports. Sometimes you can get access to what's said by listening in to analyst calls or reading press releases. You can also get information from road shows, which I briefly describe later in this chapter, but you usually don't have access to them unless you're a major investor.

Analyst calls

Each time a company releases a new financial report, it usually schedules a call with analysts to discuss the results. Usually, these calls include the chief executive officer (CEO), president (if not the same as the CEO), and chief financial officer (CFO), as well as other top managers.

Individual investors can listen in on many of these calls between companies and analysts. The calls typically start with a statement from one or more of the company representatives and then are opened up to listener questions. However, as an individual investor, you may not be able to ask any questions. In most cases, only the analysts, and sometimes the financial press, are allowed to ask questions. But even if you can't ask questions, you can learn a lot just by listening.

The biggest advantage of listening to these calls is that analysts ask questions of the executives that help you focus on the areas of concern in the financial reports. Turn to Chapter 22 to find out more about analyst calls.

TIP

You can find out about upcoming calls or listen to calls already completed at two websites: 24/7 Wallstreet (`http://247wallst.com/companies/analyst-calls/`) and Investor Calendar (`www.investorcalendar.com/IC/index.asp`).

In the past, calls between analysts and companies were a way for analysts to get insider information about a firm before the news was broadcast to individual investors. The SEC stopped that practice in 2000 with a new rule called *Fair Disclosure (Regulation FD)*. This rule makes it mandatory for companies to inform everyone at the same time about major financial announcements. Sometimes analysts find out information in a conversation with officers or employees of a corporation during a private interview. If analysts receive information that others aren't aware of, the company must release a press release about the information within 24 hours of any company outsider getting the information. Regulation FD has certainly leveled the playing field for individual investors.

Press releases

Companies often feed information to analysts through press releases. Luckily, individual investors can easily access these press releases on financial websites. But remember that press releases are always going to contain exactly what the company wants you to know. You need to read between the lines and ask questions of the company's investor relations department if something concerns you.

Press reports, which are written after a press release is issued, are probably a more important source of information. Companies put out a lot of press releases, and not every one makes it into the newspaper as a story. In fact, most press releases end up in the garbage because a financial reporter determines the information isn't worth a story.

TIP

You can easily track press releases online. One of my favorite spots for following not only a company's press releases, but also any stories mentioning the company, is Yahoo! Finance (finance.yahoo.com). You can find out about any recent press coverage for a company by searching the website using the company's stock ticker, which is a multiletter abbreviation for the company's stock. Links to recent press coverage and press releases appear in a section called "Headlines." If you want to go further back in history, most companies post at least three years' worth of press releases in the press section of their websites.

Mobile apps

Some companies now provide mobile applications to communicate with their investors. It's a relatively new phenomenon at the time of this writing, but a leader in developing these is theIRAPP (`www.theirapp.com/`). You can find out which companies offer these apps at theIRAPP website. I checked the investor sections of companies offering a mobile app, and many had not yet listed the app as available; you may have to do some digging to find these apps.

Road shows

Companies use road shows (which I discuss in greater detail in Chapter 3) to introduce new securities issues, such as initial stock or bond offerings. *Road shows* are presentations by the company and its investment bankers to the analyst community and other major investors, in the hope of building interest in the new public offering. As an individual investor, you're not likely to be able to attend these shows; invitations are usually reserved only for people who can put up significant funding.

IN THIS CHAPTER

» Attending annual shareholder meetings

» Looking at the responsibilities of the board of directors

» Keeping abreast of corporate special events

» Listening perceptively to analyst calls

» Getting information from company websites

» Investing through company incentive programs

Chapter 22

How Companies Communicate with Shareholders

Happy shareholders don't necessarily make for a happy company, but they're a good start. Although a company collects most of the money generated from stock transactions when the stock is first sold to the public during an initial or secondary public offering, shareholders still hold a bit of power over management. Angry shareholders showed what their wrath could do when their lack of support for Disney CEO Michael Eisner helped oust him from the chairmanship of the board in 2004. In August 2013, at the time of this writing, another very public fight to oust the chairman of the board and interim CEO of J.C. Penny Company was being led by a hedge fund manager, among others.

Sending out quarterly and annual reports aren't the only strategies companies use to keep their shareholders informed and happy. Other activities include analyst calls, special meetings, website services, e-mails, stock-investment plans, and individual investor contact. In this chapter, I review the steps companies take to inform their investors of operations and to respond to any investor concerns.

Making the Most of Meetings

At the very least, a company must hold an annual meeting for its shareholders. These events are often gala affairs that are more like a carefully orchestrated pep rally than a place where you can get solid information. The company's top officers make presentations highlighting what they want you to know and put on a show that closely resembles what you find in the glossy portion of an annual report.

TIP

The big advantage of being at the company's annual meeting is that you can ask questions, which you can't do if you just read the financial reports at home. Prepare yourself before the meeting by reading the recent financial reports, as well as annual reports from the past couple years, so that you're fully armed with details about what has gone on in the past. Make a list of questions that you want answered by the company's executives so that you're ready to ask them when the opportunity arises. Note that if shareholders are unhappy with the corporation's board or its executives, annual meetings can turn into major shouting matches when the floor is opened to questions and comments.

If you're a shareholder, the company notifies you about the date and location of the meeting. In addition to asking questions, shareholders vote on any open issues. Almost every annual meeting includes the election of at least some members of the board of directors. Most companies stagger the election of board members over a number of years so that the entire board doesn't change in one year. Other issues that involve major changes to the way the company does business are also voted on, such as a change in executive compensation.

Sometimes shareholders add their own issues to the agenda. For example, environmentalists who own stock in a company may seek a shareholder vote on how the company gets rid of its waste (to ensure that controls to protect the environment are in place) or how it develops land it owns near a wildlife preserve (to be sure wildlife is protected during and after construction).

Sometimes a corporation calls a special meeting if the shareholders must vote on a significant issue before the next annual meeting. A possible merger is one of the most common events to spur such a special meeting.

REMEMBER

Innovative companies see annual meetings as a way to communicate effectively with their investor base. The problem for many firms is that most shareholders don't show up. But the Internet can help reach them — some companies place all their meeting materials on a website, and companies may even webcast the meeting itself and archive it for shareholders to watch at their leisure.

Checking Out How the Board Runs the Company

Corporate governance is the way a board of directors conducts its own business and oversees a corporation's operations. Ultimately, the board of directors is liable for every decision the company makes, but in reality, only major shifts in the way the company operates make it to the board for decision. For example, if executives recommend that the company take on a new product line that involves a large investment of cash, they consult the board for this decision. However, most day-to-day decisions are left to the company's executives and managers.

Watching the directors

The shareholder landscape changed dramatically after the corporate scandals of the 2000s exposed severe corporate governance problems, beginning with the collapse of Enron. Today shareholder groups — many led by institutional investors such as pension plans and mutual funds that own large blocks of shares in various companies — closely watch the following four major issues in the companies in which they own shares of stock.

Composition of the board of directors

Shareholder groups monitor the makeup of the board, how board members are chosen, and how many members serving on the board are truly independent — meaning that they're not directly involved in the day-to-day operations of the company. Outsiders prefer that a majority of the board members be independent because independent board members can be more objective (they aren't protecting their own jobs and their own income).

Compensation packages for board members and CEOs

These details are on public record now. In addition, shareholders must approve of or be notified of any major benefits or compensation offered to the company's executives, such as *stock option plans* (offers to buy company stock at prices below market value). Shareholders complain bitterly if they believe executives are receiving excessive compensation.

Takeover defenses and protections

In some cases, board members place defenses against the possibility of a company takeover. For example, Comcast unsuccessfully attempted a hostile takeover of Disney during the battle between shareholders, led by Roy Disney, who was attempting to oust Michael Eisner. Sometimes these defenses help protect shareholders from a corporate raider who wants to buy the company and sell off the pieces, which can leave shareholders with stock that's worth very little.

Other times these defenses prevent a takeover by some other company that may benefit the shareholders but not the current management team and board of directors (especially if the leadership ranks would change under the new owners and they could lose their jobs). Shareholder groups watch whatever takeover defenses or protections the board puts into place to be sure their best interests are protected, not just the best interests of the directors and the management team.

Audits

The primary responsibility of the board of directors is to review the audits of the company's books to be certain that both the internal accounting team and the external auditors are accurately handling them. Today the Securities and Exchange Commission (SEC) requires that independent board members make up the audit committees.

Before the Enron scandal, many audit committees weren't as independently run, which allowed company insiders to control not only how money was spent, but also how it was recorded in the company's books and how the financial results were reported to outsiders. This insidious practice allowed top executives to more easily hide any misdeeds or misuse of funds.

CEOs GET BETTER RAISES

Most working Americans would be delighted if they received pay raises anywhere near the ones that CEOs got in 2012. According to Executive Paywatch, the average total compensation for a Fortune 500 CEO was $12.3 million. That's up from $10.8 million in 2006. The average pay for workers is just $34,645. You can check out how much the CEOs of companies you're interested in tracking are paid at the Executive Pay Watch database, run by the AFL-CIO online (`www.aflcio.org/Corporate-Watch/CEO-Pay-and-You/Trends-in-CEO-Pay`).

Speaking out at meetings

Shareholders can voice their opinions during annual meetings and during any special corporate meetings the board of directors calls to address a specific issue. At these meetings, shareholders cast weighted votes, called *proxy votes*, based on the number of shares they hold. If board members aren't responsive to shareholder concerns on any of the issues in the preceding list, they may find themselves defending a major challenge at the annual meeting.

Before the Enron scandal, a shareholder rarely brought forth an issue for the rest of the shareholders to vote on; most often, the corporation's board of directors controlled what the shareholders voted on. If a shareholder issue even made it to the point of being voted on by the other shareholders, it rarely had a chance of passing. Today shareholders are more successful at getting issues on the agenda to be voted on at an annual meeting; sometimes they win the proxy vote, and sometimes they lose.

A proxy fight can cost a corporation millions of dollars, no matter who wins, as illustrated by Hewlett-Packard's pricey battle in 2001 and 2002 (see the sidebar "Hewlett-Packard's costly clash").

HEWLETT-PACKARD'S COSTLY CLASH

REAL WORLD EXAMPLE

Walter Hewlett, son of one of the cofounders of Hewlett-Packard, led one of the most costly battles against a CEO and a board of directors when he tried to stop a merger with Compaq. Hewlett lost the fight when the final vote of the shareholders ended in approving the merger.

Hewlett reported that he spent $32 million on his attempt to stop the merger. Financial analysts speculate that Hewlett-Packard's board of directors, led by CEO Carly Fiorina, spent at least twice that much on advertising in the major media markets where most of Hewlett-Packard's shareholders live, plus on other actions, to defend its merger decision.

In addition to the costly advertising, Hewlett-Packard's board racked up about $70 million in expenses to defend its merger decision, including an estimated $3 million to individually call its shareholders and another $25 million in mailings to its shareholders. Hewlett-Packard also paid $33.5 million to investment banker Goldman Sachs, which handled the merger deal. Analysts guesstimate that Hewlett-Packard's total cost for this fiasco was $100 million to $125 million, and a good portion of that money was necessary only because of the shareholder battle.

Moving away from duking it out

Since the success of the shareholder fight to oust Michel Eisner from the chairmanship of Disney's board of directors in 2004, corporations have been finding ways to negotiate with unhappy shareholders to avoid fighting it out in a proxy vote.

To avoid a costly proxy fight, boards of directors negotiate with unhappy shareholders by meeting with them quietly behind closed doors and discussing the issues on which they disagree, with the hope that they can find a solution that both sides can accept. If the shareholders and the board fail to find common ground, a proxy fight is likely. Knowing that a proxy fight can cost millions, more corporations are wising up to the fact that they need to listen to their shareholders.

One of the major leaders of proxy fights is large institutional shareholders, along with the help of other state retirement systems and some mutual funds. These large institutional investors hold large blocks of stock in their pension or mutual fund portfolios, so they have a lot to lose if a company doesn't do what they believe it should do.

Many times, the issues include how the board of directors operates and how many independent directors serve on the board and its various committees, particularly the audit committee. New rules about independent directors were adopted after the Enron scandal. Under revised SEC Rule 10A-3, a public company must appoint independent directors to the audit committee, and the committee must establish procedures for complaints regarding accounting, internal accounting controls, or auditing matters, including procedures for employees to confidentially and anonymously submit concerns regarding questionable accounting or auditing issues.

Sorting through Reports

Mailing out reports on an annual and quarterly basis is the primary way a corporation informs its shareholders about its performance. Many companies allow shareholders to opt for electronic reporting. Instead of sending a paper report, they notify their shareholders that the report is available online. Not only does this save money for the company, but it also enables shareholders to access the report more quickly. Some companies are experimenting with mobile apps, but as of this writing, it was not yet prevalent.

The corporation usually mails the annual report before the annual meeting, along with information on the proxy votes that will take place at the meeting. Proxy information is a critical part of the annual report package because voting by proxy is the primary way shareholders get to voice their position on board decisions. Many companies also provide for online voting at their website.

The mailing also includes information about the board's position on any issues that will be presented at the annual meeting. If the board brings an issue to the shareholders for a vote, the board explains the issue and its position. If a group other than the board brings the issue to the shareholders, the board states the issue and discusses why it's in favor of or opposed to the issue. In most cases, the board opposes issues brought by outside sources.

An outside group raising or opposing an issue is also likely to mail its position to the shareholders. Walter Hewlett spent about $15 million mailing information to Hewlett-Packard shareholders in an attempt to stop the merger with Compaq, which I discuss in the earlier sidebar "Hewlett-Packard's costly clash."

Catching Up on Corporate Actions

Corporations must report special events to their shareholders as soon as the event can *materially impact* the company's results (affect the profits or losses of the company). The most common special events include the following:

- **Acquisitions:** Before a company can finalize plans to acquire another company, it must report those plans to its shareholders.
- **Class-action lawsuits:** If a company is the defendant in a class-action lawsuit that can have a material impact on its results in the future, the company must report the lawsuit and discuss its potential impact with shareholders.
- **Mergers:** If two firms plan on merging, the firms' management must inform shareholders and also ask them to vote on the merger. If shareholders in either company vote against the merger, the deal is likely cancelled. Sometimes companies may revise the deal and attempt a second shareholder vote.
- **Dividends:** Whenever the board decides to pay dividends, it has to report that information to the shareholders. Of course, dividends are one of the few items boards enjoy reporting, so they usually make a very public announcement to shareholders about the dividend payments.

- **SEC investigation:** If a company discovers that the SEC is investigating it, the company must report this knowledge to its shareholders in a timely manner.
- **Stock splits:** A *stock split* occurs when the board decides to make one share of stock worth more than one share. For example, a stock split may be two shares for one, which means that each shareholder gets two shares of stock for each share that he holds. Most times, a company announces a stock split when it believes the price of its stock has gotten too high for the market. So a stock that sells for $100 before a two-for-one stock split sells for $50 a share after the split.

REMEMBER

In short, a company must give its shareholders the lowdown on anything that materially impacts the business's value. In fact, companies must report to the public and to financial analysts within 24 hours of telling any company outsider about a major event, such as the ones I list in this section, that may impact a company's net income materially.

TECHNICAL STUFF

INTRODUCING FAIR DISCLOSURE

Today the SEC requires that a company release all information that can significantly impact its financial position to shareholders and analysts at the same time or within a reasonable period (usually 24 hours) after the first company outsider gets the information. This practice began in 2000 after the adoption of the Fair Disclosure Rule (Regulation FD), which mandates open disclosure to everyone as soon as possible after one person outside the company gets the information. The information can be something as simple as the expected net income for the quarter or something as dramatic as the decision to buy another company.

Before the SEC rule calling for fair disclosure, companies often told financial analysts several days before the general public about upcoming key events or other financial data. When this occurred, the analysts could tell key investors who depended on their analysis (and, by the way, paid them big bucks for their services) to buy or sell stocks before the general public even knew anything about what was happening. Individual investors could lose a major part of their stake in the company before they even knew what was driving down the stock price. Regulation FD killed that practice and leveled the playing field for individual investors. Today individual investors must get information at the same time as analysts and portfolio managers for large institutions (such as pension and mutual funds).

Culling Information from Analyst Calls

Today investors get information not only by reading press releases or newspapers, but also by attending company calls for analysts, which used to be open only to financial analysts and institutional investors. Companies usually sponsor these calls when they release their annual or quarterly earnings reports. But special events — such as a change in company leadership or the purchase of another business — can also prompt companies to set up analyst calls. By listening in on these calls, you usually get more details about whatever issues are being discussed.

The company CEO, president, and chief financial officer (CFO) typically participate in these calls. They usually start the call by discussing the recently released financial reports or by explaining the impact that the special event has on the company; then they usually open the call to questions.

The question-and-answer part of the call is often the most revealing, as you can judge how confident senior managers are about the financial information they're reporting. Questions from the audience usually elicit information that press releases or the annual or quarterly reports haven't revealed. Most times, analysts and institutional investors ask the questions; in many situations, individual investors don't have an opportunity to ask questions at all, but you can still learn a lot by listening to these conversations. And don't hesitate to write or call the company's investor relations department to get an answer to a specific question you may have about the financial report or the special event discussed during an analyst call.

TIP

The language participants use in an analyst call differs from the language you use every day. Familiarize yourself with the most commonly used terms before listening to your first call. I list most of the key terms and abbreviations used during analyst calls in Part 3 of this book, where I discuss analyzing the numbers. Get comfortable with terms like *earnings per share (EPS), EPS growth, net income, cash,* and *cash equivalents.* Check out the sidebar "Decoding analyst-call-speak" for more on analyst call lingo.

TIP

If you hear a term you don't understand, write it down and research it after the call. Then the next time you listen in on one of these calls, you'll have a better understanding of what's being discussed.

DECODING ANALYST-CALL-SPEAK

In addition to the financial terms I use throughout this book, you're likely to hear a few colorful descriptions when listening in on an analyst call, such as the following:

- **Hockey stick:** Management may say that company revenue came in like a *hockey stick,* meaning that most of the revenue occurred in the final days of the quarter. In this situation, the revenue charts actually look like a hockey stick because they're flat most of the month and then shoot up in the last few days. Listen for explanations about why sales jump up at the end of a month or quarter. It may be normal for the type of business or it may be related to some outside factor, such as a storm that closed stores for part of the month.
- **Lumpy:** Senior management refers to uneven sales in a given quarter as being *lumpy.* During some weeks, the order rates were low, and during other weeks, the order rates were high; these results make the revenue charts look lumpy. If you hear this term, listen for explanations about why sales were lumpy and whether this result is normal for the company.
- **Run-rate:** Senior management uses the term *run-rate* when talking about how to project a company's current performance over a period of time. For example, if the current quarter's revenue shows a $1 million monthly run-rate, you can expect the annual revenue to total $12 million. This type of projection may work for firms with steady earnings, but it doesn't work for businesses that have primarily seasonal products. For example, if a retail company reports a run-rate for the fourth quarter that includes holiday sales of $1 million per month, you can't expect that performance to carry over for the entire year. So you must be certain that you understand a company's revenue picture before counting on run-rate numbers.

Listening between the lines

Pay attention to how the executives handle the call and to the words they use. When management is pleased with the results, you usually hear very upbeat terms, and they talk about how positive things look for the company's future. When management is disappointed with the numbers, they're more apologetic, and the mood of the call is more low key. Instead of talking about a rosy future, they'll probably explain ways they can improve the disappointing results.

TIP

You most likely need to listen to more than one call hosted by a particular company before you start picking up the nuances and moods of the executives. Try attending as many of these calls as you can or listening to a recording of a call after it occurs. Many companies actually post recordings of their analyst calls on their websites, just like they post press releases.

Take the time to read the financial reports before the call so you're at least familiar with the key points that management discusses during the call. After you listen to a few calls for the same company, you'll find that the information management discusses is much clearer.

Earnings expectations

All calls about a company's financial results include information about whether the firm has met its own earnings projections or the projections of financial analysts. If a company misses its own earnings projections, the mood of the call will be downbeat, and the stock price is likely to drop dramatically after the call.

TIP

Of course, you don't have to sell the shares you own if you happen to be a shareholder. If you're listening to the call because you're thinking about buying the stock, you may want to do so after the bad news drives down the stock price. The key for you as a shareholder or potential shareholder is to analyze what's being said and whether you think the company has a good chance of turning around the bad news. Good news, on the other hand, can drive the stock price higher. Be careful not to jump on the bandwagon right after major good news is announced. Usually, the stock price falls back down to a more realistic price after the initial rush to buy is completed.

Revenue growth

Listen for information about the company's revenue growth and whether it has kept pace with its earnings growth. Growth in revenue is the key to continued earnings growth in the future. During an economic slowdown, watching revenue growth becomes very important because a company can play with revenue numbers to make them look better. In fact, some companies practice what's called *window dressing* (using accounting tricks to make a company's financial statements look better) to make sure their earnings meet expectations. Earnings growth is easier to manipulate than revenue, so earnings usually become part of that window dressing. I talk more in Chapter 23 about how a company can manipulate its results.

WARNING

If you hear numerous questions from the analysts about revenue growth figures, it may be a sign that they suspect a problem with the numbers or are disappointed with the results. When you repeatedly hear analysts' questions about revenue or any other issues, take a closer look at these numbers yourself. Do further analysis and research before you decide to buy or sell the company's stock.

Analysts' moods

Listen carefully to the analysts' tone as they ask their questions. Take time to assess their moods. Do they seem downbeat? Are they asking very probing questions, or are they upbeat and congratulating the executives on their performance?

When analysts are disappointed with a company's results, they dig for more information and ask for more details about the areas where they see a problem. The call's discussion focuses on past results and how management can improve future results. When analysts are happy with the results, they encourage further discussion about future results and plans.

You may find it difficult to judge the mood of the analysts or company executives when you listen to your first call, but as you listen to more calls for the same company, you'll be able to judge more easily how the mood differs from that of previous calls.

The right facts

You can judge whether the executives are confident in their reporting by how quickly they answer the questions. When executives are comfortable and confident in the numbers, they answer questions quickly, without rustling through papers. If they're cautious with their answers and are constantly taking time to look through their papers, you can be sure they're not comfortable with the report and must carefully check themselves before answering the questions.

WARNING

If company executives seem unsure or respond slowly, take this as a red flag that you need to do a lot more homework before making any decisions about buying or selling that company's stock.

An eye to the future

Listen to the vision that the company's executives portray for the future. Does the vision they present inspire you, or are they unclear about their vision for the company's future and how they plan to get there? If you find the executives uninspiring, they may not be doing a good job of inspiring their employees, either. If you see a downward trend in the company, this may be one of the reasons for that trend. When executives lack inspiration for the company's future, you have good reason to stay away from investing in that firm.

Employee satisfaction

Keeping employees happy is important for the future of any company. During the call, you can judge whether employees are satisfied by listening for information about the success or failure the company's having attracting new employees or retaining existing ones. If the business reports a problem with either of these two areas, trouble may be on the horizon. High employee turnover is bad for the growth of any company, and a firm that has trouble finding and recruiting qualified employees may also face a difficult future.

WARNING

Don't ever plan to buy or sell stock based only on what you hear during analyst calls. Use the calls as one more way to gather information about a stock that you're thinking of buying or for tracking stocks that you already own.

Knowing when to expect analyst calls

To find out when a company plans to host an analyst call, check out the investor relations section of its website. Some companies just post a recording of the call on their website. A few companies don't even mention the calls; in this case, you can call the investor relations department and ask whether you can attend their analyst calls. Some firms do ban investors from analyst calls.

TIP

Some companies offer investors a service that alerts them to upcoming events. If the companies you plan to follow don't offer these services, your best way of tracking upcoming analyst calls or listening to previous calls is through one of two websites: Yahoo Finance (`http://biz.yahoo.com/cc/`) and Earningscast (`www.earningscast.com/`).

Staying Up-to-Date Using Company Websites

The Internet provides an excellent way for companies to stay in touch with their investors. Companies can include an unlimited number of pages on websites that investors can access whenever it's convenient for them. Because investors can print multiple copies of the information provided online for free, businesses can save the expense of providing thousands of pages of information to their investors.

TIP

In addition to basic information — such as company headquarters, mailing address, phone numbers, and key executives — many companies post their firm's history, market share, vision and mission statements, credit ratings, and stock dividend history. Many companies also post all the information from their annual meetings, financial reports, press releases, and key executives' speeches, and they allow investors to order paper copies of previous annual and quarterly reports up to five years old. So the Internet is a handy tool that gives investors greater access to company activities and helps the firm keep its investors better informed — which improves the company's long-term relations with its investors.

Regarding Reinvestment Plans

Another way a company can build better relations with its investors is to offer them stock directly so they can avoid broker costs on every share they buy. Some companies offer their investors dividend reinvestment plans and direct stock purchase plans. Both plans provide companies effective ways to maintain direct contact with their shareholders instead of going through a broker.

Dividend reinvestment plans

Dividend reinvestment plans give current investors a way to automatically reinvest any dividends toward the purchase of new shares of stock. To take advantage of this plan, shareholders must register their stock directly with the company instead of opening an account with a broker.

Shareholders can reinvest all or just part of their dividends through the reinvestment plans. Many times, these plans offer investors the opportunity to buy additional shares by using cash, check, or a debit that's automatically taken from the investor's bank account. This option gives small investors a way to steadily increase their ownership in the company. Many firms also allow investors to access their dividend reinvestment plan on the company website, making maintaining accounts and managing transactions even easier.

Direct stock purchase plans

Through *direct stock purchase plans*, companies can offer stock directly to the public so that investors don't have to contact a broker to purchase even the first share of stock. Prior to these programs, investors had to buy stock through a broker before they could participate in a dividend reinvestment plan.

Today shareholders can buy all their stock directly from a company, if it offers the service, and avoid paying any broker fees. Direct stock purchase plans also provide the same features as dividend reinvestment plans, such as the ability to reinvest dividends.

TIP

Depending on how a company sets up its program, the shareholder or the company may pay the direct stock purchase plan's fees. Some companies offer this service for free; others charge a fee for every transaction, which can amount to more than what a broker charges. Be sure you understand the fees involved if you buy directly from a company, and compare those fees with the cost of buying through your broker to make sure you're getting a good deal.

» Discovering the methods of creative accounting

» Finding massaged company earnings

» Recognizing beefed-up revenues

» Spotting expense-cutting strategies

» Detecting cash flow games

Chapter 23

Keeping Score When Companies Play Games with Numbers

Companies cooking the books — and I don't mean throwing them in a raging fire in disgust — fuel an ongoing game of hide-and-seek among company outsiders that results in millions, and sometimes billions, of dollars of losses for investors every year. In some cases, company insiders use numerous tactics to deceive their shareholders and pad their own pockets. The mortgage mess in 2007, when mortgage-related securities were held off the books, destroyed the stock value of many major financial institutions, such as Citigroup and Merrill Lynch.

Throughout most of this book, I concentrate on reading financial reports that accurately portray the financial status of a company, but unfortunately, not all reports fall into this category. The pressure companies face to meet the quarterly expectations of Wall Street drives many firms to play with their numbers. When a company doesn't meet expectations, its stock price is beaten down, which lowers the company's market value. Sometimes this game to meet expectations goes beyond legal methods to fraud and deception.

In this chapter, I review the primary tools that companies use to hide their financial problems and to deceive the public and the government.

Getting to the Bottom of Creative Accounting

Enron, once the world's largest energy trader, now lives in infamy as the host of one of the world's largest accounting scandals. After the company declared bankruptcy in 2001, Congress enacted legislation to correct the flaws in the U.S. financial reporting system and protect investors and consumers from misleading accounting practices. But corporate lobbyists are powerful, and Congress continues to get pressure to weaken the legislation passed after the Enron scandal because the companies think the new laws are too burdensome.

In the meantime, the public's faith in corporate financial accounting has taken a nose dive, in large part because of the glut of creative accounting that came to light during the late 1990s and continued to rear its ugly head in 2007 during the scandals related to the mortgage mess. More rules for Wall Street were added with the passage of the Dodd-Frank Wall Street Reform and Consumer Protection Act of 2010.

Companies that practice creative accounting deviate from generally accepted accounting principles (GAAP). The financial reports they issue use loopholes in financial laws in ways that are, at the very least, misleading and, in some cases illegal, to gain an advantage for the company over the users of those financial reports.

Defining the scope of the problem

In the hundreds of cases in which companies *restated their earnings* (that is, when companies changed the numbers they originally reported to the general public to correct "accounting errors"), company insiders used creative accounting techniques to cook the books. And when trying to unearth the accounting problem, you have to be creative yourself.

In these scandals, some company insiders used corporate accounts for personal purposes, such as buying expensive cars or numerous houses and taking luxury trips — all at the expense of shareholders. Instead of using profits to grow the company and increase the stock's value for the stockholders, these insiders lined their own pockets. How did they get away with that? Well, most board members were closely tied to the corporate chiefs, which means that no one was really watching the cookie jar — or the hands going into it. In some cases, these close ties were members of the same family who didn't question their father or brother. In other cases, the board members were close friends and didn't want to question a buddy. You can find more details about these scandals in Chapter 24.

WARNING

Company insiders use different techniques to cook the books. In some cases, earnings are *managed*, meaning that companies use legitimate accounting methods in aggressive ways to get the bottom-line results they need. Other companies present revenues that are pure fiction. Still others toy with how they handle their capital financing, or overvalue their assets, or undervalue their liabilities. Insiders who want to deceive company outsiders can use a variety of these tactics.

Seeing through cooked books

Former Securities and Exchange Commission (SEC) chairman Arthur Levitt groups these creative techniques — which he calls "accounting hocus-pocus" — into the following five categories.

REMEMBER

I discuss how company insiders use these various techniques, but too often, you don't find out about the deception until someone inside the company decides to blow the whistle or the company seeks bankruptcy protection.

Big-bath charges

Company insiders use this technique to clean up their balance sheet by giving it a "big bath," meaning they wash away past financial problems. When earnings take a big hit, some executives hope that Wall Street will look beyond a one-time loss and focus on future earnings.

A good time to use this practice is when the company decides to restructure some parts of its business — for example, when two divisions of a company merge or a single division is split into two. During the restructuring process, executives can clean up any problems in previous reporting. This cleaning process may include hiding past financial reporting problems. The accounting problems washed off the books can be deliberate or nondeliberate accounting errors made during previous reporting periods.

Creative acquisition accounting

Levitt also calls this category "merger magic" because it includes the technique in which companies use acquisitions to hide their problems. It's particularly useful when the acquisition is merely a stock exchange rather than a cash exchange. By setting a stock price for an acquisition that enables a company to hide previous problems, a lot of past accounting problems can disappear like magic because the higher stock price covers up the problems, such as previous losses that the company didn't accurately report. Most times, company insiders can erase the problems in a popular write-off called *in-process research and development,* which is a one-time charge mentioned in the notes to the financial statements detailing an acquisition. Getting rid of problems with this charge removes any future earnings drag, and future earnings statements look better.

Miscellaneous cookie jar reserves

Companies that use liabilities rather than revenue to hide problems do so by using what Levitt calls "cookie jars." When using this technique, company insiders make unrealistic assumptions about company liabilities. In a good year, a firm assumes that its sales returns will be much higher than they have been historically. These higher assumptions are "banked" as a liability, which means they're added to an accrual account that can be adjusted in a later year. When a business has a bad year and needs to manage its earnings, it can massage those earnings by reducing the actual sales returns, using some of the banked sales returns from the cookie jar.

Materiality

In accounting, the generally accepted principle is to report only financial matters that can have a material effect on a company's earnings. Whether an item has a material effect on the company's bottom line is purely a judgment call made by company executives and the auditors. For example, a $1 million loss in inventory may have a material effect on a company's bottom line if the company's total profits are $10 million. But that same million-dollar loss for a company that reports multibillion-dollar earnings may not be considered material because that loss has less impact on the company's bottom line.

Firms that play the materiality game set a percentage ceiling under which errors don't matter because they're not material. For example, the multibillion-dollar company may decide that as long as errors reflect less than 5 percent of any department's revenues, the error isn't material to the company's results. But those little errors can add up when spread carefully across a firm's financial reports. Sometimes small errors can help a business make up for the 1- or 2-cent loss per share that may miss Wall Street expectations and cause the stock price to drop. Anytime a company misses Wall Street expectations — even by pennies — the stock price takes a drop, and the company's overall value on the market may also fall by millions of dollars.

Revenue recognition

Companies using this technique boost their earnings by manipulating the way they count sales. For example, these companies recognize a sale before it's complete or count something as sold even though the customer still has options to terminate, void, or delay the sale.

Unearthing the Games Played with Earnings

All companies manage earnings to a certain extent because they want their bottom lines to look as good as possible, and they use whatever accounting method gets them there. For example, a company can improve its earnings by using different methods for valuing assets and costs. As I discuss in Chapter 9, the accounting policies and methods that a company uses can have a great impact on its bottom line.

REMEMBER

In accrual accounting, revenue is recognized when it's earned (when the sale of the product or service is complete and payment for the product or service is due), and expenses are recognized when they're incurred (when the purchase is complete, even if cash hasn't yet been paid). See Chapter 4 for more details. Cash doesn't have to change hands for revenue to be earned or expenses incurred. The key is whether the revenue is actually earned and the expenses are actually incurred or whether a company is reporting them prematurely or fictitiously.

The generally accepted accounting principles (GAAP; see Chapter 18) that govern reporting practices are pretty flexible. Managing earnings becomes abusive when it involves using tricks that distort a company's true financial picture to present the desired view to outsiders. And the games that companies play along those lines are numerous. The only limit to these games is the creativity of the people who manage the company's finances.

Companies usually play with numbers that impact revenue recognition or expense recognition. The bottom line for any company is really the amount of revenue that a company takes in or the amount of expenses that it pays out to generate that revenue. All the other numbers that a company reports are based on either its revenue or its expenses.

Reading between the revenue lines

In this section, I cover the gamut of revenue recognition games, from slight misrepresentations to gross exaggerations. Unfortunately, many of these problems are difficult for readers who are company outsiders to find. Still, if you're an investor, you need to be familiar with the terms I discuss in this section so you can understand news reports about problems that may exist inside a company.

Goods ordered but not shipped

In some cases, a company considers goods that have been ordered but not yet shipped to be part of its revenue earned. In the long term, this system can create not only an accounting nightmare, but also a nightmare for managers throughout the company. Orders can get severely backlogged, and ultimately, the company may have a lot of problems satisfying its customers.

Additionally, this practice can have a big impact on a company's bottom line. Accrual accounting is specifically designed to match revenue with expenses each accounting period. As more goods build up that are ordered but not shipped, financial reports overstate the firm's revenue and understate expenses until the deception is exposed. Eventually, the firm has to admit its game-playing and restate its net income, which then likely results in a profit reduction or possibly even a loss.

Executives and managers just delay the inevitable when they practice this game. Some do it to maintain their bonuses as long as possible. Others do it because they don't want to face the reality of the company's financial position. And I'm sure companies make many more excuses when the game is finally exposed.

Goods shipped but not ordered

Some companies get even more aggressive with their deception, counting goods that they've shipped but that customers haven't ordered yet. Companies that use this technique commonly ship items for inspection or demonstration purposes in the hope that customers will buy the product. This tactic can help a company meet its revenue for the upcoming reporting period because it counts these unordered goods as sales, even though the products haven't really been sold. However, if some customers receive the goods, decide not to purchase them, and return the merchandise, the company must subtract these sales from its revenue during the next period.

As the problem snowballs, the company has to ship more orders without actually having the sales to meet its revenue expectations. Each month, it has to reverse a greater percentage of its revenue, and as a result, it has to make up the shortfall by shipping an even greater number of units without actual orders. Eventually, the company can't keep up the deceptive practices and must correct its financial statements, lowering the amount it reported as revenue and reducing its net income. That correction usually sends shockwaves through the stock market, and the stock price drops dramatically.

Extended reporting period

Some companies try to meet Wall Street's revenue expectations by keeping their books open for a few days — or even a few weeks — into the next reporting period to generate last-minutes sales. This tactic eventually creates major financial reporting problems for the company because it takes the sales from what should have been reported as income during the next reporting period. Eventually, the company has to reveal its deceptive practices because it has to leave its books open longer and longer each period to meet the next period's expectations.

Pure fiction

The most outrageous acts are the ones that involve reporting purely fictional sales. How do companies do this? Well, they recognize revenue for sales that were never ordered and never shipped. Company insiders fill financial records with false order, billing, and shipping information. Eventually, the lack of actual cash forces the company to reveal its games, and the business probably goes bankrupt.

Channel stuffing

Channel stuffing is a way for companies to get more products out of their manufacturing warehouses and onto distributors' and retailers' shelves. The most common method is to offer distributors large discounts so that they stock up on products. Distributors buy more product than they expect to sell because they can get it so much cheaper. Then distributors sell the product to their customers; however, several months or even a year may pass before they sell all the products. If the products don't sell, in some cases, companies are given the right to return the product.

Although this strategy is a legitimate type of revenue, it can come back to haunt the company in later accounting periods, when distributors have so much product on their shelves that they don't need to order more. At some point in the future, new orders drop, which means fewer sales and a drop in revenue reported on the income statement. Less revenue translates to lower net income, which Wall Street sees as a bad sign, and the stock price takes a dive.

Side letters

Sometimes companies make agreements with their regular customers outside the actual documentation used for the corporate reporting of revenue. This agreement is called a *side letter*. The side letter involves the company and customer changing terms behind the scenes, such as allowing more liberal rights of return or rights to cancel orders at any time that can essentially kill the sale. Sometimes these agreements go as far as excusing the customer from paying for the goods.

In all cases, the side letter terms eventually result in turning revenue that was recognized on a previous income statement into a nonsale, either by the return of goods or by the extension of credit beyond a 12-month payment period. This practice makes revenue from these sales look better initially, but the revenue is later subtracted when the goods are returned.

Rights of return

Giving customers liberal return rights is another way of getting them to order goods, even when they're not sure whether they'll be able to resell them. By offering distributors or retailers terms that allow them to order goods for resale that they can return as much as 12 months later if they don't sell, the sales, in essence, aren't really sales and shouldn't be recognized as revenue on a company's financial report. Rights of return are offered to most customers, but when payment for goods depends on the need for the distributor or retailer to first resell the goods, the recognition of that revenue is questionable.

Related-party revenue

Related-party revenue comes from a company selling goods to another entity in which the seller controls the management of operating policies. For example, if the parent company of a tissue manufacturer sells the raw materials needed for manufacturing that tissue to its subsidiary, the parent company can't count that sale of raw materials as revenue. Whenever one party to the transaction can control or significantly influence the decision of the entity that wants to buy the goods, a company can't recognize the sale as revenue.

TECHNICAL STUFF

These related-party sales don't meet the SEC's requirement for an *arm's-length transaction*, which is a transaction that involves a buyer and a seller who can act independently of each other and have no relationship to each other. The SEC does require that companies recognize only sales with third parties that are at arm's length and that can't be controlled by the party planning to recognize the sale as revenue. Companies aren't permitted to record sales to their affiliates or other related entities as part of their recognized revenues.

Bill-and-hold transactions

Sometimes a buyer places an order but asks the company to hold on to the goods until it has room in its store or warehouse. So the company has sold the goods but hasn't shipped them yet. This sale is called a *bill-and-hold transaction*.

TECHNICAL STUFF

The SEC has a set of criteria that a company must meet for it to recognize revenue for items it hasn't shipped yet. These criteria include the following:

- **The seller passes the risks of ownership to the buyer:** If anything happens to the goods while the seller is holding them, the loss is the buyer's responsibility, not the seller's.
- **The customer makes a fiscal commitment to purchase the goods:** This commitment should preferably occur in writing.
- **The buyer, not the seller, requests the bill-and-hold transaction:** The buyer must have a business purpose, such as planning a future sales event and not wanting to receive the goods until just before the event, to justify ordering the goods on a buy-and-hold basis.
- **The buyer and seller set up a fixed schedule for the delivery of the goods:** Determining dates for delivery indicates that the sale is real and not a scam.
- **The seller separates the ordered goods from its inventory so that it won't use the goods to fill other orders:** If it doesn't clearly separate these goods and hold them, the company can't prove that the goods were actually bought, so the sale can't be counted.
- **The seller has the goods complete and ready for shipment:** Only goods being held and ready for shipment can be counted as a sale.

Up-front service fees

Companies that collect up-front service fees for services that they provide over a long period of time, such as 12, 24, 36, or 60 months, must be careful about how they recognize this revenue. If the company collects fees to service equipment up front, it can't count these fees as revenue when the money is collected. The SEC requires that such companies recognize their revenue over time as the fees are earned. Companies that recognize this type of revenue all at once are prematurely recognizing revenue.

Detecting creative revenue accounting

With so many tricks up so many corporate sleeves, you may feel that you're at the mercy of the tricksters. You can get to the bottom of many of the common creative accounting tactics by carefully reading and analyzing the financial reports, but you have to play detective and crunch some numbers.

Reviewing revenue-recognition policies

The financial report section called the *notes to the financial statements* is a good source for finding out at what point a company actually recognizes a sale as revenue. Some companies recognize revenue before they deliver the product or before they perform the service. If you come across this scenario, try to find details in the notes to the financial statements that indicate how the company really earned its revenue. If you can't find this info, call the company's investor relations department to clarify its revenue-recognition policies, and be sure that you understand why it may be justified in recognizing revenue before delivery or performance has been completed.

When a firm indicates in the notes to the financial statements that it recognizes revenue at the time of delivery or performance, that timing may seem perfect to you, but you must look further to find other policies that may negate a sale. Dig deeper into the revenue-recognition section of the notes to find out what the company's rights-of-return policy is and how it determines pricing. Some companies may allow a price adjustment or have a liberal return policy that may cancel out the sale.

TIP

Take note if you find that the company recently changed its revenue-recognition policies. Just the fact that the company is changing those policies can be a red flag. Many times this change comes about because the firm is having difficulty meeting its Wall Street expectations. It may decide to recognize revenue earlier in the sales process, which may mean that more of this revenue reported on the income statement may have to be subtracted in later reporting periods. Scour the revenue-recognition section of the financial report until you understand how the change impacts the company's revenue recognition. You may want to review the annual reports from the past few years to compare the old revenue policies with the new ones.

Evaluating revenue results

Reported revenue results for the current period don't tell the whole financial story. You need to review the revenue results for the past five quarters (at least) or past three years to look for any inexplicable swings in seasonal activity. For example, extremely high numbers for retail outlets in the last quarter of the year (October to December) aren't unusual. Many retailers make about 40 percent of their profits during that quarter due to holiday sales.

TIP

Be sure you understand the fluctuations in revenue for the company you're investigating and how its results compare with the results of similar companies and the industry as a whole. If you see major shifts in revenue results that normal seasonal differences can't explain, an alarm needs to go off in your head. Take the time to further investigate the reason for these differences by reading reports by analysts who cover the company and by calling the company's investor relations office.

Monitoring accounts receivable

Accounts receivable tracks customers who buy on credit. You want to be sure that customers are promptly paying for their purchases, so closely watch the trend in accounts receivable. In Chapter 16, I show you how to calculate accounts receivable turnover. Compare the *turnover ratio*, which measures how quickly customers pay their bills, for at least the past five quarters to see whether a major change or trend has occurred. If you notice that customers are taking longer to pay their bills, it can be a sign that the company is having trouble collecting money, but it can also indicate revenue management. Either way, this raises a red flag for you as a financial report reader.

While you're investigating, check the percentage rate of change for accounts receivable versus the percentage rate of change for net revenue over the same period. For example, if the balance in accounts receivable increases by 10 percent and net revenues increase by 25 percent, that would be a sign of game playing. Normally, these two accounts increase and decrease by similar percentages year to year unless the company offers its customers a significant change in credit policies. If you see significant differences between these two accounts, it may be another sign of revenue management.

TIP

Check to see if the changes you're seeing match trends for similar companies or the industry as a whole. If not, ask investor relations people to explain what's behind the differences. If you don't like the answers or can't get answers that make sense to you, don't buy the stock, or consider selling the stock you already have.

Assessing physical capacity

Evaluating *physical capacity*, the number of facilities the company has and the amount of product the company can manufacture, is another way to judge whether the company is accurately reporting revenue. You need to find out whether the firm truly has the physical capacity to generate the revenue it's reporting. You do so by comparing the following ratios:

- **Revenue per employee (Revenue ÷ Number of employees):** If the annual report doesn't mention the number of employees, you can call investor relations or find it in a company profile on one of the financial websites, such as Yahoo! Finance (finance.yahoo.com).
- **Revenue per dollar value of property, plant, and equipment (Revenue ÷ Dollar value of property, plant, and equipment):** You can find the dollar value of property, plant, and equipment on the financial report's balance sheet.

» **Revenue per dollar value of total assets (Revenue ÷ Dollar value of total assets):** You can find the number for total assets on the financial report's balance sheet.

» **Revenue per square foot of retail or rental space, if appropriate (Revenue ÷ Square foot of retail space):** You can find details about retail or rental space in the managers' discussion and analysis or the notes to the financial statements, or in the company's profile on a financial website.

TIP

Compare these ratios for the past five quarters, and also compare the ratios to ones of similar companies and ones for the industry as a whole. If you see major differences from accounting period to accounting period or between similar companies, it may be a sign of a problem. For example, if revenue per employee is much higher, or if revenue per dollar value of property, plant, or equipment far exceeds figures for similar companies or for previous periods, it may be a sign of abusive revenue management.

Exploring Exploitations of Expenses

If a company is playing games with its expenses, the most likely place you'll find evidence is in its capitalization or its amortization policies. You can find details about these policies in the notes to the financial statements. For further explanation of amortization, see Chapter 4.

Companies that want their bottom lines to look better may shift the way that they report depreciation and amortization, which are the tools they use to account for an asset's use and to show the decreasing value of that asset. To make their net incomes look better, companies can play games with the amounts they write off. They do so by writing off less than they should and lowering expenses.

In addition to depreciation and amortization schedules, companies can play games with expenses when reporting some types of advertising, research and development costs, patents and licenses, asset impairments, and restructuring charges. In some cases, companies can capitalize (spread out) their expenses over a number of months, quarters, or years. Spreading out expenses can certainly improve a company's bottom line because the expenses will be lower in the first year they're incurred, and lower expenses mean more net income.

REMEMBER

So the key question is whether a company is spreading out its expenses properly or is improperly managing its bottom line. You can find details in the accounting policies section in the annual report. I point out the key policies to review, but if the company is playing games, detecting anything out of the ordinary is difficult to do by using the annual reports. You have to depend on reports in the financial press or from the SEC to see if problems are detected or exposed by a whistle-blower.

Advertising expenses

Companies report most advertising expenses in the accounting period when they're incurred. However, for some types of advertising, such as direct-response advertising, companies can spread the expense over a number of quarters. *Direct-response advertising* is mailed directly to the consumer. For example, when a business sends out an annual catalog, it can legitimately spread out the costs for that direct-mail piece over the year, as long as it can show that it receives orders from that catalog throughout the year. To find out a firm's policy on advertising expenses, look in the notes to the financial statements.

Research and development costs

Companies are supposed to report research and development (R&D) costs in the current period being reported on the financial statements, but some companies try to stretch out those expenses over a number of quarters so the reduction in net income isn't necessary all in the same year. If fewer expenses are subtracted from revenues, net income is higher, which makes the company look more profitable. However, the SEC has ruled that because these expenditures are so high-risk and a company isn't certain when the R&D activities may benefit its revenue, the company must immediately report R&D expenses rather than spread them out over months or years. One notable exception occurs when a company is developing new software, in which case it can spread its expenses over a number of periods until the software development is technically feasible.

TIP

To see how the company expenses its R&D, read the notes to the financial statements. If you're uncertain about the accounting policies that the notes present, don't hesitate to call investor relations and ask questions until you understand what you're reading.

Patents and licenses

Understanding the accounting for patents and licenses can be difficult. Most times, the expenses a company incurs during the research and development phase — before it receives a patent or license — must be written off in the year when they occurred, and the expenses can't be capitalized (written off over a number of years). But the company *can* capitalize some expenses — for instance, those it incurs to register or defend a patent. The company can also list a patent or license it purchases as an asset at the purchase price and capitalize it. Companies like to capitalize a patent or license because such a large purchase can significantly reduce their net income; most prefer to write it off over several years, if they can, to reduce the hit.

All patents and licenses that a company purchases are listed as assets on the balance sheet. In addition, the balance sheet lists the costs of registering patents or licenses for products developed in-house. The value of these patents and licenses is amortized over the time period for which they're *economically viable* (meaning for as long as the company benefits from owning that patent or license).

Companies can play games with the value of patents and licenses, as well as with the time periods for which they'll be considered economically viable. To see what a company says about its patent and license accounting policies, read the notes to the financial statements. Compare its policies with the policies of similar companies to see whether they appear reasonable or whether the company may be overstating its value or capitalizing its expenses in a way that differs from its competitors. For example, if Company A makes widgets and says the patent for its type of widget is good for 10 years, and Company B makes a different kind of widget and says its patent is economically viable for 20 years, you probably want to call investor relations and find out why Company B believes it has an economically viable widget for so much longer than its competitor.

Asset impairment

Tangible assets depreciate based on set schedules, but not all intangible assets face a rigid amortization schedule. For example, goodwill is an intangible asset that's no longer amortized each year. This line item on the balance sheet has long had potential for creative accounting practitioners. Today most companies have goodwill on their balance sheets because many large public companies are formed by buying smaller companies.

Any company that acquires another company can list goodwill on its balance sheet. A firm's value of goodwill is based on the amount of money or stock that it pays for the acquisition, over and above what the net tangible assets were worth.

In the past, companies amortized goodwill and wrote off its expenses each year. Today a company must prove that the value of its goodwill has been impaired (worth less than it was in a previous year) before it can write it off. The SEC requires that companies test goodwill before they write off any value to see if any impairment to its value has occurred.

The value of goodwill is tested based on a number of factors, including

- Competition and the ability of competitors to negatively affect the profitability of the business that a company acquires
- The current or expected future levels of industry consolidation
- The impact that potential or expected changes in technology may have on profitability
- Legislative action that results in an uncertain or changing regulatory environment
- Loss of future revenue if certain key employees of the acquisition company aren't retained
- The rate of customer turnover, or how fast old customers leave and new customers arrive
- The mobility of customers and employees

TIP

If you see that a company has written off goodwill or any other asset under the rules of impairment, look for an explanation about how it calculated that impairment in the notes to the financial statements. If you don't understand the explanation, ask the investor relations office questions.

Restructuring charges

Restructuring charges is one of the primary ways companies can hide all sorts of accounting games. A company can *restructure* itself by combining divisions, having one division split off into two or more, or dismantling an entire division. Any major change in the way a company manufactures or sells its products usually entails restructuring.

Whenever a company indicates restructuring charges on its financial statements, carefully scour the notes to the financial statements for reasons behind those charges and how the company determines how much it will write off. Find out what costs the firm allocated to the restructure, and carefully read the details for those costs. The restructuring method is a great way for a company to get rid of losses in one-time charges and clean out the books. Luckily, this is a red flag that the SEC closely watches for, and SEC staff question company reports if they believe a company's charges and its explanations seem fishy.

In the notes to the financial statements, you usually find a note specifically detailing the restructuring and its impact on the financial statements. You may also find mentions of restructuring charges or plans in the management's discussion and analysis section of the financial report. Many times when a company restructures, it incurs costs for asset impairment, lease termination, plant and other closures, severance pay, benefits, relocation, and retraining, giving creative accountants a lot of room to fiddle with the numbers.

The company must specify costs not only for the current period, but also costs for all future years in which the company anticipates additional costs and any related write-offs in periods prior to the one being reported. The SEC watches these charges very closely, too, and tries to close any loopholes that allow companies to charge recurring operating expenses to their restructuring, which companies do to improve the appearance to outsiders of the earnings results from business operations.

Finding Funny Business in Assets and Liabilities

Overvaluing assets or undervaluing liabilities can give a distorted view of a company's earning power and financial position. These practices can have a devastating impact when the company must finally admit to its game playing.

Recognizing overstated assets

Overstated assets make a company look financially healthier to annual report readers than it truly is. The company may report that it has more cash due than it really does, or that it holds more inventory than is actually on its shelves. The company may also report that the value of its inventory is greater than it really is.

Accounts receivable

The accounts receivable section of the financial report is the place where you may find an indication of premature or fictitious revenue recognition. One way a company can overstate its accounts receivable is to post sales to customers who will return the items early the following month without paying for them. The dollar value of those goods reduces the accounts receivable during the next accounting period, but the deception makes the current period look like more revenues were received than should actually have been counted because the sales are premature or fictitious.

That deception isn't the only way a company can overvalue its accounts receivable. Another account attached to accounts receivable is the allowance for doubtful accounts. At the end of each accounting period, the company identifies past-due accounts that probably won't get paid and adds the value of these past-due accounts to the allowance for doubtful accounts, which reduces the value of accounts receivable.

A company that wants to play with its numbers and indicate that its financial position is actually better than it appears reduces the amount it sets aside for doubtful accounts. Gradually, the number of days the company takes to collect on its accounts receivable goes up as more late- or nonpayers are left in accounts receivable. Eventually, the number of days it takes for the company to collect on its accounts receivable goes up, and the amount of cash it takes in from customers who are paying off their purchase bought on credit slows down.

TIP

You can test the trend for accounts receivable by using formulas I explain in Chapter 16. Test the trend by calculating days in accounts receivable for the past three to five quarters. If you see the number of days in accounts receivable gradually rise, it's a sign of a problem, and it may represent an attempt to recognize revenue prematurely or fictitiously. But it may also represent a problem of credit policies that are too liberal. I discuss that issue in greater detail in Chapter 16.

Inventory

As I discuss in Chapter 15, companies can use one of five different inventory valuation methods, and each one yields a different net income for the company. Inventory policy isn't the only way a company can shift the value of its inventory on the balance sheet. Other common methods used include the following:

- **Overstating physical count:** Although this method is absolute fraud, companies take this route to improve the appearance of their balance sheets. Sometimes they alter the actual count of their inventory; other times they don't subtract the decrease in inventory from the physical count. Companies may also leave damaged goods in the inventory count, even though they have no value.
- **Increasing reported valuation:** Some businesses don't even bother messing with their inventory counts. A simple journal entry increasing a firm's inventory valuation and decreasing its costs of goods sold can improve appearances on both the balance sheet and the income statement. The assets side of the balance sheet looks better, and the net income figure improves, too — which ultimately raises retained earnings to hide the existence of the journal entry and keep the balance sheet in balance.
- **Delaying an inventory write-down:** Company management periodically writes down the value of inventory when it determines that the products are obsolete or slow moving. Because the decision to write down inventory is purely up to management, during a rough year, the company may delay writing down inventory to make its numbers look better.

TIP

Any time you suspect that inventory may be the object of financial game playing, you can test your theory by calculating the number of days inventory sits around the company (I show you how to test the number of days inventory sits around in Chapter 15). Look for trends by running the numbers for the past three years. If you see that the number of days that inventory sits around gradually increases, definitely suspect a problem. The problem may not be creative accounting; it may be a sign of other problems, such as reduced consumer interest in the product or a bad economic market. The only way to find out is to ask your questions to the company's investor relations department.

Undeveloped land

Land never depreciates. But shareholders don't have any details about where the land that a company owns is located, so they can never truly assess the value of undeveloped land on a balance sheet. This fact allows a lot of room for creative accounting and leaves the financial reader in the dark when it comes to finding this problem. Unfortunately, in a sketchy situation like this one, all you can do is wait for a whistle-blower to expose it.

Artwork

As is the case with undeveloped land, financial reports don't detail the value of artwork that a company holds, so a lot of room exists for doctoring the numbers. Unless you're looking at the financial statements for a company that regularly sells artwork, be wary when you see a large portion of its assets listed on the balance sheet in a line item called *artwork*. This line item shouldn't be a major one for most companies that aren't in the art business.

TIP

If you see a non-art business with a significant level of assets tied up in artwork, ask investor relations why the company is spending so much money on art. Frankly, a firm that ties up its money in art instead of using it to grow the business is not one I'd want to own stock in.

Looking for undervalued liabilities

Undervaluing liabilities can certainly make a company look healthier to financial report readers, but this deception is likely to lead the company down the path to bankruptcy. Games played by misstating liabilities frequently involve large numbers and hide significant money problems.

Accounts payable

Most times, an increase in accounts payable is directly related to the fact that the company is delaying payments for inventory. To test for a problem, you need to calculate the accounts payable ratio, which I show you how to do in Chapter 16. If you find a trend indicating that the number of days the company takes to pay its accounts payable is steadily increasing, test the number of days in inventory, as I show you in Chapter 15.

If the company fails both tests, investigate further. Even though the company may not be playing games with its numbers, take these signs as an indication of a worsening problem. With the trends you're noticing, definitely call investor relations and ask for explanations about why the company has been paying its bills more slowly or why the inventory has been sitting on the shelves for longer periods of time.

WARNING

If investor relations doesn't answer the questions to your satisfaction, don't buy the stock. If you already do own the stock, you may want to consider selling it if you believe the company is hiding the truth.

Accrued expenses payable

Any expenses that a company hasn't paid by the end of an accounting period are *accrued* (posted to the accounts before cash is paid out) in the current period, so these expenses can be matched to current period earnings. This amount is added to the liability side of the balance sheet.

Unpaid expenses can include just about any expense for which the company gets a bill and has a number of days to pay, such as these expenses:

- Administrative expenses
- Benefits
- Insurance
- Salaries
- Selling costs
- Utilities

If the bill arrives during the last week before a company closes its books, the company most likely will accrue it rather than pay it. Most firms cut off paying bills several days before they close their books so the staff can concentrate on closing the books for the period.

If a firm needs to improve its net income, it can manage its numbers by not accruing bills and instead paying them in the next accounting period. The problem with this strategy is that the next accounting period has more expenses charged to it than the company actually incurred during that accounting period. The expenses will be higher, and therefore, the net income will be lower in the next reporting period.

TIP

You can test for this particular game by watching the trend for accrued expenses payable. Check to see whether accrued expenses payable is going up or down from accounting period to accounting period. Usually, accrued expenses payable stay pretty level from year to year. If you see a steady decline, the company may be doing some creative accounting, or maybe the company's decrease in expenses is simply due to discontinued operations or other changes. If you see a declining trend, look deeper into the numbers to see whether you can find an explanation. If not, call investor relations to find out why the trend for accrued payables shifts from accounting period to accounting period.

Contingent liabilities

Contingent liabilities are liabilities that a company should accrue when it determines that an event is likely to happen. For example, if the company is party to a lawsuit that it lost and the winner was awarded damages, the company should accrue the liability as a contingent liability.

A company must determine two factors before it can list a contingent liability on its balance sheet. Factor one: The company deems it probable that it will be held liable. Factor two: The company can reasonably estimate the costs that it will incur.

If the company hasn't determined these two issues, you'll probably find a note about the contingency in the notes to the financial statements. Read the notes about contingencies and research further any items you think the company may not be fully disclosing. You can do so by reading analysts' reports on the company or by calling the investor relations department to ask questions about any issues mentioned in the notes to the financial statements.

Pay-down liabilities

Another way that the firms involved in the scandals of the past three years played with their numbers was by indicating that they paid down their liabilities when they actually didn't. To make its balance sheet look better, a company may transfer debt to another entity owned by the company, its directors, or its executives to hide its true financial status.

You probably won't have any way of knowing whether this is happening until a company insider decides to expose the practice or the SEC catches the company.

Playing Detective with Cash Flow

The statement of cash flows (which I discuss in detail in Chapter 8) is derived primarily from information found on a company's income statement and balance sheet. You usually don't find massaged numbers on this statement because it's based primarily on the numbers that have already been shown on these other documents. But you may find that the presentation of the numbers hides cash flow problems.

Discontinued operations

Discontinued operations occur when a company shuts down some of its activities, such as closing a manufacturing plant or putting an end to a product line. Many companies that discontinue operations show the impact it has on their cash in a separate line item of the financial report. Companies that have cash flow problems with continuing operations may not separate these results on their cash flow statements. Because the accounting rules don't require a separate line item, this strategy is a convenient way to hide the problem from investors — most of whom don't do a good job of reading the small print in the notes to the financial statements anyway.

If discontinued operations have an impact on a company's income statement, you see a line item there listing either additional revenue or additional expenses related to the shutdown. You can find greater detail about those discontinued operations in the notes to the financial statements. Anytime you see mention of discontinued operations on the income statement or in the notes to the financial statements, be sure that you also see a separate line item in the statement of cash flows. If you don't, use the information you glean from the income statement and the notes to calculate the cash flow from operations.

To calculate the *cash flow from operations* (cash received from the day-to-day operations of the business, usually from sales), subtract any cash generated from discontinued operations (which you find noted on the income statement) from the net income reported on the statement of cash flows. When looking at a company's profitability from the cash perspective, you want to consider only cash generated by ongoing operations.

When you take on the role of detective, you may uncover a cash flow problem that the financial wizards carefully concealed because the rules allow such a misleading presentation. In Chapter 17, I show you numerous calculations for testing a company's cash flow.

Income taxes paid

Just like with discontinued operations, the amount of income taxes that a company pays can distort its operating cash flow. The reason is that, in some situations, companies pay income taxes as a one-time occurrence, such as taxes on the net gain or loss from the sale of a major asset. The income taxes a company pays for these one-time occurrences shouldn't be included in your calculations related to operating cash flow.

By reviewing the sections on investing or financing activities in the statement of cash flows, you can find any adjustments you may need to calculate the operating cash flow. Here are two key adjustments you need to make to find the actual net cash from operations (the amount of cash generated from the company's day-to-day operations):

- **Gains from sales of investments or fixed assets:** If a company gains from the sale of investments or fixed assets (for example, buildings, factories, vehicles, or anything else the company owns that it can't quickly convert to cash) that weren't part of operations, add back in the taxes paid on a gain from the sale of an investment or fixed asset. Taxes paid on one-time gains distort the true cash flow from operations.
- **Losses from sales of investments or fixed assets:** If a company loses from the sale of investments or fixed assets, the tax savings the company gets from the loss increase its cash flow. You need to subtract these tax savings from the net cash so your operating cash flow accurately reflects the cash available from operations.

TIP

SEEKING INFORMATION ON QUESTIONABLE REPORTING

If you want to find more information about companies that may be playing games with their numbers, a good place to turn is Accounting and Auditing Enforcement Releases (AAERs), posted on the SEC website. You can use the search features to find any releases that the SEC may have issued.

AAERs detail criminal actions, civil actions, or cease-and-desist proceedings and explain how the company or individual must correct their current reporting practices. The AAERs also detail any penalties the SEC imposes. To find the list of current and past releases filed by the SEC, go to `www.sec.gov/divisions/enforce/friactions.shtml`.

6

The Part of Tens

IN THIS PART . . .

Take a look at financial scandals and the world's biggest cheaters, scammers, and faulty bookkeepers.

Discover how to identify clues that a company is in trouble.

- » Checking in with cheats
- » Taking a look at foul play
- » Finding fallout from faulty bookkeeping

Chapter 24
Ten (+1) Financial Scandals That Rocked the World

I'm sorry to have to say this, but the hard part of writing this chapter was narrowing the list to ten. Too many candidates were competing for a spot on this list. Since 2000, more than 500 companies had to restate earnings after company executives, the board of directors, or the Securities and Exchange Commission (SEC) found problems with their financial statements. Because of these misstated earnings, stock prices dropped and investors lost billions of dollars on the stocks they held in their portfolios; some even had their entire retirement savings wiped out. Clearly, our entire financial reporting system needs a major overhaul.

Although the Sarbanes-Oxley Act of 2002 (you can find details about the changes that bill requires in Chapter 3) improved things a little, the mortgage mess of 2007 showed how much more needs to be done as financial institutions around the world shocked their shareholders when they lost billions due to mortgage-backed securities. Some of these securities were held on the books, but others were held off the books, Enron style. Corporate lobbyists are still trying to get Congress to weaken Sarbanes-Oxley, but the 2007 banking scandals probably made their job more difficult. Instead of weakening Sarbanes-Oxley, Congress passed another important piece of legislation, the Dodd-Frank Wall Street Reform and Consumer Protection Act of 2010.

Drum roll, please! And the winners are . . .

Enron

Was there ever a doubt that Enron wouldn't make this list? Enron (once the world's largest energy trader) has practically become synonymous with "corporate scandal." Sure, some major scandals occurred before Enron, but the downfall of this company in 2001 rattled the markets with the massive scope of the misdealings that came to light. The final word on how much Enron misstated its earnings is still to come, but Enron definitely overstated its profits and improperly used *off-the-books* (not shown on its financial statements) partnerships to hide more than $1 billion in debt and give investors a false impression about its financial position. You can follow the ongoing cases at The Enron Fraud (www.enronfraud.com).

Enron's misdeeds didn't stop with only misleading investors; company insiders also manipulated the Texas power market and the California energy market and bribed foreign governments to win contracts abroad. Enron's lead in the energy-trading scandals exposed the manipulation of the energy market by other key energy companies, including CMS Energy, Duke Energy, Dynegy, and Reliant Energy.

The Enron scandal also took down one of the big five accounting firms, Arthur Andersen, which was convicted of fraud for its role in the scandal. I talk more about Arthur Andersen later in this chapter.

Enron declared bankruptcy at the end of 2001. Now the bankrupt company is facing about $100 billion in claims and liabilities from shareholders, bondholders, and other creditors.

Some executives pleaded guilty to felony charges. A federal jury in Houston indicted two of Enron's former chief executives, Kenneth L. Lay and Jeffrey Skilling, on charges of fraud and insider trading in 2004. Former Enron finance chief Andrew S. Fastow, who allegedly pocketed $60 million in company money without the board's knowledge, pleaded guilty and cooperated with the investigation. He was sentenced to ten years in prison on one count of conspiracy to commit wire fraud and one count of conspiracy to commit securities fraud. Lay died before the criminal case was completed, but Skilling was sentenced to 24 years and is serving his time in the Waseca, Minn., Federal Correctional Institution.

Today the company is much smaller and is operating under the supervision of a bankruptcy court. Its new name is the Enron Creditors Recovery Corporation. It's liquidating its remaining assets to reorganize and pay off creditors. After the creditors are paid from the asset sales, the corporation will cease to exist.

Madoff

While Bernard Madoff did not run a major corporation, I include him because his Ponzi scheme was (and still is) the largest ever in history. He was caught in 2008 and is now serving prison time. By the time his Ponzi scheme became public, $65 billion was missing from clients' accounts. The number actually representing client losses was much smaller: $18 billion. The reason the number was so much less is that most of the missing money was only paper transactions of phony growth, not actually money put on deposit with Madoff's firm. It is has come to light that most of the reports Madoff sent to his clients were purely fictitious. Madoff's Ponzi scheme helped to fuel the fire, as the public became convinced that the world's financial system was terribly run and that major new and better regulation was needed.

Citigroup

Financial institutions certainly didn't learn anything from the Enron scandal, and Citigroup made the biggest mistakes of all. Citigroup hid its problems from shareholders by keeping a large portion of its questionable mortgage-backed securities holdings off the books.

In December 2007, Citigroup brought $49 billion in these mortgage assets back onto the books, and as of July 2008, it was still trying to recover from the mess it created — and it probably will be for years to come. Shareholders had no idea that Citigroup was so deeply invested in subprime mortgages until after the damage was already done.

Citigroup's board finally pushed its chairman and CEO, Charles Prince, out the door in November 2007. In May 2007, Citigroup's stock was selling for $51.01 a share. By December 2007, when Citigroup finally fessed up and took the bad debt back onto its books, shares were selling for $28.24. As more information came to light, Citigroup's stock continued to drop like a stone and was at $18.69 in July 2008.

While shareholders lost billions, Prince walked out with a $40 million severance package and still has an office and an assistant in Citigroup's headquarters. He also has a car and driver.

Adelphia

Adelphia (a broadcasting and cable TV company) makes the top-ten list because of its greedy top executives: John Rigas, founder of the company, and his son, Timothy Rigas. The Rigases used the corporation as their personal piggy bank, stealing $100 million from the company and using it for luxurious personal residences, trips, and other items so they could live a life of luxury.

In 2004, John and Timothy were found guilty of concealing $2.3 billion in loans, which were hidden in small companies left off Adelphia's books. The SEC charged that, in addition to hiding debt, Adelphia inflated earnings to meet Wall Street expectations between at least 1998 and March 2002. Adelphia also falsified statistics about the company's operations and concealed blatant self-dealing by the Rigas family, which founded and controlled Adelphia.

Two other executives from Adelphia were arrested in 2002 after the scandal broke. Michael Rigas, another son of John Rigas, and Michael Mulcahey, the company's former director of internal reporting, were both found not guilty.

Adelphia went bankrupt and is currently liquidating real estate assets and handling bankruptcy and litigation issues.

WorldCom/MCI

WorldCom (a telephone company) overstated its cash flow by improperly booking $11.1 billion in company assets, but the total turned out to be a lot higher when all the pieces were put together. Some put the total loss to investors at $79.5 billion.

In addition to sloppy and fraudulent bookkeeping, the post-bankruptcy audit found two important new pieces — WorldCom had overvalued several acquisitions and lost $48.9 billion, including a $47 billion write-down of impaired assets. So instead of a $10 billion profit in 2000 and 2001, WorldCom had a combined loss for the years 2000 through 2002 (the year it declared bankruptcy) of $73.7 billion. When you add $5.8 billion of overvalued assets, the total fraud at WorldCom amounted to $79.5 billion.

Bernard Ebbers, WorldCom's founder, was given $400 million in off-the-books loans by the company. Criminal fraud charges were filed against Ebbers and the former chief financial officer (CFO), Scott Sullivan. Sullivan pleaded guilty to three criminal charges related to the fraud as part of a deal to cooperate with prosecutors in their case against Ebbers. Ebbers was sentenced to 25 years in prison and is serving his time at Oakdale, Louisiana, Federal Corrections Institute.

Investor groups filed a class-action case against WorldCom's former directors and executives, 18 banks, and former outside auditor Arthur Andersen. A few of these plaintiffs settled out of court in 2004; the settlement included a $50 million payment by some former WorldCom directors and a $2.65 billion settlement by Citigroup, the bank that had promoted WorldCom's stocks and bonds as good investments, even though it had concerns about WorldCom's rocky financial position.

WorldCom filed for bankruptcy protection in 2002. The company emerged from bankruptcy as MCI in 2004, which is the name of a company it bought along the way to building its kingdom. As part of the bankruptcy settlement among the company, the courts, and the creditors, the company's debt was reduced by 85 percent to $5.8 billion, still leaving many creditors with little or nothing. Shareholders also were left with nothing, and their shares were worthless after the company emerged from bankruptcy. In December 2005, Verizon bought MCI/WorldCom.

Sunbeam

Sunbeam (once a household name for electric appliances and camping equipment) was one of the first companies exposed for its questionable accounting gimmicks and fraud, which involved overstating earnings and jacking up the stock price.

In the 1990s, Sunbeam CEO Albert Dunlap ordered the company's managers to get the stock price up. They did so by overstating sales. The company's board of directors caught them after the firm reported robust sales of electric blankets during the summer months — how many people buy electric blankets in the summer? Another clue was increasing barbecue grill sales in late autumn, just in time for winter cookouts — yeah, right! What the managers were really doing was *channel stuffing* — selling these goods at significant discounts to distributors and middlemen so company sales looked better than they really were. (I discuss channel stuffing in greater detail in Chapter 23.)

Sunbeam's board of directors finally caught on to these deceptive practices in 1998 and ousted Dunlap. The board also replaced the company's auditor, Arthur Andersen. In May 2001, the SEC filed a complaint alleging that Dunlap and former finance chief Russell Kersh had perpetrated a fraudulent scheme to create an illusion that they had successfully restructured the company to sell Sunbeam at an inflated price. The SEC also alleged that Sunbeam's scheme resulted in overstating its earnings by $60 million.

Sunbeam declared bankruptcy in 2001, and the stock is no longer trading. Arthur Andersen paid $110 million to settle a shareholder lawsuit against the firm for its role in the deception. In 2002, the SEC started an investigation of Dunlap and his cohorts, but no indictment was ever filed.

Tyco

Tyco (a diversified manufacturing and service company) was used as a personal piggy bank by some of its executives, according to charges filed by the SEC. In 2002, former chairman and CEO L. Dennis Kozlowski, former CFO Mark Swartz, and former chief counsel Mark Belnick allegedly stole more than $600 million from Tyco, which they deny.

The SEC says that they took out hundreds of millions of dollars in loans and paid excessive compensation to key executives, which they never disclosed to shareholders. In addition to the SEC charges, Tyco sued Kozlowski, seeking backpay and benefits since 1997 totaling $244 million, as well as forfeiture of all his severance pay. A 2004 trial based on the SEC charges ended in a mistrial after a juror received a threatening letter from an unknown source. In 2005, they were found guilty. Kozlowski was convicted on charges of grand larceny and sentenced to up to 25 years. He's serving his time in Mid-State Correctional Facility in Marcy, N.Y.

Fortunately, Tyco has gotten past this scandal and is on the road to recovery with a new management team that's getting high marks from analysts for reviving cash flow and implementing new corporate rules to prevent similar mismanagement in the future. On June 29, 2007, Tyco shareholders received shares in two new companies: Covidien (Tyco's healthcare unit) and Tyco Electronics.

Waste Management

Waste Management (a waste services company) restated its earnings by $1.7 billion in 1998 after an SEC investigation found that the firm's former top executives had inflated earnings, which allowed them to take home millions in personal profits and other benefits while duping the company's shareholders and giving them the impression that the company's earnings were higher than they actually were.

Their scheme unraveled in 1997 when a new CEO ordered a review of the company's accounting practices. In 1998, the company restated its earnings based on financial statements that inflated earnings from 1992 to 1997. In this case, the company prepared a corrected financial statement that showed the differences for each of the years in question. The impact these differences had on the firm's earnings was reflected in the restatement of earnings filed with the 1998 financial reports.

Arthur Andersen and three of its partners, which were the auditors for Waste Management during the period, were fined $7 million in 2001 for their roles in the scandal. In 1999, Arthur Andersen settled a $220 million lawsuit filed by shareholders who bought Waste Management stock between 1994 and 1998. In 2001, Waste Management settled a shareholder lawsuit by paying shareholders $457 million.

In 2002, the SEC filed fraud charges against former Waste Management executives, including founder and former CEO Dean Buntrock, former president and chief operating officer Phillip Rooney, former CFO James Koenig, former controller Thomas Hau, former general counsel Herbert Getz, and former vice president of finance Bruce Tobecksen. These charges were settled out of court in 2005 with no admission of wrongdoing.

Bristol-Meyers Squibb

Bristol-Meyers Squibb (a pharmaceutical company) stuffed its channels with drugs and improperly booked about $1.5 billion in revenue from the first quarter of 2000 through the last quarter of 2001, according to the SEC. The SEC filed a civil fraud action against the company in 2003. To meet Wall Street expectations, Bristol-Meyers Squibb shipped a lot of inventory to its distributors in consignment-like sales near the end of each quarter so its numbers would look better. This channel-stuffing practice built up inventory at distributor levels and risked the company's ability to sell additional drugs in the future, which ultimately would lower its earnings.

Without admitting or denying the allegations, Bristol-Meyers Squibb settled the civil fraud action with the SEC in August 2004 by agreeing to pay a civil penalty of $100 million plus $50 million for a shareholder fund. On August 20, 2008, a judge ruled in favor of shareholders and decided that the company had made false or misleading statements about pending litigation regarding Canadian generic drug maker Apotex. The judge refused to dismiss the class action suit, which is still pending.

In addition to the fines Bristol-Meyers Squibb paid to the SEC, the company consented to a permanent injunction against future violations of certain antifraud and booking rules and agreed to appoint an independent adviser to review its accounting practices and internal control systems.

Halliburton

Between 1998 and 2000, Halliburton (an oil-field services company) changed its accounting policies for booking revenues from its contracts, boosting its paper profits by about $300 million and giving investors a misleading view of the company's true earnings.

This change in accounting policies, which the company didn't report to its investors, related to when and how Halliburton included on its income statement revenue that it expected to earn from *cost overruns* (costs that exceed the contract price) on contracts. The company usually gets part of those overruns reimbursed and can include that part as additional revenue on its income statement after it receives the reimbursement. The contracts in question were *cost-plus contracts*, which means the company could negotiate for additional revenue based on cost overruns. Before 1998, Halliburton didn't book any of these cost overruns as revenue until it settled with the purchaser of its services and knew exactly how much the purchaser would pay toward the overruns.

After the change in accounting policy, Halliburton booked revenue from the cost overruns immediately upon completing the job, to improve its earnings reports to investors. But Halliburton had no guarantee that the purchaser would pay the full amount in overruns that it was asking for. In fact, the purchaser often reduced these amounts in negotiations, and Halliburton had to adjust its revenues downward after it had reported the higher earnings to investors. Halliburton's auditor during this period was Arthur Andersen. (I know. It's shocking, isn't it?)

Counting revenue before final settlement is an aggressive accounting method, and the company should have reported the change to its investors immediately. The SEC filed a civil action against Halliburton charging that because the company didn't disclose the accounting changes, it deprived investors of the information they needed to assess the firm's earnings and compare them with earnings of prior years, before the accounting change was made. The change allowed the company to report higher earnings and hide losses. In September 2004, Halliburton agreed to a $7.5 million settlement with the SEC.

Halliburton's accounting system faces regular federal scrutiny from the Pentagon. The Pentagon has charged Halliburton with overbilling millions of dollars for services in Iraq that it never provided. These disputes will probably continue throughout the course of the Iraq war.

Arthur Andersen

One name that has shown up all over this list is Arthur Andersen. Once one of the top five accounting firms, this company is now defunct because of its role in assisting Enron with its deceptive practices. In March 2002, a grand jury indicted Arthur Andersen on charges of obstruction of justice, including charges of withholding documents from official proceedings and destroying, mutilating, and concealing documents.

Arthur Andersen was convicted on these charges in June 2002 and could no longer audit financial statements or provide CPA guidance, which essentially ended the firm's ability to earn money from its accounting activities. The Supreme Court overturned its conviction on May 31, 2005, because of problems with the instructions to the jury. Yet this was a hollow victory because the company was no longer a viable business.

The staff of Arthur Andersen fell from a high of 28,000 people before the conviction to just 200 in 2008. The remaining staff is responsible for dealing with the legal issues still pending in 2008 and working on an orderly dissolution of the company.

More than 100 civil lawsuits are still making their way through the courts against Arthur Andersen and its accounting practices related to Enron and other companies. In June 2008, Arthur Andersen was socked with $23 million in damages in one of those pending lawsuits in Oregon.

- » **Keeping an eye on a company's financial numbers**
- » **Examining a company's methods and procedures**

Chapter **25**

Ten Signs That a Company's in Trouble

If you don't recognize traffic signs, driving is going to be pretty hairy. By the same token, if you don't recognize a company's danger signs by reading the financial reports, your investment decisions may not be the best ones.

Many companies put out glossy financial reports more than 100 pages long with the most graphically pleasing sections providing only the news about the company that its managers want you to read. Don't be fooled. Take the time to read the pages in smaller print and the ones without the fancy graphics, because these pages are where you find the most important financial news about the company. The following are key signs of trouble that you may find within these pages.

Lower Liquidity

Liquidity is the ability of a company to quickly convert assets to cash so that it can pay its bills and meet other debt obligations, such as a mortgage payment or a payment due to bond investors. The most liquid asset a company holds is cash in a checking or savings account. Other good liquid sources are holdings that a company can quickly convert to cash, such as marketable securities and certificates of deposits.

Other assets take longer to turn into cash, but they can be more liquid than long-term assets, such as a building or equipment. Take, for instance, accounts receivable. Accounts receivable can often be liquid holdings, provided that the company's customers are paying their bills on time. If customers are paying their bills late, the company's accounts receivable are less liquid, meaning that it takes longer for the company to collect that cash. I show you how to test a company's accounts receivable management in Chapter 16.

Another sign of trouble may be inventory. If a company's inventory continues to build, it may have less and less cash on hand as it ties up more money in the products it's trying to sell. I show you how to test a company's inventory management in Chapter 15, and I show you how to measure a company's overall liquidity in Chapter 12.

Low Cash Flow

If you don't have cash, you can't pay your bills. The same is true for companies. You need to know how well a company manages its cash, and you can't do that just by looking at the balance sheet and income statement, because neither of these statements reports what's actually happening with cash.

REMEMBER

The only way you can check out a company's cash situation is by using the cash flow statement. I show you numerous ways to test a company's cash flow in Chapter 13. After doing the calculations in Chapter 13, if you find that a company can't meet its cash obligations or is close to reaching that point, this situation is a clear sign of trouble.

Disappearing Profit Margins

Everyone wants to know how much money a company makes — in other words, its profits. A company's profit dropping year to year is another clear sign of trouble.

Companies must report their profit results for the current year and the two previous years on their income statements, one of the three key financial statements that are part of the financial reports. (See Chapter 7 for more information about income statements.) When investigating a company's viability, looking at the past five years or more — if you can get the data — is a good idea.

TIP

Luckily, finding a company's historical profit data isn't hard. In the investor relations section on their website, most companies post financial reports for the current year and two or more previous years. The Securities and Exchange Commission (SEC) also keeps previous years' reports online at Edgar (`www.sec.gov/edgar.shtml`).

WARNING

Anytime you notice that a company's profit margins have fallen from year to year, take it as a clear sign that the company is in trouble. Research further to find out why, but definitely don't invest in a company with falling profit margins unless you get good, solid information about an expected turnaround and how the company plans to pull that off. To find out more about how to test whether a company is making a profit, turn to Chapter 11.

Revenue Game Playing

A day rarely goes by when you don't see a story about company bigwigs who've played with their firm's revenue results. Although the number of companies being exposed for revenue problems has certainly fallen since the height of scandals set off by the fall of Enron in 2001, a steady stream of reporting about the games companies play with their revenue continues.

Problems can include managing earnings so results look better than they really are and actually creating a fictional story about earnings. I talk more about how companies play games with their revenue numbers in Chapter 23.

Unfortunately, the only way that a member of the general public can find out about these shenanigans is from the financial press. If the SEC or one of the country's state attorneys general begins an investigation, you likely won't know about it until the financial press decides to report on it. The SEC does post details about its investigations at `www.sec.gov/litigation.shtml`. Usually, by the time that info is posted, the financial press has already done a story.

The initial stages of an investigation usually involve private inquiries between the SEC and the company regarding financial information filed on one of the SEC's required forms. (For more information about those forms, see Chapter 19.) These initial inquiries aren't discussed publicly. Only after the SEC decides that a company isn't cooperating does it start a formal investigation. When the SEC does start a formal investigation, the company must put out a press release to inform the general public (as well as its investors, creditors, and others interested in the company) that the SEC has some questions about the company's financial reports.

Too Much Debt

WARNING

Borrowing too much money to continue operations or to finance new activities can be a major red flag that indicates future problems for a company, especially if interest rates start rising. Debt can overburden a company and make it hard for the business to meet its obligations, eventually landing it in bankruptcy.

TIP

You can test a company's debt situation by using the ratios I show you in Chapter 12. These ratios are calculated using numbers from the balance sheet and income statement. Compare a company's debt ratios with those of others in the same industry to judge whether the company is in worse shape than its competitors.

Unrealistic Values for Assets and Liabilities

Some firms can make themselves look financially healthier by either overvaluing their assets or undervaluing their liabilities. *Overvalued assets* can make a company appear as if its holdings are worth more than they are. For instance, if customers aren't paying their bills but the *accounts receivable* line item isn't properly adjusted to show the likely bad debt, accounts receivable will be higher than they should be. *Undervalued liabilities* can make a company look as though it owes less than it actually does. An example of this is debts moved off the balance sheet to another subsidiary, to hide the debt. That tactic is just one of the ways Enron and other scandal-ridden companies tried to hide their problems. If a firm hides its problems well to offset the overvaluing of assets or the undervaluing of liabilities, equity is probably overstated as well.

WARNING

If you suspect a company of either possibility, it's a clear sign of trouble ahead. Certainly, you can begin to suspect a problem if you see stories in the newspapers about the SEC or state authorities raising questions regarding the company's financial statements. You may be able to spot problems sooner by using the techniques I discuss in Chapter 23.

A Change in Accounting Methods

Accounting rules are clearly set in the generally accepted accounting principles (GAAP) developed by the Financial Accounting Standards Board (FASB). You can find details about the GAAP at the FASB's website (`www.fasb.org`). Sometimes a company can file a report that's perfectly acceptable by GAAP standards, but it may hide a potential problem by changing its accounting methods. For example, all firms must account for their inventory by using one of five methods. Changing from one method to another can have a great impact on the bottom line. To find out whether this kind of change has occurred, read the fine print in the financial notes. I talk more about accounting methods in Chapter 4 and delve deeper into inventory control methods in Chapter 15.

Questionable Mergers and Acquisitions

Mergers and acquisitions can be both good news and bad news. Most times, you won't know whether a merger or acquisition will actually be good for a company's bottom line until years later, so be careful buying into the fray when you see stories about the possibility of a merger or acquisition.

If you don't already own the stock, stay away until the dust settles and you get a clear view of how the merger or acquisition will impact the companies involved. If you do own shares of stock, you'll be able to vote for or against the merger or acquisition if it involves the exchange of stock. You can get to know the issues by reading what the company sends out when it seeks your vote. Follow the stories in the financial press, and read reports from analysts about the merger or acquisition.

You don't see much about mergers and acquisitions in the three key financial statements (income statement, balance sheet, and statement of cash flows); they rarely take up more than a line item. The key place to find out about the impact of mergers and acquisitions is in the notes to the financial statements, which I talk more about in Chapter 9.

WARNING

I can't tell you how to read the tea leaves and figure out whether a merger or acquisition is ultimately a good idea, but I can warn you to stay away if you don't already own the stock. If you're a shareholder who will eventually have to vote on the merger or acquisition before it can be approved, I urge you to read everything you can get your hands on that discusses the financial impact the merger or acquisition may have on the company.

Slow Inventory Turnover

One way to see whether a company is slowing down is to look at its *inventory turnover* (how quickly the inventory the company holds is sold). As a product's life span nears its end, moving that product off the shelf tends to be harder.

WARNING

When you see a company's inventory turnover slowing down, it may indicate a long-term or short-term problem. Economic conditions, such as a recession — which isn't company specific — may be the cause of a short-term problem. A long-term problem may be a product line that isn't kept up-to-date, causing customers to look to other companies or products to meet their needs. I show you how to pick up on inventory turnover problems in Chapter 15 by using numbers from the income statement and balance sheet.

Slow-Paying Customers

Companies report their sales when the initial transaction occurs, even if the customer hasn't yet paid cash for the product. When a customer pays with a credit card issued by a bank or other financial institution, the company considers it cash. But credit issued to the customer directly by the company selling the product isn't reported as cash received. The reason is that the customer doesn't have to pay cash until the company that issues the credit bills him. For example, if you have an account at Office Depot for charging your office supplies, Office Depot doesn't get cash for those supplies until you pay your monthly statement. If, instead, you buy those same supplies using a Visa or MasterCard, the credit card company deposits cash into Office Depot's account and then works to collect the cash from you.

Businesses track noncash sales to customers who buy on credit in an account called *accounts receivable.* Customers are billed for payments, but not all customers pay their bills on time. If you see a company's accounts receivable numbers continuing to rise, it may be a sign that customers are slowing their payments; eventually, the company may face a cash flow problem. See Chapter 16 to find out how to detect accounts receivable problems.

Appendix

Glossary

accounts payable: An account that tracks the money a company owes to its suppliers, vendors, contractors, and others who provide goods and services to the company.

accounts receivable: An account that tracks individual customer accounts, listing money that customers owe the company for products or services they've purchased.

accrual accounting: An accounting method in which a company records revenues and expenses when the actual transaction is completed rather than when cash is received or paid out.

accrued liabilities: The expenses a company has incurred but not yet paid for at the time the company closes its accounting books for the period to prepare its financial statements.

amortize: To reduce the value of an intangible asset by a certain percentage each year to show that it's being used up.

arm's length transaction: A transaction that involves a buyer and a seller who can act independently of each other and have no financial relationship with each other.

assets: Things a company owns, such as buildings, inventory, tools, equipment, vehicles, copyrights, patents, furniture, and any other items it needs to run the business.

audit: The process by which a certified public accountant verifies that a company's financial statements have met the requirements of the generally accepted accounting principles.

auditors' report: A letter from the auditors stating that a company's financial statements have been completed in accordance with the generally accepted accounting principles; the company includes this letter in its annual report.

balance sheet: The financial statement that gives you a snapshot of a company's assets, liabilities, and shareholders' equity as of a particular date.

buy-side analysts: Professionals who analyze the financial results of companies for large institutions and investment firms that manage mutual funds, pension funds, or other types of multimillion-dollar private accounts.

C corporations: Separate legal entities formed for the purpose of operating a business and to limit the owners' liability for actions the corporation takes.

capital expenditures: Money a company spends to buy or upgrade major assets, such as buildings and factories.

capital gain: The profits a company makes when it sells an asset for more than it originally paid for that asset.

cash-basis accounting: An accounting method in which companies record expenses and revenues in their financial accounts when cash actually changes hands rather than when the transaction is completed.

cash-equivalent accounts: Asset accounts that a company can easily convert to cash, including checking accounts, savings accounts, and other holdings.

cash flow: The amount of money that moves into and out of a business.

cash flow from operations: Cash a company receives from the day-to-day operations of the business, usually from sales of products or services.

Chart of Accounts: A listing of all a company's open accounts that the accounting department can use to record transactions.

common stock: A portion of a company bought by investors, who are given the right to vote on board membership and other issues taken to the stockholders for a vote.

consolidated financial statement: A report that combines the assets, liabilities, revenues, and expenses of a parent company with the assets, liabilities, revenues, and expenses of any companies that it owns.

contingent liabilities: Possible financial obligations that a company needs to report when it determines that an event is likely to happen.

convertibles: Shares of stock promised to a lender who owns bonds that can be converted to stock.

corporate governance: The way a board of directors conducts its own business and oversees a corporation's operations.

cost of goods sold: A line item on the income statement that summarizes any costs directly related to selling a company's products.

current assets: Things a company owns that it will use up in the next 12 months.

current liabilities: Payments on bills or debts that a company owes in the next 12 months.

depreciate: To reduce the value of a tangible asset by a certain percentage each year to show that the asset is being used up (aging).

discontinued operations: Business activities that a company halts, such as the closing of a factory; can also refer to the sale of a division within a company.

dividends: The portion of a company's profits that it pays out to investors according to the number of shares that the investor holds.

double-entry accounting: An accounting method that requires a company to record every transaction using debits and credits to show both sides of the transaction.

durable goods: Goods that last for more than one year.

earnings per share: The amount of net income that a company makes per share of stock available on the market.

EBITDA: An acronym for *earnings before interest, taxes, depreciation, and amortization,* which is a line item on the income statement.

equity: Claims, such as shares of stock, that investors make against the company's assets.

expenses: Any costs not directly related to generating revenues. Expenses fall into four categories: operating, interest, depreciation/amortization, and taxes.

Financial Accounting Standards Board (FASB): A private-sector organization that establishes standards of financial accounting and reporting that the Securities and Exchange Commission and the American Institute of Certified Public Accountants recognize.

financial statements: A company's reports of its financial transactions over various periods, such as monthly, quarterly, or annually. The three key statements are the balance sheet, income statement, and statement of cash flows.

fixed costs: A company's expenses for assets it holds long term, such as manufacturing facilities, equipment, and labor.

fraudulent financial reporting: A deliberate attempt by a company to distort its financial statements to make its financial results look better than they actually are.

generally accepted accounting principles (GAAP): Rules for financial reporting that dictate that companies' financial reporting is relevant, reliable, consistent, and presented in a way that allows the report reader to compare the results to prior years, as well as to financial results for other companies.

going-concern problem: An indication in an auditors' report that the auditors have substantial doubt that a company has the ability to stay in business.

goodwill account: An account that appears on the balance sheet when a company has bought another company for more than the actual value of its assets minus its liabilities. Goodwill includes things such as customer loyalty, exceptional workforce, and a great location.

gross margin: A calculation of one type of profit based solely on sales and the cost of producing those sales.

gross profit: The revenue earned minus any direct costs of generating that revenue, such as costs related to the purchase or production of goods before any expenses, including operating, taxes, interest, depreciation, and amortization.

income statement: A document that shows a company's revenues and expenses over a set period of time; an income statement is also known as a *profit and loss statement* or *P&L.*

initial public offering (IPO): The first time a company's stock is offered for sale on a public stock market.

insolvent: No longer able to pay bills and debt obligations.

in-store credit: Money lent directly by a company to its customers for purchases of its products or services.

intangible assets: Anything a company owns that isn't physical, such as patents, copyrights, trademarks, and goodwill.

intellectual property: Works, products, or marketing identities for which a company owns the exclusive rights, such as copyrights, patents, and trademarks.

interest expenses: Charges that must be paid on borrowed money, usually a percentage of the debt.

internal financial report: A summary of a company's financial results that's distributed only inside the company.

liabilities: Money a company owes to its creditors for debts such as loans, bonds, and unpaid bills.

liquidity: A company's ability to quickly turn an asset to cash.

long-term assets: Holdings that a company will use for more than a 12-month period, such as buildings, land, and equipment.

long-term debt or liabilities: Financial obligations that a company must pay more than 12 months into the future, such as mortgages on buildings.

majority interest: The position a company has when it owns more than 50 percent of another company's stock.

managing earnings: Using legitimate accounting methods in aggressive ways to get the bottom-line results that a company needs.

marketable securities: Holdings that companies can easily convert to cash, such as stocks and bonds.

material changes: Changes that may have a significant financial impact on a company's earnings.

material misstatement: An error that significantly impacts a company's financial position.

net assets: The value of things a company owns after the company has subtracted all liabilities from its total assets.

net business income: Business income or profit after a company has subtracted all its business expenses.

net marketable value: The book value of securities, adjusted for any gains or losses.

net profit: A company's bottom line, which shows how much money the company earns after it deducts all its expenses.

net sales or net revenue: Sales a company makes minus any adjustments to those sales.

nonoperating income: Income from a source that isn't part of a company's normal revenue-generating activities.

notes to the financial statements: The section in the annual report that offers additional detail about the numbers provided in those statements.

operating cash flow: Cash generated by company operations to produce and sell company products.

operating expense: Any expense that goes into operating a business but isn't directly involved in selling the product, such as advertising, dues and subscriptions, or equipment rental.

operating lease: A rental agreement for equipment that offers no ownership provisions.

operating margin or profit: A company's earnings after it subtracts all costs and expenses directly related to the core business of the company — its sales of products or services.

operating period: A specific length of time — which may be a day, month, quarter, or year — for which financial results are determined.

parent company: A major corporation that controls numerous smaller companies that it has bought in order to build the company.

partnership: A business that's owned by more than one person and isn't incorporated.

physical capacity: The number of facilities a company has and the amount of product the company can manufacture.

preferred stock: A type of stock that gives its owners no voting power in the company's operations but guarantees their dividends, which must be paid before common stockholders can get theirs.

profit: The amount of money the company earns.

proxies: Paper ballots sent to shareholders so they can vote on critical issues that impact the company's operations, such as members of the board of directors and executive compensation programs.

receivership: A type of bankruptcy in which a company can avoid liquidating itself and, instead, work with a court-appointed trustee to restructure its debt so it can emerge from bankruptcy.

recognize: To record a revenue or expense in a company's books.

related-party revenue: Revenue that comes from a company selling to another entity where the seller controls how the company operates and makes a profit.

restate earnings: To correct "accounting errors" by changing the numbers originally reported to the general public.

restructure: To reorganize business operations by means such as combining divisions, splitting divisions, dismantling an entire division, or closing manufacturing plants.

retained earnings: Profit that a company doesn't pay to stockholders over the years it accumulates in the retained earnings account.

revenue: Payments a company receives for its products or services.

royalties: Payments a company makes for the use of intellectual property owned by another company or individual.

secondary public offerings: The sale of additional shares of stock to the general public by a company that already sells shares on the public stock market.

secured debt: Money borrowed on the basis of collateral, which is usually a major asset such as a building.

securities: Stocks and bonds sold on the public financial markets.

shareholders' equity: The value of the stocks held by company shareholders.

short-term borrowings or debt: Lines of credit or other debt that a company must repay within the next 12-month period.

side letters: The agreements a company makes with its regular customers outside the actual documentation it uses in a formal contract to purchase or sell the goods.

sole proprietorship: A business started and owned by an individual that's not incorporated.

solvency: A company's ability to pay all its outstanding bills and other debts.

statement of cash flows: One of the key financial statements, a document that reports a company's performance over time, focusing on how cash flows through the business.

stock incentives: Shares of company stock that a company offers as part of an employee compensation package.

stock option plan: An offer a company gives to employees and board members to buy the company's stock at prices below market value.

tangible asset: Any asset that you can touch, such as cash, inventory, equipment, or buildings.

tax liability account: An account that tracks tax payments that a company has made or must still make.

trading securities: Securities that a company buys primarily as a place to hold on to assets until the company decides how to use the money for its operations or growth.

unrealized losses or gains: Changes in the value of a holding that hasn't sold yet but has a market value that has increased or decreased since the time it was bought.

variable costs: Costs that change based on the amount needed, such as raw materials or employee overtime.

venture capitalist: A person who invests in start-up businesses, providing the necessary cash in exchange for some portion of company ownership.

volume discount: A reduced rate received by a business that agrees to buy a large number of a manufacturer's product.

wholly owned subsidiary: A company whose stock is purchased in full by another company.

working capital: A company's current assets minus its current liabilities; this figure measures the liquid assets the company has at its disposal to continue building its business.

Index

Numerics

A

B

C

D

E

F

G

H

I

M

N

O

Q

R

S

T

U

V

W

Y

About the Author

Lita Epstein ran the accounting lab when she worked as a teaching assistant while completing her MBA at Emory University's Goizueta Business School. After earning her MBA, she managed finances for a small nonprofit organization and the facilities management division of a large medical clinic.

Now she enjoys helping people develop business and personal financial and investing skills. She designs and teaches online courses on bookkeeping, accounting, and how to start your own business. She is the author of more than 30 books, including *Bookkeeping For Dummies, Trading For Dummies, The Business Owner's Guide to Reading and Understanding Financial Statements,* and *Surviving a Layoff: A Week-by-Week Guide to Getting Your Life Back Together.*

Lita was the content director for a financial services website, MostChoice.com, and also managed the website Investing for Women. As a Congressional press secretary, Lita gained firsthand knowledge about how to work within and around the federal bureaucracy, which gives her great insight into how government programs work. Lita has also been a daily newspaper reporter, a magazine editor, and an associate director of development at The Carter Center.

For fun, Lita enjoys scuba diving and is a certified underwater photographer. She hikes, canoes, and enjoys surfing the web to find its hidden treasures.

Dedication

To my father, Jerome Kirschbrown, an auditor and savings and loan examiner, who helped hone my financial skills and taught me to be leery of what I see in financial reports.

Author's Acknowledgments

I would like to thank all the people at Wiley who helped make this book possible, especially my acquisitions editor, Stacy Kennedy, who first discussed this topic with me; my project editor, Tracy Brown Hamilton, who did a wonderful job of steering this book through the entire process; and my copy editor, Krista Hansing, for her excellent work cleaning up the copy. And a special thank you to my husband, H. G. Wolpin, who has learned to stay away as I rush to meet deadlines.

Publisher's Acknowledgments

Acquisitions Editor: Stacy Kennedy
Project Editor: Tracy Brown Hamilton
Copy Editor: Krista Hansing
Technical Editor: Sukriti Nayar
Art Coordinator: Asia Jureczko
Project Coordinator: Patrick Redmond
Cover Photos: © Zorabc/Shutterstock

PERSONAL ENRICHMENT

9781119187790
USA $26.00
CAN $31.99
UK £19.99

9781119179030
USA $21.99
CAN $25.99
UK £16.99

9781119293354
USA $24.99
CAN $29.99
UK £17.99

9781119293347
USA $22.99
CAN $27.99
UK £16.99

9781119310068
USA $22.99
CAN $27.99
UK £16.99

9781119235606
USA $24.99
CAN $29.99
UK £17.99

9781119251163
USA $24.99
CAN $29.99
UK £17.99

9781119235491
USA $26.99
CAN $31.99
UK £19.99

9781119279952
USA $24.99
CAN $29.99
UK £17.99

9781119283133
USA $24.99
CAN $29.99
UK £17.99

9781119287117
USA $24.99
CAN $29.99
UK £16.99

9781119130246
USA $22.99
CAN $27.99
UK £16.99

PROFESSIONAL DEVELOPMENT

9781119311041
USA $24.99
CAN $29.99
UK £17.99

9781119255796
USA $39.99
CAN $47.99
UK £27.99

9781119293439
USA $26.99
CAN $31.99
UK £19.99

9781119281467
USA $26.99
CAN $31.99
UK £19.99

9781119280651
USA $29.99
CAN $35.99
UK £21.99

9781119251132
USA $24.99
CAN $29.99
UK £17.99

9781119310563
USA $34.00
CAN $41.99
UK £24.99

9781119181705
USA $29.99
CAN $35.99
UK £21.99

9781119263593
USA $26.99
CAN $31.99
UK £19.99

9781119257769
USA $29.99
CAN $35.99
UK £21.99

9781119293477
USA $26.99
CAN $31.99
UK £19.99

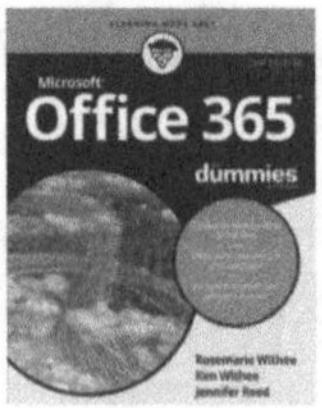

9781119265313
USA $24.99
CAN $29.99
UK £17.99

9781119239314
USA $29.99
CAN $35.99
UK £21.99

9781119293323
USA $29.99
CAN $35.99
UK £21.99

dummies.com

dummies®
A Wiley Brand